The
One to One
Fieldbook

The One to One Fieldbook

THE COMPLETE TOOLKIT FOR
IMPLEMENTING A 1TO1
MARKETING PROGRAM

Don Peppers,
Martha Rogers, Ph.D.,
and Bob Dorf

CURRENCY

DOUBLEDAY

New York London Toronto Sydney Auckland

A Currency Book

published by doubleday

a division of Bantam Doubleday Dell Publishing Group, Inc.

1540 Broadway, New York, New York 10036

Currency and Doubleday
are trademarks of Doubleday, a division of
Bantam Doubleday Dell Publishing Group, Inc.

Book design by Chris Welch

Library of Congress Cataloging-in-Publication Data

Peppers, Don.
The one to one fieldbook: the complete toolkit for
implementing a 1to1 marketing program / Don Peppers, Martha
Rogers, and Robert Dorf.
p.   cm.
Includes index.
1. Market segmentation.   2. Consumers' preferences.
3. Relationship marketing.   I. Rogers, Martha, Ph.D.   II. Dorf, Robert.
III. Title.
HF5415.127 .P469 1998
658.8′12—ddc21
98-38165
CIP

isbn: 0-385-49369-X

TO ALL THE 1TO1 PIONEERS

Contents

INTRODUCTION

Chapter One   One-to-One Marketing: What It's All About

THE FOUR IMPLEMENTATION STEPS OF A
1TO1 MARKETING PROGRAM   /   1

Companies in all industries today are faced with rising customer disloyalty and shrinking margins. But some firms are enjoying surprising successes by focusing on individual customers, using technology to create long-term, individualized, one-to-one (1to1) relationships. In as few words as possible, 1to1 is based on the simple idea of *treating different customers differently.* Companies initiate 1to1 marketing programs in order to create more loyal, profitable customers, and to protect their unit margins from erosion. The actual, detailed mechanics of a 1to1 marketing strategy depend on understanding the various ways customers are different, and how these differences should affect the firm's behavior toward particular, individual customers.

There are four key steps in implementing a 1to1 marketing program. These steps, which are only roughly sequential, represent progressive stages of implementing the basic principles of 1to1 marketing. Any company wishing to implement a 1to1 marketing program must be able to (1) identify its customers, (2) differentiate them one from another, (3) interact with them, and (4) customize some aspect of its product or service to meet their individual needs. These steps are so important for understanding the 1to1 marketing process that they form the basis for the rest of the *Fieldbook*.

Chapter Two   Quick Start

HOW TO GET IMMEDIATE RESULTS WITH ONE-TO-ONE MARKETING   /   15

There are many reasons why 1to1 marketing will be difficult to implement. But there are also many ways to generate short-term, significant results. Before getting overly involved in the theory and practice of 1to1 marketing, with all its implications for your enterprise, you might want to take a look at a few Quick Start ideas for getting a jump on the process. Even with a Quick Start, of course, you'll need to be able to tie the results of the program back to some quantifiable measure of profit or benefit. The basic idea of a Quick Start initiative is to ensure that a large part of the upfront costs of implementing more comprehensive 1to1 marketing strategies can be funded by the short-term profits of immediately practical tactics.

DESIGN

Chapter Three   Identify Your Customers

HOW TO OBTAIN MORE INDIVIDUAL INFORMATION
ABOUT A GREATER NUMBER OF
YOUR CUSTOMERS / 24

This is the first of the four implementation steps. Unless you can identify a healthy proportion of your Most Valuable Customers in enough addressable detail to distinguish one from another, individually, you cannot be a 1to1 marketer. Addressable details might be postal address, account code, e-mail address, phone number, or any other unique identifier. But in many consumer businesses, especially those that depend on large distribution systems or retailing, it is difficult to gain access to individual customer identities and, even if access is gained, it is just as difficult to track an individual customer from transaction to transaction. It is often difficult, also, to identify an individual customer who does business with different divisions, or locations. While business-to-business firms usually have less problem identifying the companies they deal with, they often do have difficulty tracking the individual executives with authority for, or influence over, the purchasing decisions at these firms.

Chapter Four   Differentiate Your Customers

HOW TO UNDERSTAND WHAT DIFFERENT CUSTOMERS
ARE WORTH TO YOU AND WHAT THEY NEED
FROM YOU / 56

In order to do things cost-efficiently, it's important to know which customers are most valuable and which are least valuable. Defining the value of a customer is the tricky part, but once you do it, your plan should be to rank your customers by this variable and allocate different strategies to different tiers of customers. If the concept of "value" itself is difficult, when applied to your customers, you can substitute "importance to your enterprise." After ranking your customers by their value, the next task is to differentiate them by their needs. Concentrating on your most valuable customers first, you should be able to identify a number of needs-based groups by examining transactional patterns, but often your understanding of customer needs will be aided by some type of interaction with the customer as well.

Chapter Five   Interact with Your Customers

Assuming you can identify your customers individually, rank them by their value, and differentiate them generally by their needs, then the next step is to work on your interactions with these customers. Interacting with a customer is the first *visible* sign (to the customer) of your 1to1 marketing program. The interaction itself can take place in a variety of forums and media. Two things are important here. First, you want to drive more and more of your interactions with customers into more cost-efficient media, such as the Web, point-of-purchase (for retailers), or EDI. And second, you must concentrate on acquiring more useful information during every interaction—information that can help you make decisions or implement new strategies with respect to your customers. If the customer is to be presented with a "rational" view of your enterprise during the interaction process, then many of the conflicts that now exist, with respect to handling individual customers, must be resolved—so interaction serves as a crucible in which many of these integrative issues will be hammered out.

Chapter Six   Customize Your Product or Service

If you don't change how you actually treat a customer based on what you know about that customer, then what would be the point of even calling it a "one-to-one" relationship? When the customer tells you something about how he or she wants to be treated and you *act* on it, you are, in fact, customizing. But the only way you'll be able to make customized products and services more generally available to your own customer base is by adopting at least some form of mass customization. In addition, treating different customers differently will mean that your enterprise pushes for a greater degree of integration than ever before. Functional integration is required if the production or service delivery department is going to be able to do for your customer what the sales or marketing department learned that this particular customer wants. Eventually, the push for a greater degree of integration will also lead the firm to seek out strategic alliances with other, noncompeting firms.

BUILD

Chapter Seven   The One-to-One Gap Analysis

The first step at most firms, before launching into any new initiative, is to gain an understanding of how far there is to go with the initiative, what and how much needs to be done, and how easy or difficult it's likely to be. This chapter consists of three activities for assessing your own firm's situation, and its current readiness to launch a 1to1 marketing initiative:

1. A "Quick Start Self-Assessment," composed of only four basic questions, which parallel 1to1 marketing's four implementation steps.
2. A "Gap Tool" to provide a more comprehensive look at your firm's organizational and cultural ability to launch and sustain a 1to1 marketing initiative.
3. A "Strategy Map" designed to help you better understand your customer base and its current capabilities. It also will help you plot a "migration" toward 1to1 marketing.

Chapter Eight   Information Systems

Many books have already been written about information management systems. Ignoring all but the most vital technical issues, what this chapter tries to do is help you design and manage an information infrastructure that is "one-to-one friendly." We'll point out those characteristics of a database and information system that are supportive of, rather than a roadblock to, a continuous cycle of improving your enterprise's 1to1 marketing programs. The entire 1to1 information system, regardless of hardware and software, must be constructed to facilitate rapid-fire, individualized interactions with customers at increasing frequency and depth. But few, if any, companies junk their existing systems entirely, so the limitations of your firm's own legacy systems must also be considered. Gaining access to individual customer data, storing it, and making it accessible to every entity within your enterprise is the ultimate goal. The result is likely to lead to a truly revolutionary cultural and organizational transformation of your business.

Chapter Nine   Infrastructure

Treating different customers differently doesn't just happen. The organization has to be ready for it. Getting the information necessary to run a good 1to1 marketing program is important, but you also have to decide what your enterprise is actually going to do with that information, and who will have access to it. Functions and divisions have to work together better, and people have to know what's expected of them. What kind of people will you need, and how will you train them? Should your compensation systems change to reflect the enterprise's emphasis on increasing customer value? What cultural values should your firm aspire to once it becomes technically capable of treating different customers differently?

MANANGE

Chapter Ten   Channel Management

EVALUATING CHANNEL MEMBERS IN THE
ONE-TO-ONE ORGANIZATION / 225

In order to thrive in today's competitive markets, companies must build strong, interactive relationships with their channel partners. Such partners often control the relationships with end-user customers and deep collaboration is vital if everyone is to succeed. This chapter documents a step-by-step procedure for creating the tightest, most mutually beneficial relationships with channel members. It suggests that companies identify all relevant channel members and rank order them by value. As with 1to1 customer relationships, it then becomes important to learn the channel partners' needs and preferences, and act on them, in order to establish and strengthen the partners' commitment to mutual success.

Chapter Eleven   The One-to-One Sales Organization

NEW DIRECTIONS FOR SALES IN THE
1TO1 ENTERPRISE / 247

If you are trying to manage your transition to a 1to1 enterprise, the sales force will almost certainly lie at the very center of your organizational plans, either as an asset, an obstacle, or both. Companies must recognize the critical role of the direct sales force not only in acquiring new customers but in strengthening and expanding relationships with existing ones. In this chapter, we discuss issues such as sales compensation and incentives, suggesting that if companies want to improve customer loyalty and growth, then they must begin to reward sales people for finding loyal, growable customers. We also discuss trends in sales force automation and customer relationship management technology that promise to transform the role of the sales force and enable it to become more intelligent in terms of addressing the needs and preferences of customers.

Chapter Fourteen   Advertising and Marketing Communications for the One-to-One Enterprise

HOW TO USE TRADITIONAL MASS MEDIA
TO GENERATE BETTER
CUSTOMER RELATIONSHIPS   /   328

Mass media may be falling in importance relative to more direct and interactive forms of communication, but it will continue to be with us for a long time. Nonaddressable, noninteractive media—ranging from television and radio to print—remains an important force in the strategies of many companies to attract the attention of unknown prospects. Smart companies will find ways to use such media to complement the more powerful and engaging interactive strategies that they develop to win their customers' lifetime loyalty. This chapter reviews how to use broadcast, print, and outdoor media, as well as direct mail, brochures, collateral, kiosks and other forms of non-mass media to further the goals of a 1to1 marketing campaign. We'll also cover how some of the more traditional marketing tasks—such as product launches—should be adjusted to account for your 1to1 marketing program.

Chapter Fifteen   Next Steps

WHERE TO GO FROM HERE   /   348

You are just at the beginning of a challenging journey, but one that promises tremendous rewards. In this chapter, we provide a ten-step plan for putting the ideas in this book into practice. We recommend an iterative approach, beginning with department-specific or division-specific projects, progressing gradually to a broader and more ambitious set of initiatives, then circling back to expand your program. We also outline the steps you will need to take in order to get support for your efforts, and manage them in a coherent and effective fashion.

Appendix   The One-to-One Nonprofit

In the not-for-profit universe, there are all sorts of organizations, including foundations and associations, colleges and universities, health care institutions, and government agencies. Each has its own particular constituencies. Each has special opportunities to individualize its offerings. And while such organizations are not focused on generating profit, they do face tough competition. Therefore, 1to1 approaches are as critical to their long-term success as they are to firms in for-profit businesses. This chapter offers some ideas to help nonprofits explore their own opportunities for implementing 1to1 principles to strengthen relationships with their customers and constituents.

Acknowledgments

Don and Martha hadn't yet met Bob in 1993 when *The One to One Future* was published. By the time *Enterprise One to One* appeared in 1997, the whirlwind had started in earnest. Don and Martha had founded Peppers and Rogers Group (originally known as marketing 1:1, inc.), and Bob was running it. *The One to One Future* presents the what-to and why-to of 1to1 marketing. Soon after its publication, it became apparent that 1to1 was not just about marketing and that any suggestions about how-to would involve the entire enterprise. So *Enterprise One to One* offers some real-world examples, many drawn from projects we had worked on with clients grappling with the real challenges of putting 1to1 to work. This book is the result of more of that kind of work—in the trenches—with clients, audience members, visitors to our Web site. It sets out to answer this question: But *really*—**how** do we turn our organization into a 1to1 enterprise? We worked together on this book—Don and Martha continuing to confront the role of new technology in business strategy, and Bob as the head of Peppers and Rogers Group's consulting practice.

But this book is a collaboration of more than the three people named as its authors. It is really the work product of inventive and intelligent clients and other business leaders who are slogging through the tough transition from traditional marketing to 1to1—the movers and shakers of a new way of doing business. And of the others who are devoted to developing a way to harness new technologies to improve relationships between businesses and customers—thinkers and writers working together to shape the new marketing. And of the wonderful partners and staff of Peppers and Rogers Group, who have served as a powerful sounding board for ideas, as a gentle inspiration to keep going and meet deadlines, and as the trustees of the myriad details that, we hope, make a book like this useful to a reader. Much of what works best about this book is because of them. The authors take credit for any errors.

We are indebted in many ways to the best and brightest wrestling with business issues today—those who have walked hand in hand with us as we all invent the best response to explosive developments in information processing and interactivity. Working with them as clients or colleagues (and often both), we have learned a lot—not only about how to build long-term Learning Relationships with an organization's Most Valuable Customers but also how to define and overcome the very real obstacles of culture, organization, compensation, and how to make use of the living human beings who bring their own experiences and issues to the transition process. Lane Michel at Hewlett-Packard, Steve Blank at Epiphany, Joe Pine and Jim Gilmore at Strategic Horizons LLP, Dr. Pehong Chen at BroadVision, John Acton at BellSouth, and Steve Smoot at Owens Corning—all have helped us to advance our thinking.

We also thank Bruce Hamilton at 3M, Dave Euson at Carlson Marketing Group, Collin Bruce and David Radoff at Chordiant, Nick Noyes at Executive Perspectives, Gayle Christensen at FedEx, Sandra Nicholls and Dave Ropes at Ford Motor Company, Pat Kennedy at Guestnet, Andy Danver of Hewlett-Packard, Gordon D. Shank and Sanjay Choudhuri at Levi Strauss & Company, Scott Randall at Media Designs Interactive, Inc., Jack Mitchell at Mitchells of Westport and Richards of Greenwich, Peter Boulter at NCR, Greg Padovani at Northwestern Medical Faculty Foundation, Anne Lockie at Royal Bank of Canada, and Seth Godin at Yoyodyne.

Special thanks to those who commented on specific chapters or shared specific insights and expertise, especially for issues surrounding database management, sales-force automation, and infrastructure. Besides Lane Michel and Steve Blank, these include Christine Lenick at the Alleris Group, Neil McClumpha at Cambridge Management Consulting, Craig Wood and David King at KnowledgeBase Marketing, Inc., Richard Cross and Alan Steele of Cross World Network, Inc., Linda Dumas at Lucent Technologies, Neil Mendelson at Oracle, Bob Runge at Pivotal, Jon Anton at Purdue University, Linda Winterbottom on behalf of Sky Alland Marketing, and John Santaferraro at Compaq Computer Corporation. Special thanks, also, to NCR's D. S. (Stu) Coleman, Keith Carr, and Chris Yanik, for their early-stage work on the self-analysis program that eventually became Chapter Seven's "Gap Tool."

Thanks to all of our partners and staff—since everybody gets pulled into a project this size somehow, sooner or later. Special thanks to our partners Bruce Kasanoff, Tom Shimko, Tom Niehaus, and Trish Watson. Kudos and thanks to our strong right arms, the remarkable Mary Cavello, Deanna Lisk, and Alesa Cunningham. Special thanks to our Web team for the extensive support they have given this book: Andrew Vernal, Felicia Bates, Melissa Martinez, and Michael Vernal. Many thanks to our editorial and research team, especially Julia Johnson (now at Gartner Group), Diane Kroll, Britton Manasco, and Mike Barlow. There's a special place in our hearts for the never-tiring, always-cheerful and extraordinarily talented Stacey Riordan, who has taught us a lot about handling details with grace and accuracy.

Most of all, we thank our families, and our spouses, for their patience and support: Pamela Devenney, Stuart Bertsch, and Fran Dorf.

Don Peppers, Martha Rogers, and Bob Dorf
July 1998

Preface

BY DON PEPPERS, MARTHA ROGERS, PH.D.,
AND BOB DORF

Every day, all around the world, managers worry about the declining loyalty of their customers—customers who are being wooed ever more feverishly by competitors offering better prices, better deals. As customer loyalty declines, so does margin, because the most successful customer acquisition tactic is to cut prices, and the only defense in most firms' arsenal is to match those price cuts. Even more ominous, a number of new players in the interactive arena are opening entirely new and extremely threatening avenues for driving these margins farther downward. You can now go on the Web and find any car you want at just a few dollars over dealer invoice, or trade 10,000 shares of General Motors and pay a commission of less than $8.

As information about customers becomes more plentiful and detailed, and as customers themselves become more interactive with the companies they buy from, you and your firm face a radically different competitive landscape. It was never easy to differentiate your product or service, and today it is more difficult than ever. Instead, your competitive success hinges increasingly on using customer-level information and interaction to create long-term, profitable, 1to1 customer relationships.

The magnitude of this revolution is startling. Already the most successful firms in a wide variety of industries and disciplines are precisely those that do embrace the principles of 1to1 relationship marketing. Dell Computer is now the benchmark of success in the PC business. In the personal insurance industry, USAA is the benchmark. Cisco, FedEx, Owens Corning, American Express, Amazon.com, Hewlett-Packard, BellSouth, Royal Bank of Canada, Belgacom—each of these companies has built its success on customer knowledge and interaction.

Every day, on every continent, managers and executives are wrestling with the issue of how to deal with this revolution. CIOs worry about how better to manage and use the information now available in their new or upgraded customer databases. Product managers wonder whether it makes sense to launch yet another line extension to meet the needs of a newly identified segment of customers. Sales managers wonder how to integrate the sales force automation system with their overall marketing program. Webmasters try to figure out how to understand and benefit from the customer feedback they receive at their interactive Web sites. CEOs want to encourage cross-selling among divisions, leveraging the strong customer relationship at one division to make a profit in other places. And CFOs need to quantify the progress being made in all these efforts.

That's why we wrote this book.

You could think of *The One to One Fieldbook: The Complete Toolkit for Implementing a 1to1 Marketing Program* as a "book of lists." It is full of checklists for implementing relationship marketing programs, along with questions for evaluating a firm's progress or readiness for such programs. In this book, we've listed the tasks required to implement a successful tactical program in 1to1 marketing along with the steps to take and the order in which you should take them. We've listed the barriers to success, the obstacles you'll face, and some ways to avoid or over-come these obstacles.

So you should read this book if you've ever thought about trying to implement a relationship marketing program at your company and won-dered where to begin, how to measure its results, when to speed the ef-fort up or slow it down, and whom to hold accountable for it. Or read it if you want to make steady, incremental progress in 1to1 marketing at your company, verifying and documenting the results at each step, but not "going all the way"—yet.

Read this book if you're already familiar with the theory of 1to1 mar-keting, and you now want a simple, step-by-step guide for turning your firm into a 1to1 enterprise. Or if you've already launched one or more re-lationship marketing programs or initiatives, and you're now looking for a better way to link them into a coherent, strategically viable program.

Read this book if you're serious about implementing at least some re-lationship marketing programs at your firm and you need to know the precise steps to take in this process. Or if you need to convince the rest of your firm's management about the feasibility of the process itself. Or if you've already launched one or more relationship marketing initiatives and you now need to deal with the organizational and cultural barriers that are restricting further progress.

Or don't read this book. Just skim through it and keep it as a refer-ence guide of checklists and planning tools for implementing relation-ship marketing programs—a "safety net" for those unknown situations you haven't yet faced but know you will, sooner or later.

Fieldbook readers can go online for electronic tools, spreadsheets, discounts.

The One to One Fieldbook comes with its own set of electronic tools that you can download from the Web site operated by Peppers and Rogers Group, *www.1to1.com.* These tools include electronic versions of all the checklists and questionnaires, spreadsheets for use in model-ing your customer economics, and self-assessment tools.

In addition, you can search for specific topics from a selection of text supplements to the *Fieldbook*. These supplemental sections, which cover a variety of industries, case studies, and more specialized situations, total roughly twice as many words as we could fit into this single printed book. You won't want to read all of these sections yourself, but by signing on you'll be able to download the sections most relevant to you. The truth is, unless you retrieve some of these "extras" from our Web site, you won't be taking full advantage of the *Fieldbook*. (Note: Only *Fieldbook* readers are permitted access to this part of our Web site. At the end of Chapter One we explain how to use the unique access code enclosed with each book.)

You can think of *The One to One Fieldbook* as an instruction manual for implementing relationship marketing programs. That is essentially what it is—a manual of step-by-step instructions for planning, implementing, evaluating, and upgrading your relationship marketing program, whether that program is a purely tactical, one-at-a-time initiative, or part of a broader, more coordinated effort. Our goal is to help you identify your best customers, keep them longer, and grow them bigger—to compete successfully in the Interactive Age.

June 1998

Introduction

Chapter One

One-to-One Marketing: What It's All About

THE FOUR IMPLEMENTATION STEPS OF A 1TO1 MARKETING PROGRAM

At its root, one-to-one (1to1) marketing is a type of relationship marketing. But not everything that could be called "relationship marketing" is in fact 1to1 marketing. To be a genuine 1to1 marketer, you have to be able and willing to change your company's behavior toward an individual customer based on what you know about that customer and what the customer tells you.

So 1to1 marketing is basically a simple idea:

Treat different customers differently.

The actual mechanics of a 1to1 marketing strategy depend on understanding the various ways customers are different and how these differences should affect the firm's behavior toward particular, individual customers. While the idea is quite simple, implementing a 1to1 marketing program is not. One-to-one marketing involves much more than just sales and marketing, because the firm must be able to change how

1

its products are configured or its service is delivered based on the individual needs of individual customers.

When a firm really harnesses all its resources to address the different needs of individual customers—to implement a 1to1 marketing program—we call that firm a one-to-one enterprise. One enterprise, one customer. A true 1to1 enterprise considers the cultivation and management of customer relationships to be the single most critical issue it faces—and recognizes that the strength or weakness of those relationships is the key determinant of the enterprise's long-term profitability and success.

Smart companies have always encouraged the active participation of customers in the development of products, services, and solutions. For the most part, however, being customer-oriented has always meant being oriented to the needs of the *typical* customer in the market—the average customer. In order to build enduring 1to1 relationships, a company must continuously learn from interactions with *individual* customers. It must dynamically respond to the information those interactions elicit. The enterprise must *engage* its customers—particularly its best customers—and ensure they never want to leave.

The actual, detailed mechanics of building a 1to1 relationship depend on understanding the various ways customers are different and how these differences should affect the firm's behavior toward particular, individual customers. It's an idea that is critical to success in high-velocity, highly competitive times. It recognizes that no two customers are the same and that smart companies can capitalize on these inherent and essential differences.

Who Is the Customer?

Most companies sell not to end users or to consumers directly but to intermediaries—purchasing agents, dealers, distributors, retailers, or resellers. Whether your company sells consumer products through retail outlets or factory machinery to the contracting officers at large industrial firms, defining the nature of all your "customers" is a first step. But even if a company doesn't sell directly to the end user of its product, it still has an interest in creating a better relationship with that end user.

It is the end user—the ultimate customer or consumer—who supports everyone in a network of value-creating relationships.

Ford Motor Company sells almost all of its cars to dealers, not to consumers, but it must recognize nevertheless that the ultimate drivers of Ford vehicles think of themselves as having a relationship with Ford. Hewlett-Packard may sell expensive testing equipment to the purchasing agents at large microchip-manufacturing companies, but the ultimate users of these products are the bench engineers who develop new products and test current ones. Even companies largely thought of as consumer marketing firms usually sell their products, in actuality, to retail chains, while running tens of millions of dollars in advertising to pull consumers into these stores to buy their products.

Regardless of how the customer is actually defined, one reason so many firms are beginning to focus on 1to1 marketing is that this kind of marketing can create intense customer loyalty and, as a part of the process, help a firm protect its unit margins. These benefits appeal to firms all over the world, in every industry, because everyone's business today is threatened to some extent by declining customer loyalty and by a kind of "creeping commoditization" that steadily erodes margins.

Learning, Loyalty, and Profitability

You can make your own customers more loyal and more profitable to you—one customer at a time—by establishing a "Learning Relationship" with each of them, starting with your most valuable customers. Think of a Learning Relationship as a relationship that gets smarter and smarter with every new interaction. The customer tells you of some need, and you customize your product or service to meet this need. Then, with each interaction and recustomization you get better and better at fitting your product to this particular customer. Now, even if a competitor offers the same type of customization and interaction, your customer won't be able to get back to the same level of convenience until he reteaches the competitor what he's already spent time and energy teaching you. In effect, by implementing a 1to1 marketing program you are making your product more and more valuable to *this* customer through every successive interaction and transaction.

Four Implementation Steps for a One-to-One Marketing Program

There are four key implementation tasks that can be used as a guide for launching a 1to1 initiative: *identify, differentiate, interact,* and *customize.* These principles are roughly in order of increasing difficulty and complexity, although, as we'll see, there can be a good deal of overlap. Nevertheless, these four implementation steps can be thought of as a sequential process for putting a 1to1 marketing program to work:

1. **Identify** your customers. It's critical to know customers in as much detail as possible. Not just name and addressable characteristics but habits, preferences, and so forth. And not just a snapshot—a one-time questionnaire, say—but across all contact points, through all media, across every product line, at every location, and in every division. This is not simple "targeting." It's important to know and remember each customer individually, and to link information about that customer across the entire enterprise, throughout the duration of a customer relationship. If a company hasn't acquired the addressable identities of at least a fair number of its most valuable customers, then it isn't prepared to launch a 1to1 initiative. (Or you haven't defined your customers the right way. Your only option may be to try to create relationships, not with end users but with the intermediaries and channel members whose identities you do have.)

2. **Differentiate** your customers. Customers are different in two principal ways: They represent different levels of value (some are very valuable, some not so valuable), and they have different needs from you. So, once you identify your customers, the next step is to differentiate them so as to (a) prioritize your efforts and gain the most advantage with the most valuable customers and (b) tailor your firm's behavior to each customer based on that customer's individual needs. The degree and types of differentiation in a firm's customer base will also help you decide which 1to1 strategy is more appropriate for a particular business situation.

3. **Interact** with your customers. The next step is improve both the cost-efficiency and the effectiveness of your interactions with customers. To make interactions more efficient, drive them into more automated, cost-efficient channels. Push call-center interactions toward your Web site, and push personal sales calls more to the call center. To improve the effectiveness of each interaction, gather only relevant information, when it is needed either (a) to better grasp a customer's individual needs or (b) to more accurately quantify a customer's potential value. In addition, every interaction with a customer should take place in the context of all previous interactions *with that customer*. A conversation should pick up where the last one left off, whether the previous interaction occurred last night or last month, at the call center or on the company Web site.

4. **Customize** some aspect of your enterprise's behavior toward your customer, based on that customer's needs and value. To lock a customer into a Learning Relationship, a firm must adapt some aspect of its behavior to meet that customer's individually expressed needs. This might mean mass customizing a manufactured product, or it could involve tailoring some aspect of the services surrounding a product—perhaps the way the invoice is rendered, or how the product is packaged (we will be discussing the mechanics of mass customization in Chapter Six). In any case, in order to practice true 1to1 marketing, the production or service-delivery end of your business has to be able to treat a particular customer differently based on what *that customer* said during an interaction with the sales or marketing part of the firm.

These four principles overlap considerably. For instance, an enterprise might put up a Web site not primarily to interact with customers but simply to attract the most valuable ones and begin to identify them individually. Nevertheless, the principles are in a rough order that corresponds to increasing complexity as well as benefit for a company. So these steps can be used as a kind of macro-checklist to guide your efforts in implementing a 1to1 marketing program. If you can't identify your customers individually, you have no hope of differentiating them, much less adapting your behavior to address each individual customer's needs.

Is One-to-One Marketing an "All or Nothing" Proposition?

It's impossible to simply "strap on" a 1to1 marketing campaign and continue to do business in a traditional manner. Some companies—Dell Computer, USAA, or Amazon.com, for instance—are successful at creating 1to1 relationships with their customers because they built their businesses from the very beginning on the basis of direct customer interaction.

But while it's certainly easier to implement a comprehensive 1to1 marketing program by starting from scratch, it's not actually necessary. If your business is already up and running, you can make incremental, manageable progress toward becoming a 1to1 enterprise by concentrating on the four principal implementation steps outlined in this *Fieldbook*.

Other companies are doing it now. Large, well-established enterprises like Pitney Bowes, Wells Fargo, 3M, Owens Corning, American Express, and British Airways have begun incrementally creating stronger, more interactive relationships with their customers. They implement these strategies piece by piece, in one business unit and then another, wrestling with one obstacle at a time. But they are making substantial progress and gaining a significant competitive advantage as a result.

Or consider Hewlett-Packard, a firm with more than a hundred thousand employees in seventy-six independent business units each of which operates in dozens of countries. This vast enterprise is making substantial progress toward turning itself into a 1to1 enterprise, simply by concentrating on the individual implementation steps involved. The firm already has about a hundred separate 1to1 initiatives under way, with progress in each initiative tracked on the company's intranet.

Most firms must be able to make such progress without substantially undermining their current business, and figuring out how to make incremental progress is exactly what this *Fieldbook* is all about. The aspiring 1to1 enterprise needs a vision and a strategy. It also needs tactical, step-by-step plans for attaining its objectives.

The four implementation steps—identify, differentiate, interact, and customize—provide an extremely useful road map for the 1to1 strategist. In our own consulting practice, we use these four implementation steps as an easy guide for evaluating a particular client's strengths and opportunities in 1to1 marketing.

These four steps are useful enough that we'll be relying on them throughout *The One to One Fieldbook*. In the first half of the *Fieldbook,* we'll be asking you to consider each of these steps, one at a time, and to think about its implications for your own business. We've woven a large number of examples into the first half, in order to illustrate how completely different companies, in entirely different business situations, can still rely generally on these steps as a guide.

In the second half of the *Fieldbook* we'll examine a variety of business functions and processes, from call centers to advertising, from information systems to channel management. What we'll be looking for is how each area of activity will affect, and be affected by, the task of implementing a 1to1 marketing program using these four steps.

We've designed the *Fieldbook* as a toolkit, and we've stocked it with tools. The way we have visualized this book being used is as a transition guide. In our experience, managers who begin to implement 1to1 marketing programs soon find that they must interact and cooperate with other departments, even other divisions, at their firm. Often, a serious enterprise creates a kind of multidepartmental team of managers who are tasked with navigating the transition. This transition team should include ten to fifteen of the brightest, craziest people in your company, from a variety of departments and functions, including marketing, sales, customer service and support, finance, production, delivery and logistics, product management, and information systems.

Try to avoid the following on your guest list:

- More than one person (two, maximum) from any business function
- Anyone who's notably more senior than the rest of the crowd

- Grandstanders and meanderers (including anyone who has a major vested interest in the status quo)

We have written the *Fieldbook* explicitly to help this kind of transition team.

You could also think of the *Fieldbook* as a "book of lists." There are checklists of activities for identifying customers, or for interacting with them more cost-efficiently. There are lists of tasks and responsibilities, pitfalls, advantages, things to watch out for. There are item-by-item lists of "thought starter" ideas and concepts.

In addition, we've sprinkled a number of "scenarios" into the *Fieldbook*. Sometimes we propose alternative scenarios and ask you to select the one that best fits your own situation in order to provide a better key for your self-assessment. Other times we use them as examples of particular business situations we think it would be useful for you to think through—problems to work out.

This *Fieldbook* is—even as it goes to press—a work in progress. In the few weeks or months between the time these words are typeset and you read them in print, we are absolutely positive that many of these concepts will be updated and improved. All over the world, managers at companies like yours are constantly adding to the 1to1 marketing knowledgebase. The revolution is, if anything, accelerating, and writing the *Fieldbook* has been somewhat like trying to shoot a moving target.

That's one reason we've gone to great lengths to link the *Fieldbook* to a special section on our Web site (http://www.1to1fieldbook.com).

Notice the card included with your *Fieldbook?* Don't lose it. This special section is for *Fieldbook* owners, and in order to access it, you'll need to provide the unique access code on the card during a registration process. By going to this area, you'll have access, at no additional charge, to electronic versions of every spreadsheet, worksheet, checklist, scenario, or planning page included in this toolkit. Instead of ripping the checklists out, or photocopying them, you can download and print these files whenever you choose. In addition, as the 1to1 knowledgebase grows, we'll be updating all of these tools and adding others.

So you'll never be more than a few keystrokes away from what amounts to our latest learning with respect to the issues involved in setting up a 1to1 enterprise.

Davis, Stan, and Christopher Meyer. *Blur: The Speed of Change in the Connected Economy* (Addison-Wesley Pub., 1998).
Davis and Meyer provide some very valuable insights into the nature of the new economy and the "connectivity, speed, and the growth of intangible value" that lie at its heart. They are particularly insightful in their discussion of the changing roles and relationships of companies and customers.

Dyson, Esther. *Release 2.0: A Design for Living in the Digital Age* (Broadway Books, 1997).
Dyson offers a sweeping view of how new digital technologies can be expected to change economies and organizations as well as our social lives. She looks at an array of issues—everything from education to privacy to e-commerce.

Pine, B. Joseph II, and James H. Gilmore. "Welcome to the Experience Economy," *Harvard Business Review,* July/August 1998, pp. 97–105.
Beyond goods, products, and services lie "experiences" and "transformations" as a force in the new economy. Pine and Gilmore argue that companies must sell a compelling and memorable set of experiences if they hope to sustain their customer relationships.

McKenna, Regis. *Real Time: Preparing for the Age of the Never Satisfied Customer* (Harvard Business School Press, 1997).
An engaging and informative look at the high-tech, high-velocity trends that are shaping the new economy and the new enterprise. McKenna champions strategies based on immediacy and results, and shows us how new technologies can facilitate such efforts.

McKenna, Regis. *Relationship Marketing: Successful Strategies for the Age of the Customer* (Addison-Wesley Pub. Co., 1992).
This book helped lay the foundations for relationship marketers, demonstrating opportunities for more effectively learning customer needs and winning their loyalty. McKenna offers a wealth of stories, ideas, and practical advice highly relevant to all executives engaged in a relationship-building effort.

Recommended Reads

Newell, Frederick. *The New Rules of Marketing: How to Use One-To-One Relationship Marketing to Be the Leader in Your Industry* (Irwin Professional Pub., 1997).

This book contains practical ideas about managing and acting on customer information. Newell offers an excellent explanation of why and how to create a customer-focused marketing system that is valued by the entire company.

Novak, Thomas P., Donna L. Hoffman, and Y. F. Yung. "Modeling the Structure of the Flow Experience Among Web Users."

This is a detailed abstract submitted to the INFORMS marketing Science and the Internet Mini-Conference at MIT, March 1998. The authors argue that companies should develop Web experiences that are "seamless" and "intrinsically enjoyable" if they hope for success in the new medium. Donna Hoffman and Thomas Novak, who are directors of an ongoing Web-marketing study at Vanderbilt University called Project 2000, refer to this notion of seamless navigation as "flow." They discuss in this paper models and constructs that promise to help firms understand how to interact more effectively with customers online.

Payne, Adrian, Martin Christopher, Moira Clark, and Helen Peck. *Relationship Marketing for Competitive Advantage* (Butterworth-Heinemann, 1995).

This is a solid primer on the power and potential of relationship marketing. The authors offer an integrated approach for looking at such issues as customer retention, employee satisfaction, supplier relations, and management of service quality.

Peters, Tom. *The Circle of Innovation: You Can't Shrink Your Way to Greatness* (Knopf, 1997).

Peters delivers yet another perceptive look at the trends that are shaping the business world, urging companies to champion "perceptual innovation." Peters understands that companies must innovate—not downsize or consolidate—if they hope to thrive in today's chaotic and unforgiving markets.

Pine II, B. Joseph, Don Peppers, and Martha Rogers, Ph.D. "Do You Want to Keep Your Customers Forever?" *Harvard Business Review,* March/April 1995, pp. 103–114.

This classic article introduces the notion of a Learning Relationship for the first time as well as the concept of a Learning Broker. With case studies on Andersen Windows, Individual Inc., and Peapod, it explains the intimate link between interaction, learning, and mass customization.

Sheth, Jagdish N., and A. Parvatiyar. *Relationship Marketing: Theory, Methods and Applications* (Emory University, 1994).
Excellent overview of the challenges and opportunities facing companies as they engage in relationship-marketing efforts. This book is solidly grounded in academic research and theory.

Taylor, Jim, Watts Wacker, and Howard Means. *The 500-Year Delta: What Happens After What Comes Next* (HarperCollins Publishers, 1997).
The authors provide a sweeping view of the disruptive societal and economic changes they think will occur in the coming years. Among other things, they predict the collapse of "producer-controlled consumer markets" and the emergence of a new "Age of Possibility."

Wayland, Robert E., and Paul Michael Cole. *Customer Connections: New Strategies for Growth* (Harvard Business School Press, 1997).
The authors propose a comprehensive system for developing customer relationships in order to strengthen company profitability and growth. One of the most interesting aspects of this book is its discussion of "customer economics."

Wiersema, Fred. *Customer Intimacy: Pick Your Partners, Shape Your Culture, Win Together* (Knowledge Exchange, 1996).
With powerful examples such as Airborne Express, Nike, and Staples, Wiersema discusses the strategies and techniques that have been used to build lasting customer relationships. The book shows you how to provide complete solutions to customers' needs, create a partnering rather than vendor relationship, and differentiate your customers.

Activity 1A

Overview Issues for Your Transition Team to Discuss

Target Completion Date: _____

1. Elevator Speech:* If your boss asked you to describe the importance of transitioning to a 1to1 strategy, what would you say?

_____

_____

_____

2. What are the most serious problems and weaknesses in your industry and organization that a 1to1 initiative could address?

_____

_____

_____

3. What attracted you to the concept of building a 1to1 enterprise?

_____

_____

_____

4. What are some of the most significant hurdles that stand in the way of implementing 1to1 strategies at your organization? (Use all the paper you need, but don't be intimidated by your list; we'll help you to overcome those hurdles throughout this *Fieldbook.*)

_____

_____

_____

*An Elevator Speech is a speech that lasts no longer than about thirty seconds, the amount of time you might have a "captive audience" in an elevator. The idea is to be as concise and compelling as possible so you can make your point before the elevator doors open.

5. Project yourself five years into your organization's future as a 1to1 enterprise. If you were a customer, how should your perception of the company have changed? In other words, what do you want your organization to look like to a customer in five years?

_____

_____

_____

Ten Ways to Think About 1to1

Target Completion Date: _____

Number	Exercise
1	■ Identify four reasons to move your company toward 1to1 marketing
2	■ Name the leading direct competitors to your firm that are implementing 1to1 marketing practices ■ Identify the practices you know of
3	■ Identify the three best 1to1 marketers who affect you as a business buyer and two that affect you most as a general consumer ■ Name two activities undertaken by each that have gotten your attention
4	■ What are the biggest obstacles to 1to1 your company is likely to encounter based on what you know so far? ■ Identify the leader in your company who will help you overcome these obstacles ■ Involve him or her in the process from the beginning
5	■ What are the biggest sources of customer dissatisfaction or complaints about your company? ■ Your industry? ■ Put an asterisk next to those you think can benefit from 1to1 programs
6	■ When your customers speak positively about your company, what do they most often cite? ■ Which of these items reflects 1to1 practice as you know it?

7	■ Think about a local retailer you use: a dry cleaner, independent pharmacy, or local garage. Sketch out several ways any one of them might use 1to1 tactics, based on what you know right now, to get more business from you
8	■ Think about your favorite charity. How might it use 1to1 practices to get you more involved or to encourage you to donate contributions more frequently?
9	■ Consider the ways a commodity business, such as a large gas station, might use 1to1 relationships to grow its business with you
10	■ Which area or function at your company is weakest where customer relationships are concerned? ■ What could your company do most easily to strengthen this area?

Chapter Two

Quick Start

HOW TO GET IMMEDIATE RESULTS WITH
ONE-TO-ONE MARKETING

The basic principles behind one-to-one marketing competition might sound simple and, in the age of interactivity and mass customization, perhaps inevitable. Even so, there are numerous reasons you might consider putting off the effort to launch a 1to1 marketing program in the first place:

- Information technology plays a critical role. Customer database capabilities, one system talking to another, tracking individual customer interactivity—these requirements place the task squarely in the IT department's queue, where all the other projects are already piled up.
- Capital investment is often needed, and only certain of the most senior executives even get to wait on that line. Sales and marketing managers are seldom seen at the treasurer's door. Same with support and customer service.
- Organizational conflicts will obstruct your progress. It's easy to assign responsibility for a product, but who takes responsibility for

growing a customer across different business units at your enterprise? Which business unit "owns" the customer anyway?

- People are already too busy with their day jobs to take on another assignment. Whether it is the micromanagement of quarterly sales quotas, or the company-wide drive for "top box" quality or satisfaction scores, everyone at your company is already 110 percent employed, and squeezing another something onto the plate is very hard.

- Cultural change of the first order is required. Changing the attitudes and moment-to-moment behavior of airline flight attendants, retail clerks, or call center reps is not going to be easy, not to mention salespeople, marketing managers, or service-delivery specialists.

- You've had it with change already. Everybody at your company is up to here with change. Your firm has done all the management fads, and now skepticism rules.

The fact is that 1to1 marketing competition is so different from traditional, product-based competition that in our experience many business executives dismiss it as simply unattainable for their own company. They look at these obstacles and think the whole task is beyond the capability of their firm. We see it over and over again. An organization can become paralyzed just by thinking about the magnitude of the change it faces by choosing this route.

But the mere fact that you won't turn your company into a full-fledged 1to1 enterprise overnight doesn't mean there aren't very substantial benefits to be derived from initiating the process. We've seen many companies realize a quick payoff through a series of short-term improvements in the way they do business. Sometimes the payoff comes in the form of reduced costs, sometimes it comes in added revenue, sometimes just in a better reputation for customer service, but in every case the benefits come simply from *beginning* to reorient the firm toward 1to1 relationships with individual customers.

So before taking you any further in the *Fieldbook* we thought we would outline some ideas for doing a "Quick Start."

Your immediate goal should be to *fund* your effort, and you can do this by showing a payoff that exceeds your initiative's short-term implementation cost, while still returning long-term benefits.

The first step is to agree on what the actual cash benefits are. By what criteria will you judge your effort to be a success? The most fundamental long-term benefit of 1to1 marketing is that it will increase the overall value of your customer base. Assuming we're talking short term, however, and that you probably don't yet have the capability to measure the value of your overall customer base anyway, what are the short-term metrics by which we could judge our initiative to be a success or failure? There are several:

1. Increased cross-selling. If you can just track a few of the transactions coming through your business, you can compare the amount of added benefit you're getting from cross-selling and "up selling." This ought to result in higher unit margins, as well, provided you're tracking this metric on a per-customer basis.

2. Reduced processing or transaction costs. One-to-one marketing is a discipline that's basically oriented toward making it more and more convenient for a customer to buy. This has the added benefit, in many situations, of reducing your own processing costs, and a lot of times you can track this cost reduction more easily than you can quantify the value of increased customer loyalty.

3. Reduced customer attrition. One of the primary benefits of 1to1 marketing is that it will generate more loyalty among customers. So measure your customer defection rate, track it, and figure out how to reduce it.

4. Faster cycle times for processing purchases and other transactions. Convenience for the customer translates directly into faster time for you. If a customer has to specify fewer things this time around, then you can process the transaction faster. So measure it.

5. Higher customer satisfaction and other "soft" ratings. Granted, you can't eat customer satisfaction. But if you do your job right,

your customers will be happier with the service you're delivering. And if your management is at all oriented toward increasing customer satisfaction levels, you can probably show quick results with a 1to1 program.

If you stick to just these five metrics alone and design a few tracking mechanisms to gauge your progress, then you can put short-term programs into place that will provide measurable results. The first three items on this list of five are immediately measurable in terms of cash benefit to the enterprise, and that's how they should be measured, if at all possible. The last two items represent non-cash benefits. Faster cycle times can sometimes be converted to a cash equivalent, but customer satisfaction scores are not so easily converted, even though many firms go to great lengths to track them.

Regardless of how the dollars arrive on your doorstep, however, dollars are what really matter. And short-term benefits from applying 1to1 marketing principles are not at all hard to achieve. Consider these two simple examples:

- A well-known business-to-business catalogue merchant buys a high-speed laser printer and a modest database tool to drive individualized thank-you notes and customer-satisfaction correspondence, adding two employees to run the system. It covers its all-in costs simply by putting a P.S. on every letter making a special, discounted up-sell offer for its best customers. Result: It got its customer-database system "free."
- A major ski resort wants to make the Voice Response Unit (VRU) in its call center more customer-friendly and upbeat. It overhauls the VRU, rebuilds the "branching" to get customers the information they want more quickly, and saves forty-five seconds per phone call. Multiplied by more than half a million calls per year, the company saves six thousand hours in long-distance time, which more than pays for the $35,000 switch upgrade in the first year.

It is, in fact, possible to begin the journey toward becoming a 1to1 enterprise without having to adopt a comprehensive, all-encompassing vision. In Activity 2A we've listed dozens of Quick Start "thought starters," and categorized them according to which of the four implementation steps they support. Some of these suggestions could probably work for your business today, and others will stimulate your own thoughts. So why wait?

Activity 2A

Quick Start "Thought Starters"

Target Completion Date: _____

Activity	Steps to Consider
Identify	
Collect and input more customer names into the existing database	■ Use an outside service for scanning or data entry ■ Swap names with a noncompetitive firm in your industry or area
Collect additional information about your customers	■ Use drip-irrigation dialogue: Ask them one or two questions every time you are in touch with them
Verify and update customer data and delete departed individuals	■ Have a "spring cleaning" day for the customer-information files ■ Run your database through National Change of Address (NCOA) file
Differentiate	
Identify your organization's top customers	■ Take your best guess at the top 5% of your customers using last year's sales or other simple, readily available data
Determine customers who cost your organization money	■ Look for some simple rules to isolate the bottom 20% of your customers and reduce the mail you currently send them by at least half

Select several prospect companies you really want to do business with next year	■ Get them in your database with at least three names per company
Find the customers who have complained about your product or service more than once in the last year	■ Baby-sit their orders. Call them and check up on your progress. Get a product or quality person in touch with them ASAP
Look for last year's large customers who have ordered half as much or less this year	■ Go visit them now, before your competition does
Find customers who buy only one or two products from your firm, but buy a lot from other firms	■ Make them an offer they can't refuse to try several more items from you
Divide all customers into As, Bs and Cs	■ Decrease activities and/or marketing spending for the Cs and increase for the As

Interact

Call the top three people at each of your top 5% of corporate customers	■ Say hello and see how it's going. Don't sell—just talk and make sure they are happy
Call your company. Ask questions. See how hard it is to get through and get answers	■ Test eight to ten different scenarios as a "mystery shopper." Record the calls and critique them
Call your competitors	■ Repeat the above activity
Use incoming calls as selling opportunities	■ Offer specials, closeouts, and trial offers to generate profits
Time the voice-response unit at your customer-information center	■ Determine ways to make the recordings friendlier, more helpful, and to get customers through the system faster
Follow the interaction paper trail through your organization	■ Seek to eliminate steps, reduce cycle times to speed up your response to customers

Initiate more dialogue with valuable customers	■ Print personalized messages on invoices, statements, and envelopes ■ Have letters signed by individual sales representatives, not senior management ■ Start a regular program of having the right people in your organization call the right customer executives ■ Call all the customers your company has lost in the last two years and give them a reason to return
Use technology to make doing business with your company easier	■ Gather customer e-mail addresses and follow up with them ■ Offer nonpostal mail alternatives for all kinds of communication ■ Consider fax-back and fax-broadcast systems as first steps ■ Find ways to scan customer information into the database
Improve complaint handling	■ Plot how many complaints you receive each day, and work to improve the ratio of complaints handled on the first call

Customize

Customize the paperwork to save your customers time and your company money	■ Use regional versions of catalogues ■ Don't send the entire catalogue to customers who don't want it
Personalize your direct mail	■ Use customer information to individualize offers ■ Keep the mailings simple
Fill out forms for your customers	■ Use existing laser equipment, which saves time and makes you look smarter
Ask customers how, and how often, they want to hear from you	■ Use fax, e-mail, postal mail, or in-person visits as the customer specifies
Find out what your customers want	■ Invite small groups of customers to focus groups or discussion meetings ■ Solicit their feedback on your products, policies, and procedures

Ask your top ten customers what you can do differently to improve your product or service	■ Do what they suggest ■ Follow up and do it again
Involve top management in customer relations	■ Give them lists of questions to ask based on the individual customer's history

Activity 2B

Quick Start Brainstorming Session

Target Completion Date: _____

Objective:

The objective of this activity is to agree upon several 1to1 programs or activities to implement immediately.

Step 1: Assemble a team of bright people—including the people who are already on your 1to1 project team, or will soon be assigned to it.

Step 2: As a group, spend no more than fifteen minutes reviewing the ideas listed in Activity 2A. Identify those that could be applied easily to your organization.

Step 3: Concentrating first on "Identify," and then on each additional implementation step, one step at a time, ask each team member to spend five minutes writing down at least three *more* Quick Start ideas.

Step 4: At the end of this five-minute "thinking" period for each step, each person gets fifteen seconds to describe one idea at a time. Go all the way around the room, taking turns one idea at a time until all ideas have been shared. Ideas that are prompted by other ideas can also be shared. During this drill, list the ideas one at a time on a flip chart organized like the example on the following page. Be sure to consolidate or eliminate duplicate ideas as you go.

Step 5: Rate the ideas by writing three different scores, from 0 to 3, in the right margins. Scores should be based on the degree to which each idea
  (a) could be made to work today,
  (b) would be noticed by customers, and
  (c) would increase profitability.

A score of 0 means no chance, and a score of 3 means absolutely great. Cross off any ideas that lose support after discussion.

Step 6: Multiply the scores together and place the resulting composite score in the column on the far right. The top-scoring ideas are the ones most appropriate to implement first.

Activity 2C

1to1 Evaluation Flip Chart Sample

Identify	A	B	C	Total Score
1.				
2.				
3.				
4.				
5.				
6.				
7.				
8.				
9.				
10.				

Legend

A = Can our company make this work today?
B = Will our customers notice if we do?
C = If we do, will it make us more money?

Design

Chapter Three

Identify Your Customers

HOW TO OBTAIN MORE INDIVIDUAL INFORMATION
ABOUT A GREATER NUMBER OF YOUR CUSTOMERS

| *Identify* | Differentiate | Interact | Customize |

*IMPLEMENTATION STEP 1: Create a system that enables you to
identify customers as individuals each time
you come in contact with them.*

The first stage of a one-to-one initiative is simply identifying as many customers as possible. Until your business knows and remembers the identities of at least some portion of your individual customers, launching any kind of program that depends on treating different customers differently will be impossible. You don't have to know any individual customers to discover a better product feature desired by *most* of your customers or to come up with a better method for handling inquiries or complaints. You can still improve your overall service, or you can upgrade your product quality. But service and product improvements like these are not examples of 1to1 marketing, which involves treating different customers differently, one customer at a time. A 1to1 enterprise cannot be built without knowing the actual identities of at least some customers—the more valuable ones—individually.

"Customer identifying information" is any information you can use to separate one particular customer from another, track your transactions and interactions with the customer over time, or get in touch with the customer individually. Name, rank, serial number. Other examples include: postal address, phone number, e-mail address, position description or title, account number. This is the first and primary building block of a 1to1 marketing program.

So ask yourself these questions:

- How many customers does your firm actually *know*, individually?
- Do you have a customer database with identifying information on all your customers, or on any portion of them?
- How current and accurate is that database?
- How much information about each customer does it contain?
- Does each different business unit within your company have its own customer database?
- Are there other sources of customer-identifying information?
- Are there any simple ways to increase the amount of customer data available to your firm?

These are some of the issues we'll be considering in this chapter.

Of course, the first question is how to define the customer. Different definitions of "customer" will create different types of problems for the 1to1 enterprise and call for different strategies. Is your customer simply the next step down in your distribution channel? Or is your customer better defined as the end user of your product?

The major business within Owens Corning is the manufacture and distribution of building-materials systems through a variety of channels. The company's end user might be a small building contractor or a large construction firm, and it could reach these end users through wholesale distributors, chain retailers, or several independent dealer formats. The company has traditionally defined its customer as the "first buyer" reseller and not the end user. This has implications for its relationship-marketing strategy. The channel customers are highly skewed in their values, with large consolidating channel members accounting for an increasing first-buyer share of the business. Down the channel, however, among residential-construction customers, there is much more fragmentation, with some 250,000 licensed residential builders in the United States, and another 300,000 or so specialty subcontractors. In addition, there are literally millions of other types of agencies and influencers in the building process, ranging from architects to realtors.

The point is, for a firm such as Owens Corning (or any other business with a reasonably complex set of distribution channels), how the customer is defined can dramatically affect the types of customer-relationship programs that are most effective. In Chapter Ten we'll explore in more detail the implications of treating channel members as customers.

If the end users for the products or services you sell are other companies, rather than consumers, then the issue of identifying your customers becomes even more complex. Is the company itself your customer? Or is it the purchasing agent within that company? Or is your real customer the end user of the product, within the company you're selling to? (Correct answer: "All of the above.") The issue of identifying customers in a business-to-business situation is different enough from identifying consumers as customers that we will consider business-to-business and consumer-marketing situations separately.

Identifying Customers in a Consumer Marketing Business

In some types of consumer marketing businesses, customer identities are obtained during the natural course of doing business. If you're in the banking or the telephone business, or if you run an accounting service or a doctor's office or a health maintenance organization, then part of your business involves obtaining customer identifying information and tracking customers individually.

Even in other consumer businesses there are usually a few companies that go direct, circumventing the channels used to distribute products or services by many of their competitors. Dell Computer and Gateway sell personal-computer equipment directly to consumers via the Internet, the phone, and the mail, even though the majority of PC manufacturers sell through retailers and resellers. USAA sells insurance directly to consumers, but most other insurance vendors distribute their products through insurance agencies. Most clothing is purchased in retail stores, but L. L. Bean, Lands' End, and various others do a very healthy business by going direct to consumers.

How much customer-identifying information does your firm already have? Before setting up programs and promotions to identify your customers, it would be wise to figure out how many customer identities you already know, and how you know them.

You should follow a three-step process:

Step 1   *Take an inventory of all customer data already available in an electronic format.* Before doing anything else, you should find all the customer-identifying information at your firm that is immediately accessible at present. Look in the customer database, of course, if you have one and you're reasonably comfortable you understand its scope and limitations. But customer information gets turned over in many different programs, and as a result it can be found in a variety of other places. Perhaps you have a Web site that allows customers and prospects to register their names. Or you have a customer-service call center that collects customer identities as a routine part of handling complaints and service inquiries. You might have credit card information, either from a company-branded card or other purchase records.

Step 2   *Locate customer-identifying information that is currently "on file" but not electronically compiled.* You need to look for repositories of customer information that might not yet be in a database, or might be in a database not generally considered useful for marketing purposes—an invoicing system, perhaps, or a warranty-service or complaint-handling system. Various departments and divisions may have their own "shoeboxes" of names. Or different divisions at your enterprise might each have their own customer files, but no one's ever identified the unduplicated individual customers for the whole enterprise.

Step 3   *Devise strategies for collecting more information.* Once you've gathered all the information that's already "lying around" at your firm, you may need to devise strategies or programs for capturing more customer information on a cost-efficient and routine basis. There are third-party database firms that sell individual customer information (Metromail Corporation, for instance, or R. L. Polk in the automotive category, Carol Wright in packaged goods, or Dun and Bradstreet in business-to-business), and you may be able to sort their data in such a way as to identify your own customers. Maybe collecting and documenting more customer identities is an activity your customer-contact people could undertake, after some training. Or perhaps you'll decide to launch a contest, a frequency marketing promotion, or some other program, to turn over more names. But whatever mechanism you use to identify customers, there will be an expense involved. If you are selling to consumers, it probably won't be economical to try to identify *every* customer. Instead, you'll want to concentrate on identifying those customers who are more valuable to the firm (more about customer-valuation methods in the next chapter).

Consider, for instance, the situation of a retailer. If you are a traditional retailer, customers walk in and out of your stores every day without identifying themselves. They come in, they browse your shelves, converse with your salespeople, try on clothes or examine products, and then they buy things. You take their money, not their names. You and your best salespeople will tend to recognize very good customers and accord them extra courtesies, but because there is no identifying information tied to each customer transaction, your ability to treat even these customers differently is limited by your salespeople's individual skills and personalities.

Then again, you could design a different business model. You could decide that remembering customers individually is important enough that you need to install a system for tracking these identities. That is exactly what Bill and Jack Mitchell have done for their Mitchells of Westport clothing store business in Westport, Connecticut, and for its sister store, Richards of Greenwich. The process begins with identifying each customer who comes into their store, a task made easier because each customer is assigned a personal salesperson.

Using an IBM AS/400 computer database linked directly to the store's cashier stations, Mitchells tracks every item any customer buys and records each customer's individual preferences. (Every time you walk in, your sales assistant will discreetly manage to slip away for a second to look up your record and refresh his or her memory.) That's why your salesperson will be able to find just the right skirt to match your blouse, even four months after you bought the blouse.

Although Mitchells tends to avoid sales and discounting, most customers consider the value-added services, specifically the customized service, to be worth it. Go there regularly and within two years or so everything in your closet will match everything else. Mitchells will know your taste, work environment, travel habits, and budget, even if you stay away from the designer shelves. To make the experience even more special, Mitchells sends out personalized letters thanking customers for their business, offering special discounts on upcoming sales, and even inviting their MVCs (Most Valuable Customers) to designer clothing shows and cocktail parties.

It might take you about thirty minutes to buy two suits, three shirts, and four ties at Mitchells, but it could easily take six months to buy the same elsewhere. The company's relationship-building effort increases the share of each customer's shopping it acquires, while sustaining higher profit margins than most competitors can generate.

Zane's Cycles in Branford, Connecticut, has managed to build phenomenally loyal relationships with its customers, relying heavily on their referrals to keep new customers walking in the door. Zane's offers bike purchasers a free lifetime service warranty covering all repairs. Forever. The store even gives away items that cost less than a dollar, knowing that small touches get noticed and talked about.

Indigo, a popular restaurant in Atlanta, doesn't take reservations—except for its most frequent and loyal customers, who are given an unlisted phone number they can call to reserve their table.

But these are examples of relatively compact retail establishments, with one or two principal store locations, upscale products, and an educated sales staff easily trained to recognize most of their regular customers on sight. What about a larger, multi-outlet retail chain, selling lower-priced products with less input from on-site salespeople? Sometimes offering customers the convenience or status of a store-branded credit card will do the trick, but credit is so easy to obtain these days that most customers will decline without some incentive. Another method, especially popular in Europe, is the card-driven frequency marketing plan, rewarding your customers with points or discounts so that they will identify themselves at the cashier's station every time they come to the store. Although these are not really the "loyalty" programs they claim to be, they do successfully provide incentives to customers to give their identity at every contact.

Some current examples of this type of program:

- Groupe Casino, the $14.5 billion French chain of "hypermarkets," supermarkets, convenience stores, and cafeterias, launched a card-driven frequency marketing program for its supermarkets, called Casino, that accumulated more individual customer identities in six months than its store-branded credit card for its hypermarkets, called Géant, had accumulated in the previous six years.
- Albert Heijn, the Dutch retailer, launched a card-based program that was so popular it signed up more than two million customers within the first few weeks.
- Sainsbury and Tesco, two UK grocery retailers, have their own frequency marketing programs. In each case, a customer applies for the program, completes a brief questionnaire with identifying information, and then receives a membership card. By producing this card when checking out after each visit to the store, customers earn points entitling them to discounts, extra services, special offers.

- Dallas/Fort Worth McDonald's franchisees recently introduced a "McBreak Card" as a loyalty program in 212 of their restaurants. Customers earn redeemable points for menu items. This is a thermal card, rather than a magnetic-stripe card, so it is not only less expensive, but thinner and more convenient for the customer to carry. But the thermal technology is still capable of storing rudimentary transaction information on the card itself, in essence turning the card into a portable database. Each day the franchisees send their McBreak Card data via modem to a centralized database at McDonald's marketing department.

FREQUENCY MARKETING PROGRAMS

Frequent shopper programs, frequent flyer programs, and many other kinds of frequency marketing programs are being launched all around the world in order to strengthen ties with individual customers. But are these programs actually 1to1 marketing programs? Or are they simply promotional tactics to purchase customer "loyalty"? The answer to that question depends on the nature of the program.

A frequency marketing program should be thought of as a tactic for 1to1 marketing, but not as a strategy in itself. It is a tactic designed to help the marketer gather information from customers—customers whose identities the marketer might not otherwise have or whose transactions the marketer might not be able to link together. People come into a grocery store or a bookstore or a restaurant all the time without leaving their names or giving the business's proprietor a chance to identify them individually.

In many retail businesses the marketer has no means for determining that a customer coming in today is the same customer who came in yesterday or the day before buying something else. Therefore, the key objective of a frequency marketing program is encouraging your customers to identify themselves in return for points, mileage, cash prizes, and so on. Such customer information is essential to 1to1 relationship building.

It is the information about an individual customer's purchases—demonstrating both a customer's needs and value to the corporation—that allows the enterprise to tailor its behavior or to customize its product or service. The greater the level of customization, the more loyal customers will become.

In many firms, however, a frequency marketing program itself is thought of as the primary loyalty-generating mechanism. That is, the program is put in place with an eye toward buying a customer's loyalty by rewarding him or her for their patronage. Often this will work—at least in the short term. But in the long term it is a self-defeating tactic. If the frequency program is successful, it will be matched by competitors who will offer the same or similar rewards for similar volumes of purchases or types of behavior. The result? Frequency-marketing battles among competitors where the exchange of rewards simply becomes a sophisticated form of price competition—one customer at a time.

Instead, you'll want to create mechanisms for changing your behavior based on an individual customer's purchases. This is the best way to get the most out of a frequency marketing program, while rewarding customers for their loyalty and encouraging them to identify themselves. So, for example, a grocery store whose customers use a frequent buyer card to register their purchases every time they come into the store could compile over time a fairly good record of the grocery items in each individual customer's household. This record could be used to save the customer a considerable amount of time—assuming the store could change its behavior to match each individual customer's shopping needs.

Delivering products directly to the customer's house is one way to do so. Automatically replenishing a customer's regularly consumed products is another benefit. Creating an electronic record of the customer's shopping list and making it available for regular updates is yet another convenience.

Some of the best examples of customization to benefit an individual customer in the grocery-shopping domain are Peapod, Streamline, or NetGrocer. There are many grocery-delivery services that now allow customers to maintain and update their lists on a regular basis, thereby continuously improving the customer's grocery-shopping experience. But there's no fundamental reason groceries must be delivered to the home in order to make this possible. A grocery store could simply offer to configure a customer's groceries. If you were on your way into the grocery store, you could ask the grocery to configure your list for this week. You then make additions or changes to the list.

If you do decide to launch a frequency marketing program to identify your customers, think of the program as a form of "explicit bargain" with each individual customer. Remember that the purpose of the program is to get your customers to identify themselves, every time they deal with you.

In order to ensure that your frequency marketing program accomplishes this critical objective, here are some key issues to consider:

1. A frequency marketing program might be right for your business if you don't already know the names or identities of your customers, or if you have no easy way to link their transactions over time. In each of these cases you set up a frequency marketing program for the primary purpose of providing a reward to customers for identifying themselves every time they come into your store, or every time they purchase something from you.
2. Make it as simple as possible for the customer. If it is at all feasible, avoid the use of cards and other certificates that customers might have to carry around with them. Try to come up with a mechanism that allows you to identify the customer and call up his records at the cashier sta-

tion. Name and address are sufficient in some cases, or name and phone number, or just the phone number. The key is to lessen or eliminate the burden of self-identification.

3. Make it an automated process. Create an electronic link, if at all possible, between the actual cashier's station and the frequency program itself. Such an arrangement should eliminate manual paperwork and streamline the identification process.

4. When you put together the rules defining eligibility for the frequency marketing program, be sure that these rules impose some form of self-qualification mechanism on the overall program. That is, you don't want disloyal customers to find it beneficial to join the frequency marketing program. So, whatever incentive is offered, you should ensure that this incentive pays off only if a customer behaves in some fashion that reflects a relatively high value to you.

5. Promote the program with all customers. Ensure that everyone who comes into the store or comes into contact with any part of your enterprise is informed about the program and has a chance to participate.

6. Before launching the frequency marketing program, you must define how you will use customer information to change your behavior toward individual customers. You must always strive to enhance the customer's sense of convenience and acquired value.

It's possible that your customer-contact people will need to be trained to collect and document information about individual customers. Patrick J. Kennedy is the CEO of La Mansion del Rio, an independent luxury hotel in San Antonio, and ex-chairman of Preferred Hotels and Resorts Worldwide, of which La Mansion is a member. The Preferred Hotels brand name is attached to the pooled marketing efforts of an association of independently operated and marketed luxury hotels around the world, from The Charles Hotel in Boston, to the Grand Regency Hotel in Nairobi, Kenya. A few years ago, after being elected chairman of Preferred, Kennedy decided to focus the association's efforts on building a customer database of the names, preferences, and individual stay information on the guests of its member hotels. Preferred Hotels was founded thirty years ago to allow independent hotels to share customers among themselves, so Kennedy says a customer database should actually be the physical manifestation of that founding vision. Kennedy believes that a robust customer database would give Preferred Hotels an unbeatable strategic advantage.

The reason a hotel company like Preferred would want to have information such as this should be obvious. First, having any database of guests at all would allow each hotel in the group to identify its repeat guests. This might sound simple, but it is not easy for a hotel to collect guest identities using the production-oriented property-management computer systems that most hotels are limited to. If a hotel could build its occupancy from repeat guests by just a few percentage points, this would be more than enough to justify the cost of the system. Kennedy says this was the single most important objective of the initiative—to identify repeat guests. But going beyond that, if you know a guest's individual tastes and preferences, then you can treat different guests differently, based on how *each* guest *wants* to be treated. By keeping track of preferences, you can make it easier for the guest to check in, receive that extra down pillow that she likes, or obtain information about local golfing events that may be of particular interest.

Kennedy knew, however, that putting a database in place and using it was not going to be easy. It wasn't something that could just be pasted onto each hotel's current operating procedures. In fact, he says:

> We realized that there would be three parts to the process. The first part was collecting the information. Second, we had to implement the actual infrastructure for feeding, maintaining, and using the database. And third, we had to figure out how to communicate with guests and build our dialogue with each. In terms of the information collection process, we get in these meetings and ask ourselves, Where are all the contact points in the daily operation of a hotel where it is logical to collect information about guests? We identified those contact points, and we identified the people most likely to be involved. This was eye-opening for us. Even though I've been in the business a long time, I didn't realize how many opportunities we were missing.

Ultimately, only twenty Preferred Hotels elected to install the proprietary customer database system. So Kennedy bought the software and launched his own firm, Guest Information Network, Inc. ("Guestnet"), with the goal of providing global hotel clients with the ability to capture and access guest-specific information.

To facilitate the collection of information about individual guests and their preferences, Kennedy recommends that his clients use a system that includes, among other things, "guest preference cards," carried by every customer-contact person at the hotel. That way, whenever a guest expresses a wish, enters a complaint, or makes a suggestion, the hotel employee involved needs only to write this information on a preference card and leave the card for entering into the database at the end of his shift.

So why go to this trouble? Why create a system like this at all? Kennedy can summarize the benefit of identifying and remembering customers in a heartbeat:

> We're giving the hotel the tools and the opportunity to build guest loyalty. And we know there are a number of things that are important to building loyalty—things other than the cost of a room. One of the key elements of building loyalty among repeat guests is simply remembering things from the guest's previous stay—things that are important to him, that will enable him to enjoy his stay more the next time.

On the other hand, maybe you're not so fortunate as to have access to your customers on a face-to-face basis. Perhaps your primary consumer-sales channel is through other companies' retail outlets. A consumer packaged goods ("CPG") company, for instance, will run advertising to increase demand for its products among consumers, but the consumers themselves buy the products at retail grocery stores or drugstores and never come into contact with the company directly. Not only are these consumers' identities unknown to the CPG company, but the vast majority of them are unknown to the retailers who carry its products as well.

Of course, one strategy for the CPG firm, or for any other firm that sells to consumers through a retail channel, would be to create 1to1 relationships with the channel members themselves. But sooner or later, as technology propels all companies into a more and more interactive and information-rich business environment, you'll want to identify a greater proportion of your end users in order to cement your interactive relationships with them.

If you work at a CPG firm, it probably won't be difficult to put your hands on the customer-identifying information you already have, because chances are you won't have much. Instead, you're going to need to concentrate on generating more direct consumer contacts, in ways that don't threaten your existing retail-channel partners. Some programs that already exist, or that you may want to consider launching, include:

- Product Web sites and registrations
- Recipes and cooking clubs for food-product consumers
- Cleaning tips for soap and cleanser consumers
- Contests and sweepstakes
- Sampling programs around new product launches
- Kids' clubs
- Toll-free product-information and comment centers
- Coupon redemptions
- Automatic replenishment programs

In most multi-product companies, the primary responsibility for marketing and/or selling resides in different divisions, or with different product managers or brand groups. Often, different marketing organizations within such a firm sell to overlapping customer bases. If this is your company, then one easy way to collect more customer-identifying information is simply to coordinate the efforts of these different divisions and compare notes. "We'll show you ours if you'll show us yours."

Other than the expected territorial and political resistance, the chief obstacle to collecting information from other divisions will probably be that these different divisions will have developed their own unique and incompatible formats for collecting and storing the information about their customers. One division will identify households, while another will identify consumers within households. Or one division will collect names and phone numbers, while another will collect names and postal addresses.

It isn't necessary to have a universal customer-identity format initially, although the sooner you can agree on one the better off you'll be. What is important, however, is that you don't rush off to launch an additional customer-identifying program without first understanding exactly how the information to be collected will be integrated into your company's existing databases.

It also helps if someone at the corporate level shows an interest in unifying the disparate customer databases and formats, taking an overall enterprise point of view. Ford Motor Company consists of several different divisions, selling under different brand names, including not only Lincoln-Mercury but Jaguar and Mazda. Dave Ropes, Ford's first director of corporate advertising and integrated marketing, was hired at the corporate level to supervise the consolidation of the company's overall customer-oriented marketing efforts. The first step in "rationalizing" these efforts was simply to combine the individual customer information that is found in the firm's different and unrelated databases. According to Ropes,

> We have consolidated a majority of our individual division and company databases into one single, company-wide database of roughly thirty-five million owners and lessees of our automobiles. The database right now is limited strictly to owner and leaseholder information; it is not a prospect database. We've already run some early tests just on delivering value-added incentives to current owners of our product to upgrade them in their current car line, and the returns have been very appealing. One example of such a value-added incentive might be, if you currently own an Explorer in model years '92 through '97, we could offer you an incentive to buy a 1998 model, for instance. But soon we will be moving our owners from one label to another, within Ford Motor, and the real payoff is increasing our share of customer, over a customer's entire car-owning lifetime.

If you sell to business customers, the businesses you sell to may identify themselves differently in different countries, or when buying different products. They may do this because they are themselves highly decentralized, or they might do it specifically so that they can gain an advantage on their vendors. Either way, your firm needs to know if the customer buying from Division A in Country 1 is the same customer buying from Division B in Country 2.

At 3M a major initiative to become a more customer-centered, 1to1 enterprise is generating questions along exactly these lines. As a multi-division, global enterprise, 3M sells a wide range of products to many different types of customers. And according to Bruce Hamilton, in charge of customer focused marketing at 3M:

> We're creating new databases to allow us to get a handle on who our major customers are. Beyond that, of course, we want to know how profitable our relationship is with each customer. To be honest, we're probably two or three years away from achieving this goal because of the way we book business today. When we're selling to an IBM subsidiary in Asia that may not identify itself as IBM, we can't track it as an IBM sale. We can't track IBM's purchases even here in the United States if it's buying through a number of different channels, or different distributors. Because of the distribution channels we use today, in many cases these channel partners don't have to identify the ultimate end user, just to sell our product. But we're working hard to do so.

Deciding on a Customer Identifier

How will you "tag" your customers' individual identities? Obviously, knowing a customer's name is not always sufficient. Which Bill Smith is this anyway? And names are prone to typos and inconsistent formats. Is that Bill Smith or William Smith or William D. Smith? Is Grover J. Schmidt the same person as Grover J. Schmitt? Similar problems afflict postal addresses, although when you identify someone by name *and* address it's obviously a much more accurate tag.

And no matter how your own business unit decides to tag its customers, you have to plan for moving this data across different business units at your enterprise, comparing one unit's data to another's as efficiently as possible. Hewlett-Packard, for instance, has set a common data-gathering standard for its customer information, so that every different business unit at this very large enterprise will be gathering customer-identifying data that can eventually be shared with other business units.

Every database, at some level, will need to assign a perfectly unique and reliable account number or identifier to each individual record. Wouldn't it be great if your customers could simply *remember* their account codes off the top of their heads when they call you on the phone or come into your store? This would make account codes the perfect method for telling one customer apart from another. But of course they won't do this.

A car company that uses the Vehicle Identification Number as a customer identifier is only setting itself up for problems, as customers resist going to the trouble of looking up their VINs on their registration cards or insurance policies. And some customers will own more than one vehicle anyway.

If you're running a frequency marketing program, it might make sense to ask your customers to carry membership cards. Try to make it as convenient for the customer as possible, but realize you'll still meet resistance. Unless you're selling a badge product with a good deal of status, your customers won't appreciate having to carry an extra card around just to help you identify them when they come into your store or get you on the phone. Asking customers to carry membership cards will put off some members and, in many instances, depress the benefit of the program.

It's possible you could create a useful or convenient service for your customers to help you identify them individually and track their purchases as a matter of course. Take Mobil's Speedpass program. The Speedpass is a small device that can attach either to your key ring or back window. Each transponder "communicates" to the gasoline pump, getting you on your way faster. When you attach one to your key chain and wave it over the "Speedpass Square" located on the gas pump, or simply pull up with it on your rear window, you're able to pay for gas without using cash or credit cards. Just as a highway toll pass automatically debits your account whenever you drive through, Speedpass will simply charge the credit card of your choice. So, from the customer's standpoint, there's no need to stand at the gas pump while specifying whether to use a credit or debit card, which card to bill, and whether a receipt is desired. There's no waiting for authorization either. The advantage to Mobil is that Speedpass will provide a perfect record of customer identities and transaction histories.

Radio-frequency controlled chips like the ones that power the Speedpass program are worth considering in a variety of settings. Imagine equipping your customer with a credit card that could do at the cashier's station what the Speedpass does for Mobil's customers at the gas pump.

Another technology worth considering is the "smart card"—a credit card with a microchip rather than a magnetic strip. The microchip records information, so that the credit card itself becomes a database, carrying around information about the individual customer from location to location. In Europe, where smart cards are more highly developed and widely used than in the United States, smart-card technology might be the simplest way to create a program that encourages customers to identify themselves.

The Dutch PTT (postal and telephone company) has developed a system of kiosks that will allow users to load their smart cards with money from their bank accounts. From the kiosk (or from a home computer), a customer could review the stadium seats available at an upcoming event, electronically purchase a seat, and update the card to reflect ownership of the ticket. A few weeks later, when the customer shows up at the stadium for the event, the event organizers would recognize the ticket when he swipes the card at the turnstile. Of course, if you combine smart cards with RFI chip technology, you could easily imagine the customer simply walking through the turnstile and having the ticket "read" off his card automatically. (Don't want to carry even *one* card? Stay tuned. In just a few years, stored-value RFI microchips might come preinstalled on your watch).

But let's assume you don't have immediate access to this sort of technology, nor do you want to launch a program requiring your customers to carry membership cards. You still need *some* method for identifying your customers individually when you interact with them. Some possibilities include:

Phone number. People remember their own phone numbers easily. So when they reach a call center, the phone number itself can usually be identified in advance. If a customer is calling from home, the service rep can confirm a customer's identity fairly easily. Call Pizza Hut to get a pizza delivered and they'll ask you for your phone number. When the store enters the number into its database, it can call up your customer record, including the names of people in your household who have ordered pizza in the past and the types of pizza they've ordered.

On the other hand, some customers will resist divulging their phone numbers when you ask them, for fear that you'll just call and annoy them with some type of sales appeal. Moreover, most households have only one phone number for everyone in the family, so using a customer's phone number alone will not be sufficient to identify particular individuals within a household. The reverse is also true: The household with several phone lines and numbers might end up spread out all over your database.

Social Security number. Some firms, believe it or not, collect Social Security numbers from their consumer customers, enabling them to uniquely and positively identify individual people. MCI, for instance, routinely collects customers' SSNs in connection with signing them up for a new account. They decided to use the SSN because it is the most reliable method of tracking a customer from one location to another. The company knows that when a "new" customer signs up for its service in Abilene, it's actually the same customer who "quit" MCI when she moved out of Chicago.

However, as privacy protection becomes a more and more important issue, getting a customer to divulge an SSN can be expected to become more difficult. This is particularly troublesome because, in most situations, it will be your most valuable customers—the ones with the highest disposable incomes, spending the most money—who least want to give you this kind of information.

Combined data. The most widely used form of combined data is simply name and address. This is cumbersome if you need to process transactions rapidly. It assumes that the customer will be interacting with a human operator or a service person with immediate access to the database, allowing a quick "eyeball" verification of the information. But it is customer-friendly, natural, and reliable.

Personal passwords. Another way to allow customers to identify themselves without carrying a card is to let them assign their own user names—something Web sites and online services do today. User names don't have to be reserved for online occasions. You could ask a customer to specify last name and *any* four numbers, or three to seven letters, or an animal name, or whatever. Then the only thing you'd need to worry about is whether a customer would actually be able to remember what he specified. To make that easy, you might suggest the last four digits of a phone number, or the month/day of birth. Or you could provide a membership card anyway, but with the customer's own, made-up account identifier instead of your assigned account code.

Identifying Customers in a Business-to-Business Situation

A business-to-business marketer must still identify customers to become a 1to1 enterprise, and many of the issues are the same. However, there are some important differences that merit additional consideration in the b-to-b category. For instance, when you sell to business customers, who should be on the other side of your relationship? Should it be the purchasing manager, or the executive who signs the purchase order? Should it be the financial vice president who approved the contract? Or should it be the production supervisor who actually uses the product?

The right way to approach a b-to-b situation is to think of each of these constituencies as a part of the customer base. Each is important in its own way, and you should track each of them. With the increasingly sophisticated sales-force automation systems now available, there's no reason you shouldn't be able to do so. You just have to ensure that your sales force agrees (see Chapter Eleven).

The biggest problem for many businesses that sell equipment to other businesses is identifying the product's actual end users. Purchasing managers and contract approvers are easy. Figuring out who, within an enterprise account, actually puts your product to work—who depends on the product in order to do his or her own job—is often considerably more difficult.

Some methods for identifying end users include the following:

- If your product consumes any replenishable supplies—inks, drill bits, recording paper, chemicals—providing a convenient method for reordering these supplies is an obvious service for your end users. You get their identities when they complete the reorder forms or when they call your number or log on to your Web site to reorder.

- If your product is complicated to use, requiring a detailed instruction manual or perhaps different sets of application notes, one way to secure end-user identities is to offer such complicated instructions in a simplified, individually tailored format: "Just complete the questionnaire telling us how you will be using our equipment and we'll send you a shorter, simpler, more specific version of the application notes."

- If your product needs periodic maintenance or calibration, or if it needs regular service for any reason, you can use these occasions to identify end users.

- Consider equipping your machine with Web-enabled connectivity: "Install the machine, connect it to your LAN, and we'll be able to monitor and maintain the equipment for you, remotely."

- Ask for the machine to be "registered" upon installation, by the primary end user. You can accept registrations by phone, mail, or e-mail, but the important thing is to ensure that an end user sees some type of genuine benefit from registering the equipment.

- Include a promotional benefit for the end user. Ship your machines out with offers for catalogues of new equipment or industry best-practices information. Or include a free subscription to a user magazine.

- Build some intelligence into the machine itself that will recognize end users individually and allow them to make more productive use of the equipment.

One Hewlett-Packard division sells a complex microcircuit testing system costing half a million dollars or more. It can take anywhere from several minutes to half an hour for an engineer to adjust all the system's settings, prior to completing a single test. After the test, the engineer returns to his department and the next engineer, from another department, uses the machine. So one innovation HP will be introducing in some of its systems is a "smart" machine that recognizes and remembers individual end users, and their last settings. By providing this convenience, HP can gain access to the identities of these engineers, rather than being limited to contracting officers and purchasing managers.

Another problem unique to the business-to-business marketer is that business customers are less permanent than consumer customers. Their identities change more frequently. A manager might be transferred or promoted to a different area of responsibility, or she might leave the company altogether. This requires you to pay particular attention to the currency of information within a b-to-b customer database. The sales force must constantly reconfirm customer identities and account information.

There are many other things a sales force will want to learn from and confirm with its customers, however. So, with any reasonable level of interaction, it shouldn't be all that difficult to keep a customer database current, provided you sell direct. One good rule of thumb is that customer-identifying information should be updated or verified at least once every two years. This means updating 5 percent of the names in your database every month or so, in a "position confirmation" process that can be undertaken manually, using clerical staff and the common telephone. (If you put this type of program into practice, don't forget that there are other facts you might want to obtain from your customers simultaneously with the position-confirmation calls.)

If, on the other hand, you sell through an indirect channel, you'll need to allocate the same effort to updating your information that you allocate to identifying end users in the first place. You'll need to be extremely vigilant about keeping your data current. To the extent possible, provide your end users with incentives and mechanisms for notifying you when they change positions.

Tracking business-to-business customers can be done also by assigning particular contacts to particular executives (not necessarily all sales executives) within your firm. Every executive should have a small list of contacts at prospective and current customers whom he or she knows by first name. This is the executive's "first-name list," and maintaining all the lists can be assigned to marketing operations or to sales management. Each executive is the "sponsor" for all the people on his or her own first-name list, and your customer policy should ensure that correspondence and interaction with that person takes place only through the sponsor, or over the sponsor's signature, or with the sponsor's knowledge. This works particularly well if you have a very limited number of business customers, or with VIP customers.

No matter what your definition of "customer" is, or how you identify your customers and tag them in your database, you have to be able to account for individual situations in which your system might not work perfectly. In the end, the boundaries around each of your customers may be self-imposed—by the customer, not by you. The "customer" consists of whatever the customer says. And if you want to treat different customers differently, you'll have to accommodate individual definitions.

Stay Flexible

Schwab uses phones and online connections to do the vast majority of its business with individual customers. And because, in general, customers aren't assigned to particular brokers at Schwab, whoever fields the call must have immediate access to the customer's account, the way the *customer* sees that account. So Schwab's system allows reps to mix and combine accounts in order to pull everything together that comprises a single customer's own view of his investments. If a customer has both a personal account and a closely held business with its own Schwab account, for instance, and the name and address on the business account are different from the customer's own name and home address, then these two accounts would not be linked simply by following routine household procedures. But a Schwab rep can manually modify the relationships among accounts, so that when that customer's record is called up it shows both accounts, because he controls each one.

It's important to stay flexible. This is how you create the sense of "seamlessness" in the customer's experience that will facilitate transactions and strengthen loyalty. When you identify customers, you must go out of your way to reflect their own sense of identity in your classification scheme. The customer generally doesn't care or want to know how he or she is identified. The customer just wants to be treated as a person. Respecting the individuality of your customers—which, after all, is infinite in its depth—is the foundation of the 1to1 enterprise.

Recommended Reads

Gordon, Ian H. *Relationship Marketing: New Strategies, Techniques and Technologies to Win the Customers You Want and Keep Them Forever* (John Wiley & Sons, 1998).

Gordon is one of the pioneering voices in relationship marketing. This book includes some very practical tools and techniques to help companies implement a successful strategy. It looks at everything from technology to measurement to managing a relationship-marketing effort.

Rapp, Stan, and Thomas L. Collins. *The New Maximarketing* (McGraw-Hill, 1996).

Rapp and Collins effectively demonstrate how to address emerging marketing and advertising challenges. They explore such issues as target selection, media exploration, accountability, advertising impact, and cultivating customers.

Woolf, Brian. *Customer Specific Marketing: The New Power in Retailing* (Teal Books, 1996).

Woolf describes the eclipse of mass marketing by what he calls "customer specific marketing." It shows how retailers can shed their "one-price-fits-all marketing strategies" and offer specific prices and benefits to different customers. An indispensable primer for retailers who don't want to get left in the dust of the Information Age.

Activity 3A

Identification Issues for Your Transition Team to Discuss

Target Completion Date: _____

1. Elevator Speech: Some people at your organization may assume that "identify customers" means "target the most likely buyers," but you know that "identify" means to recognize your customer in every interaction, through every channel, across all divisions and functions. How would you quickly explain the difference?

_____

2. How does your organization go about capturing customer-identification information? If you are in a business-to-business environment, how do you capture information about key decision-makers?

_____

3. What do you and your team see as the immediate benefits of knowing your customers individually?

_____

_____

_____

_____

_____

Activity 3B

Available Identification Customer Source/Inventory

Determine which methods of customer identification and data collection apply to your organization. Assess how many criteria each list source meets. Recognize that the criteria are progressive, left to right, so the more checks you place next to a list source, the more valuable it will be.

Target Completion Date: _____

Number of names available	Method of customer identification	Is available in digital form (✓)	Applies to your business unit (✓)	Seems to be accurate (✓)
	Billing and invoicing records			
	Sweepstakes and contest entry forms			
	Warranty records			
	Coupon redemption and rebate forms			
	Customer comment and research data			
	Sales force records or other field personnel			

Repairs and service records

Local or regional mailings and
promotions

Loyalty user card/frequency
program

User groups, clubs, and affinity groups
involving your company or product

Magazines or newsletters serving
your industry

Cooperative ventures with
retailers, resellers, and distributors

Other alliances with companies
close to the customer

"List swaps" with others in
industry

Mailing list brokers and industry
data providers

Getting Started: Customer Identification Checklist

Use this list of customer-identification ideas to start your own action plan. Based on the relevance of each idea to your own situation, prioritize these ideas and your own.

Target Completion Date: _____

All Companies	
Priority (1–5)	**Task Description**
	Take steps to ensure that new customers' identities are obtained
	Identify current customers and/or end users via existing company financial records
	Identify current customers and/or end users via package inserts
	Identify current customers and/or end users via warranty card returns
	Identify current customers and/or end users via service and/or support calls
	Identify current customers and/or end users via Web site visits and registrations
	Identify current customers and/or end users via trade show attendance records
	Identify individual prospects via seminars
	Identify individual prospects via free newsletter
	Identify individual prospects via Web site
	Identify individual prospects via contest, promotion, or advertising
	Identify individual prospects via inquiries or call-ins

B-to-B Only Companies

Target Completion Date: _____

Priority (1–5)	Task Description
	Within enterprise customers (business-to-business) identify and track individual decision-makers, buyers, influencers, specifiers, or users of your product
	When individual players within an enterprise customer move to another enterprise, set up a system to track those movements and pass along their status and records to the new sales representative or service person
	Create a companywide effort to ensure you never make a customer tell you the same thing twice
	Set up "first-name lists" (see Activity 3D) of the most important individuals at your Most Valuable Customer companies so sales staff and key corporate executives focus on getting to know them better, individually
	Identify all potential first-name-list sponsors within your own organization and assign some customers to each one
	Identify and track duplicate customer and individual records. Assign someone to eliminate duplicate records and consolidate information from multiple sources
	Create newsletter with feedback devices for continual contact with prospects on first-name lists
	Create seminars and visits with prospects on first-name lists
	Create telephone programs for continual contact with prospects on first-name lists
	Create e-mail programs for continual contact with prospects on first-name lists

Activity 3D

Customer-Identification Task List

Target Completion Date: _____

Who Will Do It?	By When?	Task	Init. and Date	75% Done (✓)	100% Done (✓)
		Tasks That Apply to Consumer and Business-to-Business Organizations			
		Determine how many end-user customer identities are known to the enterprise			
		Devise programs or initiatives to increase the proportion of current customers whose identities are known			
		Establish a common format for identifying customers			
		Determine how to link a customer's ID with all of that customer's contacts and transactions across all divisions, departments, products, and functions ▪ Does this link need to happen in real time? Yes _____ No _____ ▪ If so, determine how to make it happen			
		Make it easier for employees and managers to capture customer-identification information			
		Allow customers to enter and update identifying information themselves			
		Determine how to collect nontransactional data in the database (e.g., phoned-in inquiries that don't generate a sale, refunds, etc.)			

Develop a system to ensure that contact
information is kept up to date

Identify each customer record that appears in
more than one database "silo" within your
organization and assign a sponsor to each

Track "referred to" and "referred by" parameters
for all prospects and customers

Consider programs to increase referrals by
current customers

Tasks That Apply Only to Consumer Organizations

Ensure that new customers' identities are
obtained as they become customers, via:
- Mail
- Phone
- Fax
- Web site
- At point-of-purchase via:
  - Credit card
  - Check
  - Cash/debit
  - Other: _____

Tasks That Apply Only to Business-to-Business Organizations

If you are a manufacturer, decide how you will
capture information about:
- Specifiers
- End users
- Decision-makers
- Influencers
- Affiliated companies

Develop a method to track individual players as they move within a client organization

Set up first-name lists of sales staff and key corporate executives at the client organization

- Identify people in your own organization who know each of these people on a first-name basis
- Assign one of those people as the primary first-name contact to serve as a sponsor to each of those key people at your client's organization
- Post this list in a centralized location and keep it current to ensure that it is easily accessible to professionals throughout your firm

Activity 3E

Identify: Sample Brainstorming Worksheet

The Idea:
_____

The Details:
_____

The Data Needed:

-                    ▪
-                    ▪
-                    ▪
-                    ▪
-                    ▪
- ▪

Priority Score/Rank:

Impact   _____

Affordability   _____

Profitability   _____

Potential Volume _____

High = 1   Low = 5

Benefit to organization:

_____ Short term   _____ Long term

Does it require the cooperation of others?

Corporate Management_____

Enterprise Management_____

Organization_____

Chapter Four

Differentiate Your Customers

HOW TO UNDERSTAND WHAT DIFFERENT CUSTOMERS ARE WORTH TO YOU AND WHAT THEY NEED FROM YOU

Identify   *Differentiate*   Interact   Customize

IMPLEMENTATION STEP 2: First, rank your customers by their value to your enterprise, then differentiate them by what they need from your enterprise.

Treating different customers differently. In order to do this, you have to know what makes one customer different from another. Customer differentiation is perhaps the most powerful of the four one-to-one implementation principles, because it sets the stage for how the enterprise actually behaves toward an individual customer.

Differentiating customers is such an important part of a 1to1 relationship strategy that we've already written extensively about it. In Chapter Four of *The One to One Future,* then again in Chapters Two, Three, and Five of *Enterprise One to One,* we develop the idea of customer differentiation into quite a detailed theory.

In this chapter of the *Fieldbook* we need to provide a toolkit, not just for understanding the theory of customer differentiation but also for putting the theory into practice. Our goal is to show you practical ways to use information about your customer base to differentiate your customers, as this will be critical to benefiting from building a 1to1 enterprise. So the first half of this chapter consists of a compact, summary-level review of the principles involved in customer differentiation, and the last part is a set of suggestions for using information about your customer base to put these theories into practice.

Customers are different in two principal ways—they have different values to the enterprise, and they need different things from the enterprise. The key differentiation issues, in other words, are what the customer wants and what the customer is worth. The *value* of a customer, relative to other customers, allows the enterprise to prioritize its efforts, allocating more resources to ensuring that more valuable customers remain loyal and grow in value. And catering to what a specific customer *needs* is the basis for creating a relationship and winning the customer's loyalty.

So the customer differentiation process should take place in two stages, in this order:

1. Rank your customers by their value.
2. Differentiate them by their needs.

That is, use your first effort to understand the different values your customers have. Then differentiate them by what they need, starting with your most valuable customers.

Actual value of a customer. The actual, current value of a customer to your enterprise is equal to the net present value of all future profit from that customer. The term "all future profit" includes the margin your company earns on future sales of individual products and services to the customer, reduced by any customer-specific servicing costs. In addition, this term is meant to include such factors as the profit earned on referrals made by a customer, the monetary value of collaborative assistance from the customer in designing new products or services, the

Customer Differentiation: The Theory

benefit of the customer's own reputation among other current and potential customers, and so forth.

The figure you would come up with if you were able to factor in all these variables is the customer's *actual* value, or lifetime value (LTV). You can think of it as the customer's "run rate" with your firm.

Strategic value and share of customer. There's one other critical element of the customer's value: the customer's growth potential, or *strategic* value. Strategic value is the additional value a customer could yield if you had a strategy to get it. Think of a banking customer with a checking account and savings account. Every month the customer provides a certain profit to your bank, and the net present value of this continuing profit stream represents the customer's actual value to you. But the home mortgage that same customer has at a competitive bank represents strategic value—potential value you could realize if you had a proactive strategy to obtain it. Knowing both actual and strategic value allows you to calculate your share of customer. Obviously, from a purist's standpoint, the same level of detail could drive the calculation of strategic value as goes into calculating actual value. In fact, there are even more variables to consider in calculating a customer's growth potential than need to be factored into a calculation of the customer's expected run rate and current LTV.

"Good enough" is enough. Of course, no one builds a successful business by remaining a purist. In the real world, you'll need to take shortcuts, make compromises, and settle for "good enough" measurements of customer value. It is useful to think about a customer's LTV, but recognize also that LTV itself is such a theoretical idea that no one ever has enough information and predictive insight to calculate it precisely. Instead, you create a financial model for it, try to get a better and better handle on it, and, in the end, settle for a good-enough "proxy variable"— a substitute variable.

A proxy variable is good enough if it allows you to rank your customers from top to bottom, roughly in order of their value or importance to the enterprise, because ranking your customers lets you set objectives and prioritize your efforts with respect to individual customers. So don't spend time trying to calculate some aspect of customer value that won't be very important in the end. For example, very few business managers will actually factor in the value of customer referrals when calculating LTV—unless, for their particular business, referrals are extremely important as an element of value. (A home builder, for instance, dealing in a series of one-time-only customer relationships, might consider it important to estimate how enthusiastically a customer will refer others.)

Categorizing your customers by their value. After ranking your customers, the next step is to identify which ones fall into each of three distinct types of value—MVC, MGC, and BZ. These "value types" represent customers for whom different objectives and strategies should apply:

MVCs: *Most Valuable Customers* are those with the highest LTVs. They represent the core of your current business, and your primary objective should be *customer retention*. The strategies for retaining customers range from customer recognition to quality improvement, loyalty purchasing, and Learning Relationships.

MGCs: *Most Growable Customers* are those with the most unrealized strategic value. They usually have lower LTVs than MVCs, but they often have a higher growth potential. These customers could be more profitable than they are now, and your primary objective is *customer growth*. Growth strategies are more expensive than retention strategies. At many businesses, the most important customer-growth strategy is cross-selling, while in other business situations, the most important growth strategy is increasing the customer's longevity.

BZs: *Below Zero* customers are those who will probably never earn enough profit to justify the expense involved in serving them. Every business has some of these customers, and your strategy should be to create incentives either to make them more profitable or to encourage them to become someone else's unprofitable customers.

Not all customers will necessarily fall into one of these value types, but to the extent that you can identify the customers that do, you can set your objectives and strategies for them. The process might sound complicated, but there are, in fact, many practical examples of companies that use a value-based ranking of customers to set different objectives for different types of customers:

- FedEx calculates a profitability metric for *each* of its customers, using the information to negotiate price increases with Below Zeros or to close their accounts. By concentrating its efforts on its most profitable customers, FedEx engineered an impressive burst of profit growth and sent its stock up to impressive new heights.
- Roden Electrical Supply, a full-line distributor of electrical products and services based in Knoxville, Tennessee, tiers its customers by the most recent year's actual sales volume and then appends third-party information to assess strategic value. Margins are often tight in the wholesale distribution business, and there is a constant tension between meeting customer needs and generating a fair profit, which makes it all the more important for wholesalers to differentiate their customers carefully. The sales force uses customer-tiering information to identify particular customers that deserve extra attention or services.
- In 1988, Custom Research Inc., a Minneapolis-based consulting and research business, began focusing *exclusively* on its MVCs— high-volume, repeat customers in the Fortune 500 category. Within a year, the firm had trimmed its overall client list in half, to sixty-seven clients (that's a large number of BZs being jettisoned), while increasing the population of MVCs from twenty-five to thirty-four. In implementing this new strategy, CRI has reaped extremely high retention rates and has doubled its revenues. It has also won the enthusiasm of its clients—an intangible asset that

should not be overlooked. Indeed, more than 60 percent of CRI's new business now comes via referrals from its existing clients. In 1996 CRI became the smallest firm (120 employees) ever to win the Malcolm Baldrige National Quality Award.

- Milwaukee's Harry W. Schwartz Booksellers launched the "Schwartz Gives Back" (SGB) program, to strengthen customer loyalty while benefiting a number of local causes. Customers who join SGB can designate one nonprofit organization from a list of nineteen. Their designated charity then receives 1 percent of the sale every time the member purchases a book. Meantime, Schwartz is able to identify SGB members in the store and track their purchases, determining not only which categories of books are favored by each customer but also which customers are most profitable. In addition to its monthly SGB newsletter, Schwartz now focuses its customer-recognition mailings on the top 5 percent of its list (the MVCs), and has achieved a remarkable 70 percent-plus redemption rate within thirty days when coupons are provided. The SGB program now represents one third of Schwartz's overall retail sales, and SGB members tend to spend 50 percent more per visit than nonmembers.

- Boston's Charles Hotel in Harvard Square identified its MVCs as guests who stay at the hotel six or more times per year and spend a certain amount of money during these visits. The hotel sent a letter to this group of MVCs, asking if they'd like to belong to The Charles Hotel's Distinguished Guest Program. In order to serve its Distinguished Guests appropriately, the hotel has streamlined check-in procedures so no stop at the front desk is necessary. It also assigns a room based on the individual's past preferences, places a special robe with the guest's name on it in the room, and offers preferential seating in its restaurant.

- Charles Schwab differentiates its customers based on their trading activity and investable assets. The company is especially attentive to a group it calls the "Schwab 500." These are individuals who make more than forty-eight trades a year. They are assigned a special team of six to eight people who get to know them individually and help them research and execute trades appropriate to their individual objectives.

Differentiating customers by their needs. Once you rank your customers by their value, the next step is to differentiate them by what they need, starting with your most valuable customers.

A successful Learning Relationship with a customer is built on changes in the enterprise's behavior toward that customer. The customer tells you what he needs, you tailor your service or customize your product to meet this need, and then, with every interaction, your service gets closer to that customer's individual preferences. Knowing what your customers need—understanding their individual preferences and priorities—is crucial to building a 1to1 enterprise.

Community needs. The preferences or priorities one customer has in common with a set of other customers can be thought of as "community needs"—needs that are shared by a community of customers. If you run a bookstore, for example, you might notice one type of customer who tends to read fiction and another type who reads biographies. The "fiction" community and the "biography" community each need something different from your bookstore, but the customers within each community share a common need.

Knowing a customer's community needs allows a business to anticipate what the customer wants—sometimes even before the customer knows it herself. A biography of Winston Churchill, for instance, might be of interest to someone who enjoys biographies; however, it would probably be of little interest to someone who prefers fiction. If, by interacting with a few of your biography readers, you learn that this particular biography is quite good, then you could recommend it to another biography reader, even before that customer learns that the book is available.

Individual needs. The other kind of need—the "individual need"—is one that a particular customer does not share with any other customers, or at least not with any significant number of other customers. The florist who sends you a note about your mother's upcoming birthday, reminding you that you sent roses last year, is catering to an individual need, not a community need. The date your mother celebrates her birthday cannot be "projected" onto any particular community of customers. Knowing your mother's birthday will give the florist an advantage in selling more flowers to you, not to any other customer. Nevertheless, it is useful to learn and remember a customer's individual needs, if only to save the customer the time that would otherwise be needed to explain them again and again.

Customer differentiation works because it allows you to treat different customers differently, based on information you have about each individual customer's value and needs. But it's important to recognize that usually a business will already be treating different customers differently, at least to the extent that the business serves distinctly different customer bases. A business that sells to small firms as well as to large enterprises, for instance, is likely to have different sales strategies for these two types of customers, perhaps executed in different channels with different sales forces. So the first practical step in analyzing your customers by their differences is to partition your customer base into its constituent elements.

Customer Differentiation: From Theory to Practice

Partition your customer base. If you sell to both business customers and consumers, then you almost certainly have two different sales operations. Business customers might be served by a direct sales force, while consumers get their products through retailers, or maybe via direct mail or telemarketing. Meanwhile, within the set of business customers you might have several subsets, based either on the types of businesses you sell to or on the types of products and services they buy. If you sell computer equipment, for example, you may have one type of sales effort for simple, equipment-only sales, while another sales process is for larger, more complex sales of systems and services.

If you want to differentiate your customers by value and needs, you must first decide what the different elements of the base are and then partition your overall customer base into these different subsets in order to examine each individual subset. Eventually you'll have to create a mechanism for recombining these elements and viewing the enterprise's "big picture." But for now the only reasonable way to think about customer differentiation is to start by comparing apples to apples.

There are no hard-and-fast rules explaining how to divide up your customer base. You don't actually have to partition it at all if it doesn't make sense to do so. But it definitely makes sense whenever you sell to customers who are different enough to merit different sales channels or marketing plans, and often it makes sense even though the sales channel or marketing plan is the same. If your customer base is characterized by a particularly steep value skew (with a relatively small number of high-value customers accounting for a disproportionately large portion of total customer value), then it is likely that customers with widely different values will exhibit different behaviors, as well as different levels of sensitivity to your enterprise's initiatives. An airline could reasonably expect its very frequent business fliers to respond differently to its marketing initiatives than infrequent business fliers would. So the airline might first look at business travelers and leisure travelers as two separate parts of a customer base. And even though business travelers are sometimes also leisure travelers, each individual will fall into only one group—the group that will help the enterprise serve that customer better overall. Once the airline has grouped business travelers and leisure travelers, it might then look at business travelers and think about very frequent fliers and not-so-frequent fliers as separate subsets of customers.

Create a spreadsheet model of customer value. For each separate part of the customer base, create a spreadsheet model of a customer's possible life cycle with your firm. This book is not designed to be a tutorial on financial modeling, but the best type of spreadsheet would represent a picture of the "trajectory" through your business of the "average" customer in each different customer base you've identified. You should start with the customer's initial acquisition and continue to the customer's eventual departure. Add up the profits and costs of this customer's trajectory, discounted appropriately for net present values, and you can derive a calculation of the typical customer's LTV. (Some sample spreadsheets for different businesses are available for downloading at the *Fieldbook* Web site.)

For each customer base being modeled, some of the factors that should be considered in a calculation of customer value are:

a. Initial customer-acquisition cost
b. Cost of servicing (both an allocated fixed cost and a variable, per-customer cost)
c. Profit from sales of products across all divisions and operating units
d. Profit from sales of continuing services
e. Profit from referrals of other customers
f. Likelihood and magnitude of volume growth or increased profits
g. Predictors of loyalty or attrition
h. Related customer values (sister divisions, relatives, colleagues)
i. Creditworthiness or likelihood of default
j. Dummy variable to account for prestige, influence, or nonquantifiable benefits or costs

How do you decide what numbers to plug in to your model once you've created it? You plug in whatever numbers are (1) important to the calculation and (2) reasonably predictable and understandable. Predicting these variables is a matter of science and art. The best single predictor of a customer's future behavior is his past behavior, so if you sell to a customer base of millions of consumers, and you have millions (or billions) of data points in your customer database, then your model might be very statistically sophisticated indeed. This is the science part.

On the other hand, your customers' past behavior is already history, and here you are trying to predict the future. So you have to use common sense as well. The more dialogue you have with customers, the more you'll be able to enhance the quantitative model of a particular customer's past behavior by incorporating your more subjective insights into the customer's future.

This is particularly true when it comes to trying to assess a customer's strategic value. The best source of information on a customer's growth potential is the customer's own assessment of his business. Thus, when a salesperson calls on a customer, one of the most important discussions she can have with him is a review of his upcoming spending plans, his budget for the next year, or his willingness to deal with her company again. In this type of discussion, the salesperson is probing the customer to gain a better understanding of his strategic value. But the real question is this: Will the salesperson's firm *capture* the results of this probing conversation in its customer database?

Customer dialogue and subjective evaluations of different customers are even more important if the type of business you operate isn't amenable to spreadsheet modeling at all, or if it's impossible to quantify a customer's "value," per se. Nonfinancial elements of customer value are more important if what is being examined is a not-for-profit enterprise or a profession such as health care or a governmental entity.

Rank customers by their importance to the enterprise. If a spreadsheet won't capture your customers' value accurately, or if you have a business in which the "value" of a customer is itself a difficult idea to capture, then you'll need to create a different method for ranking your customers.

Professions, for instance, often deal with "customers" whose value is diminished as the professional becomes successful. If you're a doctor charging patients fifty dollars per visit, then the longer a patient remains ill, the more monetary value that patient will have for your practice. This is, of course, why we call medicine a "profession" to begin with—because the doctor's own professional responsibility is to make patients better, regardless of any crass business implications. But what this means for the 1to1 enterprise is that there really are some businesses where it just doesn't make sense to rank customers by their monetary value.

One way to prioritize your customers in this kind of situation is to replace the word "value" with "importance." Ask yourself how *important* each customer is to the enterprise's success. Rate your customers on an importance scale, from 1 to 5, if necessary.

Some of our best customers are not "paying" customers. They are important constituents that cannot be judged meaningfully in terms of profit and loss. But while their contributions to our success are nonmonetary, they are nevertheless critical. Their opinions and actions will have a significant impact on the decisions of customers in our top tiers of value. We call them "key influencers."

At Pitney Bowes, for instance, the most visible influencers are members of the United States Postal Service and other "Posts" around the world. In fact, there is a department at Pitney Bowes, reporting to the chairman of the board, whose major objective is to address the needs and concerns of these valuable constituents.

In many industries, these influencers are consultants, association directors, conference organizers, publishers, editors, and journalists. Every time your firm sends out a press release, it is directed at an influencer. Journalists and editors are gatekeepers who determine how this information will be presented to customers and potential customers. Every time your company's president makes a presentation to the board or to some Wall Street investment analysts, the objective is to reach influencers and win their confidence. Their opinions will help set your company's future course or affect the value of your stock.

Among not-for-profit organizations, key influencers might be local civic organizations, political leaders, and volunteers. And, even though these influencers may not financially contribute to the organization, they can still deliver "intangible" value—whether in the form of a referral of a donor or by lending their own reputation to strengthen your organization's credibility.

Your organization, therefore, no matter what kind of organization it is, needs to pay close attention to these key constituents. You need to treat them as individuals, and even rank them in importance—just as you would with any other set of customers. In some cases, you may want to rank them side by side with other customers. This is not that different from a company's relying on a high-visibility customer not for profit but in order to have a "reference client" to speak of with the trade press or with prospective customers. Such forms of intangible value are becoming increasingly important in today's economy, and organizations need sophisticated ways of addressing them.

You can easily apply the four implementation steps to your handling of key influencers:

1. Identify your key influencers
- Members of the press
- Community leaders
- Reference clients
- Investment analysts

- Academics and opinion leaders
- Other

2. Differentiate your key influencers
* Rank them by their importance to your enterprise
- How many customers or prospects is this person likely to influence?
- How greatly is this person's opinion respected?
- How widely is this journalist read?
- How would you rate this particular analyst's importance in the investment community?

* Differentiate them by their needs
- Does this person need handling only by your CEO?
- Does this person want information or just reassurance?
- Does this influencer want to benefit himself from being associated with your organization?

3. Interact with your key influencers
- Do you have an e-connection to your key influencers?
- How easy is it for them to contact you and interact?
- Are you getting the right feedback from them?

4. Customize for your key influencers
- Give them an appropriate level of attention
- Who is in charge of managing the relationships you have with these constituents?
- What steps can be taken to enhance these relationships?

Key influencers can and will play a vital role in your organization's future. As you develop your 1to1 strategy, make sure such noncustomers are included, and that your relationships with them are appropriately addressed.

Your goal in ranking customers by their value, or by their importance, is to prioritize your marketing and sales efforts with respect to different customers—to put some customers first on your list, second, and so forth. This is particularly important in planning your transition toward an increasingly customer-oriented organization. Whom do you approach first? Whom do you single out for the first-order change in your level of customer service? Clearly, no organization can afford to do everything all at once, so prioritization is critical.

The multi-division enterprise. Tracking customer differences can be difficult when you have to cross divisional boundaries. A telephone company, for instance, with a "land lines" division, a Yellow Pages division, a cell-phone division, and perhaps a division that sells switches and other equipment, might find that a business customer highly valuable to one division will be of inconsequential value to the others. A large and valuable Yellow Pages advertiser may have only one or two land lines and no cell phones or switches at all.

The easiest translation mechanism, among divisions, is financial value to the enterprise. If you have a reasonably usable algorithm for estimating LTV in every different and distinct division, then a customer's LTV in the Yellow Pages division could simply be added to its LTV in each other division. In this way, the multidivision enterprise's entire customer base could be ranked in terms of each customer's overall, enterprise-wide LTV.

Making comparisons among divisions by using a financially denominated LTV figure is an ideal situation, but the truth is that few large firms will be able to do that very easily. Instead, in the short term you may want to devise a series of subjective scores. Each division could rank its own customers on a five-point scale of increasing importance, for instance, from 1 to 5. These rankings could come directly from an explicit, value-based calculation performed by a division that has access to enough data to create a statistical model, or they could come out of a more subjective evaluation of a customer's importance to a division, if quantitative calculations are more problematic. A customer who is a "5" for each of three divisions would be a "15" for the overall enterprise, and so forth. You will probably have to weight different divisions' rankings of their own customers in order to take account of the fact that there are different skews of value in each base, or that all the customers in one division's base are inherently larger and more valuable to the overall enterprise than any of the customers in another unit's base.

A more common way to rank customers across different divisional boundaries is simply to create an ad hoc, cross-divisional metric. At

Hewlett-Packard the computer organization wanted to decide which consumer customers should be on the list to receive a special, free newsletter, "HP-At-Home." In the end, the firm decided to make customers eligible for the newsletter if they had (a) bought a top-line Color LaserJet printer, or (b) bought a high-end PC, or (c) bought at least one PC, one printer, and one other type of HP equipment (including digital camera, scanner, etc.). These products all are sold by different business units at HP, and the newsletter is now distributed to some half a million consumers who for the most part deal with multiple HP business units.

Capture customer needs. If you've ever looked through a good market-research study, you might have seen examples of "needs-based clusters" of customers. Clusters like this represent communities of customers with similar needs. Marketers use this type of needs-based clustering to drive their segmented-marketing programs. If a marketer can identify three, four, or five different segments, based on needs, then the next step in a segmented-marketing program is to link these different needs to different types of media (the magazine *Outdoor Life* for the outdoor adventurer, for instance, versus *Esquire* for the fashion-conscious urban resident). Then the marketer places an ad in each magazine designed to appeal to the specific issues most important to the particular cluster, or segment, of customers most likely to read that magazine.

Knowing various types of community needs for an enterprise's customers will allow it to categorize them in such a way as to make it more cost-efficient to treat them individually. There is a useful analogy between the mechanics of mass customization and the concept of community needs. Mass customization is based on modularizing the production process, mass-producing the modules, and then combining them to meet individual specifications. Levi's manufactures 227 waist/hip sizes and 25 leg sizes in its Original Spin jeans program. By taking a customer's measurements in its store, the company can deliver one of more than 5,700 different and unique sizes of blue jeans, made to order. Dell Computer and Gateway use the same basic principle for making computers to order. Other mass customizers use the principle of modularization as well.

The more modules you build into the mass-customization process, the more "granularity" there will be to the final product, and the more exact you can be in meeting the needs of your individual customers. Community needs, similarly, can be used to "modularize" your customer base—in essence, to tailor different behavior to different customers, individually.

Differentiating customers by their needs is frequently the primary objective of marketing-research studies. It can be approached in a variety of ways by a research firm, but almost all marketing research focuses, at some level, on developing a better understanding of the different needs that customers are trying to satisfy by purchasing a particular product or service. So the first place to look for your own customers' needs-based differences is in the marketing research department. Put your hands on every market-research study available, whether conducted on behalf of your own firm or on behalf of your industry.

There is one key idea you'll be looking for in this research, however, that many such studies overlook. What you want to find, in addition to descriptions of particular customer needs types, is some clue as to how to identify each type in a direct interaction. Imagine an anonymous customer visiting your Web site or contacting your call center. In order to better serve that customer you want to know what needs *that* particular customer is trying to meet with your product or service. If she's considering your bank for a business loan, for instance, does she want to "get the best possible deal" on the loan or would she rather "work with bankers she can trust"? If he's shopping for a television, is he more interested in satisfying his family's need for big-screen entertainment or in finding a simple, easy-to-maintain box? What questions would you ask a customer in order to map that customer into one needs-based group or another?

Needs differentiation does not have to be overly sophisticated. It can be applied using common sense when thinking about the different types of customers your business serves. What's important is that you get out of the product-first mode of thinking and into the customer-first mode. Concentrate on the different kinds of customers who buy from you, rather than on the different types of products you sell.

The 1to1 initiative at 3M means that customers are sorted first into profile types. It differentiates by vertical industry, such as furniture, automotive assembly, or utilities, as well as "consumer," which is a profile applied to the type of customer that would go to a Wal-Mart or Sears. Within and among these customer profiles, the firm bundles together various product offerings designed to meet the needs of these particular customers. There is, for instance, a Construction and Home Improvement organization at 3M that bundles different sets of 3M products suitable for do-it-yourself customers and for building professionals. 3M's Bruce Hamilton says "It's not so much about the size of the customer, per se, but more about the profile of the customer as it relates to their needs."

Identify and cater to individual needs. Sometimes it just makes sense to think about your business differently. If you start with a customer's needs, rather than with your own product or program, you can often get a quick leg up on the competition. It is a simple idea, but unusual enough that whenever a firm does business this way, it is still worth a look:

Franklin University, based in Columbus, Ohio, began focusing on individual student needs in order to create a powerful retention strategy. The school, which has an enrollment of more than five thousand "nontraditional" students (85 percent of whom work full-time), assigns student service associates (SSAs) to provide a single point of contact for all enrollees. Instead of standing in lines to deal with issues like registration, credit transfer, academic advising, parking, and financial aid, each student can depend on his or her SSA to serve as a liaison to the relevant departments. Where once the university would rely on uniform policies to make decisions, SSAs now have the freedom to handle individual student needs and requests on a case-by-case basis. They have, in effect, personalized the student's relationship with the school. Franklin reports this approach has resulted in an increase in the percentage of students who remain enrolled (up from 65 percent to 70 percent), as well as growth in tuition revenues of more than $500,000.

Product expertise versus customer expertise. The more you know about your own individual customers' needs, the better positioned you'll be to earn their trust by remembering things for them or recommending particular products to them. Two kinds of expertise are vital to this task. You have to have *product* expertise, in order to understand the best type of product or service, with all its specifications and nuances. You have to "know your business," in other words—you have to be an expert in your field. But you also have to have *customer* expertise. You must know something about this particular customer's needs in order to be able to make the appropriate recommendation.

Any one of your competitors could, at any time, duplicate your product expertise. You can't prevent a competing firm from developing a better understanding of the product than you have. But no one can develop the same level of customer expertise without the customer's active involvement and assent. If your customer expertise is based on what a customer has taught you about his or her needs, then your competitor would first have to secure the participation of the customer to duplicate this level of expertise.

Time and again, when a company launches a 1to1 initiative, it finds that it must create or explicitly acknowledge these two specific areas of expertise—product and customer. Recognizing both areas is a prerequisite to rationally managing the relationship marketing program overall. Owens Corning's Steve Smoot, director of customer information services, leads the firm's interactive marketing for the building-materials business. His process organization integrates across multiple business units and has identified three different and distinct processes for managing the firm's relationships with individual customers and providing different customers with the information they need about the firm and its products:

> First, our "Communication and Fulfillment" processes represent the devices, or the "how" of interactive services delivery. We formed our organization around the need for improved integration and delivery of accurate, consistent information across all the media interfaces to the market, which include 1-800 services, Internet and multimedia communications, and print fulfillment.

Second, the process we call "Product Knowledge Management" includes the data and document management infrastructure for the "what" of our communications and services content. A key business strategy for us is integrating individual building-material products into system solutions in residential construction and remodeling, as well as other commercial markets. To do this we needed to manage the elements of our product offering and configure individual elements into multiple-material system solutions. So the scope of product knowledge includes marketing and technical information, configuration tools, and system-design tools to model thermal and acoustic performance, as well as aesthetic design for external building materials. This process provides the capabilities for mass customization of building-material solutions in the actual design and construction process.

Third, and perhaps most fundamental, is how we handle knowledge of the "who"—our customers. Behind all of the interactive, outbound, and inbound communication devices, we must be able to mine our contacts with each customer longitudinally over time, and on each subsequent service opportunity connect to the record of an individual customer's contact history. We do this at an individual level to permit "smart contact" service experiences at our call center and online services in the truest sense of customization. We also utilize aggregated data from these contacts in a "learning loop" at the customer segment level for ongoing alignment of our service offering. We call this process "Customer Knowledge Management."

3M's Bruce Hamilton says the firm will increasingly be pushing its sales efforts toward "integrated solutions" for particular customer types, including vertical industries. Right now, as is the case with most multiproduct, multidivision firms, the company's sales force is organized largely into product specialties. In the past, this has made sense because the products themselves are complex enough to require a considerable level of expertise. To operate in the abrasives area, for instance, a salesperson needed to know about sandpapers that work on metal, wood, plastic, and other materials. But when a salesperson deals with a furniture manufacturer, it isn't so important to be all-knowing about metals and plastics. Instead, it would be better for the salesperson to know about the kinds of tapes, chemicals, and adhesives used in furniture manufacturing and the safety products appropriate for a furniture plant. This would allow 3M to become more and more focused on the customer's processes and needs, not only selling a wider variety of its products and earning a higher share of customer, but probably doing so at a lower cost of sales as well. Certainly, it would make 3M easier to do business with.

For customer data to be useful, it must generally be digitized and found in a single location. And most businesses already have more of this kind of data than they use. The "front screen" of a simple contact-management database like *GoldMine* will often contain more data than a company can act on, operationally, each day.

The real challenge in building a 1to1 enterprise is evaluating and understanding the data available to you already, and then deciding how to take action based on it. The kind of information we're talking about falls into four principal categories:

1. ***Current Facts and Figures***

    Start by just lining up the facts and figures you already have on your customers. You'll almost certainly be able to draw some useful conclusions. This kind of information includes:

- Sales figures, per customer: by month, year-to-date, with comparisons to prior periods
- Products ordered: by item or SKU number, by category, by sales volume
- Ship-to locations: number of customer locations, units, or subsidiaries
- Purchase frequency
- Service/repair frequency: by product, by location, by incident type
- Payment and credit history: timeliness, creditworthiness, credit limits

2. *Imputable and Computable Customer Data*

All too often companies fail to recognize the data "hiding behind" their current facts and figures. At the Sands Casino in Atlantic City, for example, databases capture the dates a customer visits and the amount of money he puts at risk (known as "handle" or "drop")—both in static, "flat file" data fields. But further analysis of that data proves far more enlightening, providing such insights as whether individual customers have been visiting the casino with increasing or decreasing frequency and whether they put more or less money at risk on each visit. The database shows whether they gamble on weekdays or weekends, in-season or off-season.

You can easily see the opportunities here for constructing individualized marketing initiatives based on this kind of "imputed" learning—a "win back" program for customers seen to be losing interest, for example. And while there may be less gambling involved in computer sales, car leasing, hotel stays, or airline flights, the same principles apply.

So, in addition to examining your current facts and figures, be sure to check for:

- Increases or decreases in dollar volume, purchase frequency, SKUs
- Number of product end users in an enterprise, often available for hard goods, technology, and software products where user registrations are higher
- Number of business units, divisions, or subsidiaries making purchases
- Number of purchasers at each unit (often requires revisiting data such as invoices, shipping records, or purchase orders)
- Seasonality of purchase: When does the customer buy all or most of your goods or services? Seasonality usually varies by industry (schools, CPAs, greeting-card and calendar printers each have distinct purchase patterns, as do many other businesses, by type), but it can also vary by individual customer (winter vacationers versus summer vacationers).

- Unique sales or servicing costs: Does each sales call require a solo flight to an expensive city? Is after-hours service or delivery always required? Does the customer make particularly heavy use of customer service lines, trainers, or technicians?
- Ancillary services sold: Does this buyer purchase add-on, support, service, supplies, financing, or other related products or services from the firm?

3. *Observable Customer Data*

Some of the most powerful data can be gathered only through observation. Most salespeople tend to keep this data to themselves, considering it to be their personal property rather than enterprise knowledge. Capturing this data can be a challenge, but it is often worth the effort.

Remember that when observed data is buried in the "notes" field of a contact report or a telemarketing screen, as it often is, it will be of little value to the enterprise on a continuing basis. Compare the power of a "front screen" field labeled "fondness for our products: HIGH," to a sentence, buried in text, along the lines of "really likes our products a lot." The information is exactly the same, but the more you can capture observational data into a specific field or module, as opposed to forcing it into boxes of text, the more useful the information will be in terms of taking real action.

Observable data often will be highly subjective because that is its nature. But it can also be one of the most powerful mechanisms for differentiating customers by their needs. If you can systematize the observations, identifying particular community needs that various different customers have in common, your enterprise will be able to use the data to devise specific strategies for specific, needs-based types of customers. Some observable customer data to consider:

- Fan or foe: Is this individual an advocate for our company or a detractor?

- Product knowledge: Is the customer using our product or service wisely?
- Referral potential: Might this company serve as an enthusiastic reference?
- "Power of the Pen:" Is this individual the buyer, influencer, hands-on user, or researcher when it comes time to decide whether to buy?
- Company health: Does this business customer seem to be energetic and growing?

These categories are broad. The list of possible categories is virtually endless. Remember to select only those characteristics that are actionable from the standpoint of one or more individuals in your enterprise.

4. ***Obtainable Customer Data***

In addition to using outside database companies for customer-identifying data, outside vendors also can sometimes provide important customer-differentiation data. This can be particularly helpful in a business-to-business setting, where share-of-customer is one of the numbers you most want to have. Industry-research services often report, for example, on individual corporate IT budgets, photocopier purchases, travel spending, and so on. In the pharmaceutical category, drugs prescribed by individual doctors and issued by individual pharmacies are available for all competitors.

Obtainable data include things such as:

- *Company characteristics*: SIC code, growth versus peers, new-product plans, management turnover, profitability, and industry reputation are the kinds of data easily obtained from trade publications, research services, and scores of online business-information services. Smart salespeople read a company's annual report or visit its Web site before making a sales call, yet little if any of that knowledge ever reaches the customer-data file.
- *Benchmarking value*: Do other companies watch this firm's behav-

ior? Will the reputation of the selling enterprise be enhanced—or weakened—by its known involvement with the buyer? Hundreds of parts suppliers, consulting firms, and others have built their businesses on "we sell to GM" (or GE, IBM, HP, and so forth).

- *Inherent opportunities:* Does the company have other divisions or subsidiaries that might ultimately be influenced to do business with the enterprise based on this initial adoption or trial? Does the company use the enterprise as one of several suppliers, and might the other suppliers be edged out, over time, thereby increasing business?

Start with these somewhat global issues and determine the most valuable strategic data for your own enterprise's customer base. Keep it simple, and remember that data you already have is infinitely more valuable than data you still have to collect.

Even in the consumer-marketing environment, there are third-party data providers who can help differentiate customers by the type of needs the customer has. A number of data providers, using information collected in large, universal databases, can map particular consumers or households into different "clusters" that are based on the individual needs or outward characteristics of each household. When used appropriately, this kind of data can help a consumer-oriented firm get a quick handle on the different types of customers it is serving.

At Guestnet, the profile of an individual guest can be enhanced using information provided by Looking Glass, Inc., a Denver-based third-party data provider. Looking Glass has a database of some thirty-six million households that they have subdivided into twenty-seven different "cohort" classifications (married couples, single men or women) and one "omega" group for consumers who don't fit into any of the other cohorts. Using this cohort information, Guestnet can provide a hotel with a snapshot analysis of a particular guest, assuming the guest matches one of the households in the Looking Glass archive. Thus, rather than having to wait to develop feedback-driven information on a guest, based on an accumulation of stays at a hotel, the hotel can begin with at least some initial understanding of the guest. In most cases, Guestnet can provide immediate information to a hotel with respect to communicating with a new guest. Such information enables the hotel to begin the dialogue process effectively.

Needs and Values

Obviously there are a great many issues to consider with regard to differentiating your customers. You must explore the different values of your customers—actual and strategic. It's critical to recognize your best customers so that you can create strategies for retaining them. You must also develop the processes and capabilities that enable you to learn your customers' particular needs, interests, and priorities. Every customer is unique. Companies that recognize and address such inherent differences are the ones that can be expected to thrive in the years to come.

Recommended Reads

Blattberg, Robert C., and John Deighton. "Manage Marketing by the Customer Equity Test," *Harvard Business Review,* July–August 1996, pp. 136–144.
Blattberg and Deighton ask the appropriate question for judging new products and customer-service initiatives. It's not "Will this product be profitable?" so much as "Will this grow our customer equity?" The article describes how to compute an organization's optimal level of spending on such initiatives. The point is: When managers strive to grow their customer equity, they put the customer at the forefront of their strategic thinking.

Cleland, Alan S., and Albert V. Bruno. *The Market Value Process: Bridging Customer and Shareholder Value* (Jossey-Bass Business & Management Series, 1996).
This book explores why companies must address customer and shareholder value in tandem. Cleland and Bruno offer a practical, twelve-step plan for ensuring that this occurs.

David Shepard Associates. *The New Direct Marketing: How to Implement a Profit-Driven Database Marketing Strategy* (Irwin Professional Pub., 1994).
This classic book is a practical, step-by-step guide to direct marketing methods and technologies with an emphasis on the kinds of statistical analysis, predictive modeling, and technology needed to differentiate customers.

Hallberg, Garth, and David Ogilvy. *All Consumers Are Not Created Equal: The Differential Marketing Strategy for Brand Loyalty and Profits* (John Wiley & Sons, Inc., 1995).
Recognizing that mass advertising is not hitting the mark, Hallberg and Ogilvy make the case for "differential marketing"—focusing on the firm's most valuable customers—as a means of cultivating a loyal customer base. They contend that double-digit sales can be maintained through integrated marketing, database management, and one-to-one relationship building.

Heskett, James L., W. Earl Sasser, and Leonard A. Schlesinger. *The Service Profit Chain: How Leading Companies Link Profit and Growth to Loyalty, Satisfaction, and Value* (Free Press, 1997).
Heskett, Sasser, and Schlesinger lay a solid, thoroughly researched foundation for efforts to link customer and employee loyalty to growth and profit. They also offer a thorough plan for assessing and delivering results.

Reichheld, Frederick F. *The Loyalty Effect: The Hidden Force Behind Growth, Profits, and Lasting Value* (Harvard Business School Press, 1996).
Loyalty—whether it involves customers, employees, or shareholders—is now one of the primary concerns of the era. In this landmark book, Reichheld explores the business strategies that enable companies to build and maintain loyal relationships. He demonstrates that smart companies can increase their profits significantly merely by delivering a small improvement in customer and employee retention.

Activity 4A

Differentiation Issues for Your Transition Team to Discuss

Target Completion Date: _____

1. Elevator Speech: Explain why meeting individual needs is the best way to secure a long-term competitive advantage. (Your answer may include the Learning Relationship, protecting unit margins, ensuring customer loyalty, etc.)

_____

_____

_____

_____

2. Before you begin the exercises and tasks that follow, try to name a few of your Most Valuable Customers. Do they share any common characteristics? Do MVCs sometimes have similar needs? If so, what?

_____

_____

_____

3. Do you have any customers who are costing the organization so much that they are probably not worth keeping? Who are they? Do they share any characteristics?

_____

_____

_____

4. Who are your Most Growable Customers? Do they share any characteristics? Any similar needs?

_____

_____

_____

Current Customer Differentiation Inventory

Target Completion Date: _____

Contact each of the key departments at your company. Determine whether they have any formal or informal programs to provide better service to some types of customers. Formalize and expand the programs that make sense and eliminate the others.
Examples may include:

Best Customers

- Special handling for shipments
_____

- Special entertainment by company executives
_____

- More liberal payment and discount terms
_____

- Greater availability of SKUs or product volume
_____

- More flexible advertising of return policies
_____

- Liberal interpretation of warranties and service policies
_____

- Special phone numbers or people to call
_____

Worst Customers

- Surcharges on smaller orders
_____

- Slower service or sales-response time
_____

- Strict enforcement of payment terms
_____

Departments to Include

- Call center
_____

- Co-op advertising
_____

- Customer service
_____

- Direct mail
_____

- General management
_____

- Product management

- Sales

- Support

- Service and repair

Estimating Lifetime Value

Target Completion Date: _____

Every company should establish a formula to rank customers based on a workable approximation of customer Lifetime Value. (This is determined by estimating the stream of future profits over some period of time, net of costs, and discounted at an appropriate rate, back to its net present value.) Considering the challenges associated with determining Lifetime Value, most organizations will need to choose a list of "proxy variables."

Such variables include:

Proxy Variables	Used as a Proxy Variable	Consider Using for LTV Variable Later
Past and expected future customer revenue		
Past and expected future customer profit (revenue minus cost of sales and servicing)		
Expectations about future loyalty		
Opportunities for up-selling and cross-selling		
Collaborative value—willingness to communicate/engage/participate/respond to surveys, etc.		
Accounts payable—the speed at which customer pays		

Time and effort customer devotes to the relationship

Once you have chosen the variables that will help you estimate value, divide your customer base up into its constituent elements (e.g., business customers versus consumers, dealers versus distributors, etc.), and for EACH separate customer base:

- Rank order into five equal-size groups, or quintiles

- Determine the percentage of profit to your firm represented by each quintile

- Explore ways to build a "picket fence" around your top tier that will help you focus on these customers and strengthen their loyalty

Activity 4D

Linking Customer Value and Customer Loyalty

When you tackle the issue of how to improve customer loyalty and reduce attrition, the first question to ask is this: Which customers do you most want to keep loyal?

This exercise will help you concentrate your customer loyalty and antiattrition efforts on the right customers—the ones who return the most value to your business.

Target Completion Date: _____

Who Will Do It?	By When?	Init. and Date	Task	Does It Apply to Our Organizations? (✓)	75% Done (✓)	100% Done (✓)

			1. Determine if customer valuations are computed, or if customers are ranked in any way, today
			  ■ If so, find out how
			  ■ If not, determine which factors might go into the computation if better data were available			

2. Determine whether the prioritization of the firm's marketing and sales efforts provide any clue to understanding both the current and potential value of your company's various types of customers
   - Find out what practical measures exist today for rank-ordering customers by value or potential value
   - List cross-selling and/or up-selling opportunities
   - Initiate one effort to measure Lifetime Value (LTV) across different divisions in order to affect your behavior toward each customer

3. Take steps to improve customer loyalty
   - See if there is any information currently available that can predict attrition and/or loyalty
   - Analyze your "oldest" and longest-tenured customers, and list any characteristics that make them different
   - Find out if those differences are trackable
   - Place extra priority on getting more customers with characteristics like those of your longest-tenured customers

4. Analyze customers who have left your company and list the reasons they may have left
   - Consider implementing "exit interviews"
   - Determine whether attrition can be predicted ahead of time
   - Rank your defecting customers by value, if possible
   - Experiment with preventive steps to avoid attrition, concentrating first on the most valuable customers who are more likely to leave

Task List: Differentiating Customers by Value

The goal of this task list is to identify Most Valuable Customers (MVCs), Most Growable Customers (MGCs), and Below Zero Customers (BZs). Absolute predictive accuracy is not imperative. Think in terms of rank-ordering your customers by their value.

Target Completion Date: _____

Who Will Do It?	By When?	Init. and Date	Task	75% Done (✓)	100% Done (✓)
			Divide your customer base into its constituent elements (e.g., business customers versus consumers, professional dealers versus warehouse distributor, etc.). Do this exercise for each customer group. Possible components of a customer base include: ■ National or strategic accounts ■ Large enterprise customers ■ Medium or small business customers ■ Geographic regions ■ Consumers ■ Heavy users versus infrequent users ■ Other_____		
			Or rank your customers by importance to your enterprise. Groups may include: ■ Influence on others ■ Collaborative value ■ Public reputation ■ "Prestige" accounts		
			Short-term task: Using the information you have today, decide how to rank-order your customers		
			Long-term task: Begin to plan how to calculate the value of customers from this point forward		

- Have your team determine the variables that should be included and the approximate weighting of each
- Ask customers how much business they are giving to competitors
- Calculate your share of customer for each
- Consider possible customer database algorithms, screening questions asked of a customer during an interaction, the practical measures appropriate to customer rank-ordering, and how customer value will be tracked
- Optional: Complete Activity 4F, "Longitudinal Customer Snapshot"
- Optional: Contact a forward-thinking knowledge-base/research firm for help with LTV modeling. Run the data for each customer through the model, in order to calculate a value for each

Determine who your MVCs are
- What percentage of your total customers?
- What percentage of your total business?

Determine who your MGCs are
- What percentage of your total customers?
- What percentage of your total business?

Determine who your BZs are
- What percentage of your total customers?
- What percentage of your total business?

Now that you've rank-ordered your customers by value, think about some quick ways to invest more in your MVCs and less in your BZs. You may want to begin this task by considering:
- Call center (see Chapter Twelve on Call Centers)

- Customer Service
- Amount spent on dialogue
- Degree of customization
- Web site
- How customers stand in line, either literally or figuratively
- Levels of complaint resolution
- Business-to-business: Which customers get your weekend pager number?

Activity 4F

Take a Longitudinal Customer Snapshot

Target Completion Date: _____

This exercise is designed to give you a simple way to visualize and perhaps quantify the customer "trajectories" that come through your customer base. Although it will definitely involve entering data and statistically analyzing it, this is an exercise that should be completed using more commonsense judgment than mathematical analysis or modeling.

1. Go to your company's archives to obtain a large number of customer records from the distant past. Ten years ago would be sufficient, but if you can't obtain customer records for that long ago, then go back as far as you can. It's possible that these records will not be computerized—they might be on microfiche, for instance—and if they are computerized at all, they'll probably be stored off-site somewhere. That's okay, you can do this exercise by examining individual customer records and entering the data into your own PC manually, if you have to. It is a sampling-and-projection exercise.

2. Pull a *random* sample of customer records from these archives. You'll need enough records to ensure statistical accuracy, but if you're doing it manually, you can probably settle for about a thousand records to start with. Be sure your sample is randomized throughout the entire customer base.

3. Now pull the customer records for *each* of these customers in each of the successive years, up to the current year. Be sure to note when customers leave the franchise, and be careful to pick them up again if they reenter in a subsequent year, perhaps under a different account code or identifying system. If you have business customers that merge with each other, be sure to track this, too. If your business is like most, the number of customer records you pull each year will decline, as more and more of the customers in your original sample defect, go out of business, or

merge into others. Do *not* add any customer records to make up for this. That would defeat the purpose of the exercise. But you need to pull enough customer records in the very beginning so that when you get to the current year you still have perhaps two hundred.

4. Now you have a complete "longitudinal snapshot" of your customer base—a sample of the customer trajectories. You can see what percentage of customers tend to leave, what percentage tend to grow. The more customers in your original sample, the more cross-tabbing and learning you can do—what are the characteristics of customers most likely to leave, for instance, or most likely to grow significantly.

Warning: Don't go overboard in your conclusions. Remember that your market situation will have changed substantially from ten years ago, when you drew your first sample of customer records.

Activity 4G
Guidelines for Needs Differentiation

1. Think through the process of buying what your organization sells, from the buyer's point of view:

   - Initially learning about the product or service availability
   - Making the initial contact
   - Deciding what to buy
   - Deciding how it will be configured
   - Choosing size, color, etc.
   - Deciding how to price it (e.g., "Buy three for a discount")
   - Setting up financing
   - Setting up pickup or delivery
   - Learning what happens when something is wrong
   - Finding out how easy it is to make the next purchase

2. Determine how your customers differ in each of the above ways

3. Determine whether you currently have any segmentation or niche strategies in which you meet the needs of customers based on these different processes

4. Using available research or your own judgment, list all the information you already have about the different needs of your customers

   a. Find out if a customer ever designed a product with your organization
      - If so, describe how collaboration was involved

- If not, determine how collaboration *could* be involved in customizing your product or service

b. List all personal information about customers that could be used to their advantage and to your organization's advantage (e.g., children's ages, colleges attended, pets, etc.)

c. Find out whether customers have access to information about themselves that is captured or exchanged by your firm

d. Create a method to prevent customers from taking away that information and bringing it to a competitor, or to give them a reason *not to want to* do this

e. Describe all customer groups, if any, that have an ongoing relationship with your organization and how those relationships are maintained (e.g., add-on services, repeat purchases, upgrades, and product improvements)

f. Describe how these customer groups vary in terms of what needs they are meeting with your organization's product or service

Activity 4H
Relationship Strategy Matrix

We consider "segments" to be groups in which customers are not managed on an individual basis. If a group of customers is not individually identifiable and its members are not in interactive contact with the firm, it would be appropriate to call it a segment. Quite often, this is the most sensible level at which to manage certain customer relationships. We recognize that companies often must begin by developing individualized relationships with their most valuable customers. Attempting to create a 1to1 relationship with every customer, all at once, often can undermine efforts to build a 1to1 enterprise.

By contrast, a "portfolio" of customers is an unduplicated group of customers that is under the management of a customer manager. Customer-portfolio management is the kind of organizational structure necessary if you are going to hold someone accountable in a firm for keeping particular customers loyal, increasing their business, and ensuring that they become more valuable to the firm. When a company puts together a series of customer portfolios, it is assumed that the customers are individually identifiable and that they are occasionally in interactive contact with the enterprise.

Think through the characteristics of your customer base and list some segments that describe your customers. Your objective is to describe segments in terms of particular community needs that the segment members might have in common. "High-tech road warriors," for instance, might be a customer segment for a telecom company. "Self-actualizing mothers of small children" might be a segment for a toy company.

For each segment identified, complete the worksheet on the following page. Your goal is to map out ways in which your firm might begin to treat different customers differently, based on their different needs from the enterprise.

Target Completion Date: _____

Defining the Relationship Strategy	**Name of Segment** _____.
What needs would you use to differentiate this segment?	
What objective (e.g., retain, grow, divest, archive, migrate) would you establish for this segment?	
What value proposition would you create for this segment?	
What interactive, two-way communication vehicles are available with this segment?	
Can you customize—cost-efficiently—any aspect of the whole product/service for this segment?	
How would you assign marketing responsibility for this segment?	
How would you monitor your relationships with customers in this segment?	

Chapter Five

Interact with Your Customers

HOW TO GENERATE MORE CUSTOMER FEEDBACK, LESS EXPENSIVELY

Identify   Differentiate   *Interact*   Customize

IMPLEMENTATION STEP 3: Engage your customers in an ongoing dialogue that enables you to learn more and more about their particular interests, needs, and priorities.

Let's assume you can identify your customers individually and that you have enough information to rank them by their value or by their importance to your organization. Assume also that you can differentiate at least your highest-value customers by their needs, having discovered particular communities of customers with similar needs. The next thing to concentrate on is how to improve your *interactions* with your customers.

Interaction Is Visible to the Customer

Interacting is usually the first, and sometimes the *only*, one-to-one initiative that is actually *visible* to the customer. Customer identification and differentiation are totally invisible, completely beneath the surface of an enterprise's actual relationship with a customer. But interaction requires the customer's active participation and involvement. It has a direct impact on the customer, whose awareness of the interaction is an indispensable part of the process.

Customer interaction has an important side benefit that is totally separate from your 1to1 strategy. Because interaction is visible, the interacting customer gains an impression of a company interested in his or her feedback. Whether or not you actually incorporate the feedback into your organization's behavior toward that particular customer, the customer is likely to have a more favorable opinion of your company, at least in the short term.

Due to this high and immediate visibility, interaction is at the center of almost every Quick Start 1to1 initiative, as you saw in Chapter Two. If you want to dramatically and immediately improve your enterprise's 1to1 profile, go directly to the interaction step. Do not pass "Go." Do not wait until you have collected information about your customers. The four implementation steps are not exactly sequential anyway. There is already considerable overlap from one implementation step to the next. In most cases, better interaction all by itself will allow you to identify a larger proportion of your customers and differentiate them more accurately.

So why wait? Why do we put interaction third in the lineup instead of first? Because if you don't already know a good deal about the characteristics of your customers, you have no way of setting any meaningful objectives for your dialogue program and no way of telling whether you are successful. And if you aren't prepared to incorporate the dialogue itself into a broader strategy for creating an individualized, 1to1 relationship with each customer, your efforts to interact will soon deteriorate into simply a noisy and annoying waste of the customer's time—

just one more communication from a marketer trying to get a snippet of this consumer's attention.

Interaction is a good thing in general, but not always. More and more these days, companies are taking the side benefit of interaction with no intention of trying to incorporate a customer's feedback into a 1to1 strategy. The result is that customers in a wide range of industries and businesses are now being oversurveyed and overcontacted. The hotel that calls your room just to assure you that the concierge is "at your service." The credit card company that mails an "important message" to *everyone* in its customer base to inform them about a new type of card that is actually of interest to fewer than 1 percent of the customers. The car company that calls you at home three different times, interrupting your day just to make sure that last week's service was acceptable. One engineering-equipment firm actually received a call from a senior officer at one of its customers, requesting that the firm stop constantly interviewing and surveying his engineers with respect to how satisfied they were with the equipment or how service could be improved. Enough already!

The saddest effect of the recent trend toward overinteraction with customers is that many people now think this is what relationship marketing is all about. A *Harvard Business Review* article, written by three professors who probably should have known better, mistakenly identified the deluge of unsolicited junk mail offers and telemarketing calls with companies' efforts to launch relationship marketing programs.

But there is a correct methodology for interacting with a customer. Interaction should not be a random and unconnected event. If your interaction is intended to build a 1to1 relationship:

1. It should minimize the customer's inconvenience.
2. The outcome should be of some real benefit for the customer.
3. It should influence your specific behavior toward that customer.

This is why interaction is third in the sequence of implementation steps and not first. The interaction itself must contribute to your overall effort to build a 1to1 enterprise. This means the type of interaction in which you choose to engage a particular customer will be driven by what that customer needs from you and by that customer's value to you.

Why Are You Calling Me Anyway?

Then there is the question of motive. Over and above the "feel good" atmosphere you may or may not be able to generate in a relationship with a customer, what is the actual *reason* behind the interaction? What are the objectives for the interaction itself? What are you really trying to find out, and why?

In the context of building a 1to1 enterprise, there are some kinds of information that are relatively less available in the ordinary course of business, and more usefully acquired by interacting directly with your customers:

Strategic value. Unless you are prepared to interact with a customer, you can't really know much about that customer's growth potential with your enterprise. You can model the customer's past behavior and predict LTV based on a run rate. You can tap outside database sources for penetration figures and the like. But in most business situations there is no more reliable way to find out what business a specific customer is doing with a competitor, or what plans a specific customer has for expanding, unless you ask the customer directly.

If you use interaction to acquire information on a customer's strategic value, you should also be prepared to systematize your data. That is, you need to devise a *format* for estimating and documenting a customer's growth potential, so you can compare one customer to another, or one group of customers to another. At a call center, this could be a simple button on the service rep's screen to denote the level of possibility that the customer is in the market for a certain category of product. For a direct sales force, the sales force automation system should accommodate each salesperson's "best guesstimate" of the value of the next potential project, and it should be possible to record this figure not just in the "notes" field, but in a field where the figure can easily be accessed and used for comparison purposes.

Customer needs. Often you have to interact with a customer in order to gain any real understanding of the customer's needs. You can pretty much assume that obviously different customers will have different types of needs (pharmaceutical companies versus oil refineries, for instance, or single men versus families with children). And it's usually possible to gain some insight into what a particular customer needs by observing what the customer buys, particularly if you have a wide variety of products, services, and other alternatives to choose from.

But, as we learned in our discussion of needs-based differentiation in the last chapter, on any given day two very outwardly similar customers might buy the same exact product from you for totally different reasons. That is, to satisfy two completely different needs. So interaction with the customer can be helpful in defining exactly what need the customer is trying to satisfy. That's why, if you commission market research to cluster your customers by their needs, you also want to find out what questions you could ask of your customers to map them into one needs-based cluster or another.

Customer satisfaction and complaint discovery. Another kind of information, useful to have but hard to get without some form of individual interaction, is the customer's level of satisfaction with the product or service you're selling. Yes, the customer bought it, and this may in fact be the fifth time he's bought it from you, but was he actually satisfied *this time*? You can interact to find out what your firm can do to make the customer's specific experience better the next time around. We call this kind of interaction "complaint discovery" (see Chapter Three of *The One to One Future,* pages 78–87, and *Enterprise One to One,* pages 266–269), because the overwhelming majority of complainers, in both consumer-marketing and business-to-business situations, consist of "silent sufferers." They are not happy with something, but they don't take the initiative to complain to you about it, even though they may talk disparagingly about your firm with their friends or colleagues.

Interacting with a customer to learn how satisfied the customer is, or whether the customer has an unspoken complaint, is really just another way of obtaining information about that customer's needs. What the 1to1 enterprise wants to know is how to make the service better *for that customer* at the next opportunity. If you can find out how to treat a specific customer better the next time, you can begin to lock that customer into a Learning Relationship with your enterprise. If every time a customer deals with you it is more satisfying—a higher-quality experience—for that customer than it was the previous time, you are creating a Learning Relationship with the customer, and after just a few interactions the customer will become very loyal.

Warning: Do not use this type of interaction to excess, or your customers will begin to resist interacting at all. One good principle to apply is to check on a customer's satisfaction whenever anything out of the ordinary has occurred in the relationship—a particularly large or complex purchase, a problem in installation or financing, a complaint or billing dispute that was (you think) resolved, or an unusual request for information by the customer. After one of these unusual events, it's not a bad idea to have someone contact the customer just to ensure that everything is okay and to find out if there is a better way to handle the customer next time around. If feedback does indicate the need for some change, then you must have a reliable customer-response system to ensure that the change is actually implemented, *for that customer,* the next time.

RULES OF ENGAGEMENT

- Don't initiate an interaction with a customer without a clear objective.
- Don't ask a customer the same thing more than once.
- Interact in the medium of the customer's choice.
- When engaging in an interaction, start with the customer, not the product.
- Make the interaction personal, and personalized.
- Ensure that your interactions with customers are always welcomed.
- Use mass-customization principles (and technology) to reduce the cost and increase the personalization of dialogue.
- Ensure that MVCs are immediately identified and treated appropriately.
- Protect the customer's privacy.
- Invite dialogue by printing toll-free numbers and Web site URLs on everything.
- Ensure that the customer can see the value from each interaction. Deliver information or value that reflects what has been learned.
- Be sensitive to the customer's time. Don't try to learn everything about a customer at once.

As personal information becomes increasingly valuable to the success of companies, it also becomes an increasingly sensitive issue to those who provide it. Dinnertime telemarketing and voluminous junk mail—all made possible through the careless distribution and redistribution of customer lists—has fed a consumer backlash. Individuals are becoming ever more concerned about how their profile information might be used—or abused.

With this in mind, you should have an explicit privacy protection policy to ensure that your own customer's privacy will not be violated. In order to build an enduring relationship with customers, it is essential to address this issue. Customers have to feel secure in the offering of their own personal information if they are to engage in the forms of dialogue that are critical to the 1to1 enterprise.

Your privacy protection policy should explain to customers what kinds of information you need from them, how the information will be used, and how it will *not* be used. It should also spell out the benefits a customer stands to gain by sharing personal information. When a privacy policy of this sort is created, promote it with a special mailing, include it with a monthly bill, or post it on your Web site. A privacy policy will strengthen the foundation on which each customer relationship is built. Trust is essential, and a privacy policy will help build that trust.

TEN POINTS TO CONSIDER IN DEVELOPING YOUR COMPANY'S PRIVACY POLICY

Every company that maintains a Web site or collects personal information of any kind about its customers should establish an explicit privacy protection policy. You can call it a "Privacy Pledge" or a "Privacy Bill of Rights" or just your "Privacy Protection Policy," but the following points should be covered:

1. Itemize the kind of information collected about individual customers.
2. Specify how personal information will be used by the company. If your policy is to use this kind

of information only within the company on a need-to-know basis, and not to make it accessible to unauthorized employees at any time, explain this policy explicitly.

3. Make whatever commitments you can make with respect to how individual customer information will *never* be used (e.g., personal information is never sold or rented to others, or never used to change prices or insurance premiums, etc.).

4. State the benefits an individual customer can expect as a result of the enterprise's use of his or her information (faster or preferential service, reduced costs, etc).

5. List a customer's options for directing the enterprise not to use or disclose certain kinds of information.

6. State how a customer can change or update personal information you've collected. For example, can the consumer access her profile or account information online and modify it?

7. Identify events that might precipitate a notification to the customer by the enterprise. If, for instance, a court subpoenas your customer records, will you notify any customers whose information was subpoenaed?

8. Name the corporate executive whom you've assigned as the "data steward," charged with overall responsibility for assuring the adherence to company information and privacy policies.

9. Specify the situations in which your company accepts or denies liability for damages incurred through the collection and use of customer data, such as through credit card fraud or misuse.

10. Provide specific procedures allowing a customer to order you to stop collecting data about him, or to purge his information files at the company.

With the proliferation of the World Wide Web, and all the information-gathering it has entailed, many commercial sites have explicit privacy policies that cover points such as these. For some sample privacy policies, see:

- American Express at http://www.americanexpress.com/corp/consumerinfo/privacy/privacystatement.shtml
- Dell at http://www.dell.com/policy/privacy.htm
- America Online at http://www.aol.com/info/privacy.html
- Hewlett-Packard at http://www.hp.com/ahp/privacy/privacy.htm
- Peppers and Rogers Group at http://www.1to1.com/member/privacy.html

TRUSTe is an independent, nonprofit organization dedicated to the disclosure of information-gathering and dissemination practices on the Web so that users can make informed decisions about whether they want to do business with particular sites. The organization describes itself as a "global initiative for establishing consumer trust and confidence in electronic commerce."

The organization is a spinoff of the Electronic Frontier Foundation. As Esther Dyson, EFF board member and president of EDventure Holdings, explains, "This system is important both in itself and as a model of how the industry can effectively regulate itself rather than waiting for government action. It provides for flexible, decentralized enforcement and allows a maximum of choice to customers."

The TRUSTe system is built around one "trustmark," an icon linked to a site's privacy statement. The trustmark tells consumers how the information they reveal online will be used.

TRUSTe is an important step in the right direction. It provides companies with a simple and highly visible method of revealing how they will use individual information. We agree with Dyson that the key to avoiding government regulation—which would certainly slow down online innovation—is aggressive self-regulation on the part of leading companies. To that end, TRUSTe has won the support of many leading companies, including America Online, Excite, IBM, Lands' End, the *New York Times* on the Web, State Farm Insurance Companies, Wired Digital, and Peppers and Rogers Group.

Companies can license use of the trustmark by downloading an online licensing agreement and invoice from the TRUSTe Web site. Licensing costs range from about US $250 to $5,000, depending on the annual revenue of the company and the sensitivity of the information. Signatories to the TRUSTe agreement are encouraged to display the TRUSTe logo prominently on their home pages and at each location on their sites where information is collected.

Making Interaction More and More Cost-Efficient

Every interaction with an individual customer involves an expense. Even without considering the cost or hassle of occupying a customer's time and attention, there is a "transaction cost" to nearly every type of interaction imaginable, although some kinds of interactions are much more costly than others. Being able to rank your customers by their value allows you to take a more rational approach to managing the interaction process.

Relationships are the goal. But some forms of interaction are more expensive than others. Therefore, plan on using different approaches for different-valued customers. A highly valuable customer is more likely to be worth a personal sales call, while a not-so-valuable customer may not merit even an outbound phone call.

As technology has made it less and less costly, businesses are finding that they can afford to interact with a wider range of customers economically. Rich and intricate interactions no longer have to be limited to a few ultra-elite MVCs. On one hand, this opens up entirely new channels for businesses, allowing a firm to serve classes of customers it couldn't even deal with *except* for the Web. And on the other hand, it allows a firm to streamline and automate many of the manual interactions required in servicing customers, reducing costs and saving time, often quite dramatically.

Consider just a few examples:

Cisco Systems manufactures and installs highly complex computer routers and switches, requiring detailed, well-engineered configuration work. As a result, Cisco's sales force and support staff often have worked for weeks at a time on a single customer's configuration problem, going back and forth with the customer's CIO and purchasing manager, documenting their progress with reams of error-prone paperwork.

Cisco, however, has streamlined and enhanced this complex sales process through its Web site, dubbed Cisco Connection Online. The site enables customers to configure and reconfigure their own systems, gaining access to Cisco's product and system specs in seconds. The benefits they've received have often been cited as a validation of the basic idea of e-commerce. Instead of weeks, a "clean order" can now be entered and slotted into Cisco's own back-end production and delivery system in as little as fifteen minutes. And Cisco makes it easy for customers to register their own system configurations for later upgrades. This saves time and cuts transaction costs, but it also ensures that no customer ever has to reenter configuration information. The site now facilitates several billion dollars' worth of transactions annually, while eliminating several hundred million dollars' worth of servicing costs. It also strengthens relationships with customers and reduces their propensity to defect.

Owens Corning uses its Web site to address multiple audiences, and increasingly to interact with builders and contractors, equipping them with tools to build their own businesses. According to Steve Smoot, director of customer-information services:

> . . . the only way a builder or contractor can significantly improve sustainable profits is by keeping tighter control over the building processes, particularly in scheduling and cost estimating, to get rid of waste and inefficiency. In collaboration with industry experts, notably BuildNet, Inc., our focus is on integrating with the construction business's project-management process. The tools we are developing will utilize the online technologies as a platform to deliver greater productivity to the way our professional customers work, and we bundle the access to those services with other business-management and marketing tools under a series of membership programs to strengthen our franchise, one customer at a time.

Hewlett-Packard makes, in addition to computer equipment, a wide variety of testing and measurement instruments, ranging from $400 oscilloscopes to $500,000 microchip-testing systems. Some of these test and measurement machines require regular maintenance and calibration, and HP provides this service to its customers as well. In Australia, HP's Test and Measurement Organization maintains a Web site on which it allows customers that own many pieces of test equipment to track their equipment, by site, forecasting the calibration and maintenance schedule for each machine, and even contacting HP to schedule a field engineer's visit. The company also allows customers to register and track non-HP test and measurement equipment on the site.

Ford Motor Company is developing a Web site for its car owners. In addition to making it easier for customers to communicate with Ford and its dealers, the Web-based services Ford is contemplating include configuration and pricing of new car purchases, financing and leasing services, and documentation of each car's service history. One problem Ford has, like other car companies, is finding out exactly when a customer is "in the market" for a new car. This is "strategic value" information. While there are algorithms and statistical techniques for making gross estimates as to when a particular person might be in the market for a new car, the only reliable way to know is to ask the customer directly. To do this, however, the company first has to create a cost-efficient mechanism for supporting the dialogue, as well as a relationship with the customer that is already based on regular interaction.

And of course there are a whole panoply of totally new businesses that have been launched on the Web. Such businesses usually revolve around some very cost-efficient or automated form of interaction. You can search for a car or execute a trade. You can purchase books, CDs, software, videos, vitamins, cats, dogs, saddles, heat pumps, contact lenses. You can get your groceries delivered or your horoscope read, diagnose your fax machine, make a long-distance call. You can also schedule shipping containers, configure a water-treatment plant or purchase a complex array of computers, software, and networking equipment for the office.

But the Internet is just one technology for interacting with customers, and it is the interaction itself that creates a relationship. There are other technologies. Many businesses have used call centers to create interactive relationships. USAA, the insurance firm, has built a multi-billion-dollar business almost entirely on the basis of call-center interactivity, as has Dell Computer, Gateway, 1-800-FLOWERS, and others.

With any form of interaction, however, including phone interactions, it is critical to emphasize the importance of cultivating a *relationship* with the customer. First Direct, the telephone-only bank based in the UK, built an extremely successful financial-services business by catering to customers over the phone, letting them make cash transactions at other banks' cash machines. The bank underscores the importance of relationships with an interesting exercise administered to all new phone employees. Each recruit is blindfolded and then issued a lemon—an ordinary, yellow lemon. The recruit is given time to hold the lemon, get to know its size and feel, memorize its various bumps and flaws, its shape, its unique texture. Then all the lemons are placed in a bowl and each recruit, still blindfolded, is asked to retrieve the lemon he or she just got to know so intimately. This is how the bank emphasizes the importance of getting to know each individual customer, each uniquely different personality, even though the interaction itself is limited to talking on the phone, and the employee will never get to meet the customer in person or look directly into the customer's face.

Direct mail can also be helpful in cultivating individualized relationships with customers, although it is important to supplement postal mail with faster, electronic forms of interaction to enable customers to make more immediate contact with the marketer. AT&T and other sophisticated direct mailers often carve up a mailing population into literally hundreds of different "clusters" of customers, based on whatever the company knows about these customers—their tastes, their price sensitivity, their brand preferences.

One thing that's important to recognize, however, is that customers have communication preferences, too. Different customers will probably *want* to use different media to interact with you. In fact, on any given day, even the *same* customer may choose to interact with you differently. So being able to ensure that your various interactive channels can actually communicate with each other is a vital part of setting up genuine 1to1 relationships with individual customers. According to Schwab's Mary Kelley:

> Our customers both want and use multiple ways to reach us—they don't all use the Internet. Even those who use the Internet by preference don't use it all the time. They might not have their laptop with them, or they might have their cell phone and want to use our Touch-Tone services, or our speech-recognition services. They may need to get help face to face with a broker, in person, perhaps to resolve a problem. Or maybe they need a check today, not tomorrow. Or they have paperwork they need help with. So our system has to accommodate these differences, not just from customer to customer, but with one customer from time to time.

Recognizing Interaction Opportunities

Setting up a Web site, a call center, or a comprehensive direct mail program involves launching an entirely new activity or department centered on customer interaction. But in the natural course of business you already interact with your customer, at least once in a while. You send customers invoices, and they send money to you. A customer might ask you for more information or for faster delivery. You ship them products, process their service requests, receive complaints, handle disputes.

There are so many potential opportunities to interact with customers that simply identifying and cataloguing all the possible "touch points" your firm has with them can be difficult. In *Enterprise One to One* (pp. 259–264) we suggested taking an interaction inventory, comparing all the different interactive media that might be used and all the reasons a firm or a customer might use them. Conducting such an inventory will allow you to spot immediate opportunities to improve interaction. Conducting an interaction inventory is a critical part of any Quick Start program.

However, regardless of the purpose of the interaction or the type of interactive media employed, your customer has the right to be "known" to you and to have this knowledge used to streamline the interaction. Customers today expect no less, and if you want to create better relationships with them, you'll have to meet certain minimum standards. This means, for example, that when a car owner calls, the auto-dealer service desk should have immediate access to the make, model, year, last service date, and any open issues. Catalogue merchants should know previous shipment dates, the status of returns or credits, and size, shipping, credit, and payment information. Ideally they'll know of special offers or even upcoming sales on products purchased repeatedly by an individual customer. Service industry "inbound" interactions should reflect knowledge of open, pending, and upcoming issues, as well as of new or emerging issues and opportunities that may be of interest.

There is much talk these days about the glut of available information. The point is that customers don't want to receive *more* information. They want to receive *better* information—customized to their personal needs. There are many opportunities to accomplish this objective. Greg Padovani, director of marketing for the Northwestern Medical Faculty Foundation (NMFF) in Chicago, has figured out how to use the humble medical bill as a vehicle for highly personalized communications.

Each month his medical group sends out bills that include individually customized newsletters, dubbed "Health Notes." Using the medical group's enormous storehouse of demographic and treatment-related customer data, Padovani's two-person marketing group is matching the content (and even the priority in which the content appears) with the inferred needs and interests of the individual customer. Out of a total of fifty thousand newsletters published monthly, "no two are alike," he explains.

The newsletters serve as a direct-response vehicle whereby medical specialists of all kinds can inform potential customers of the procedures they provide. The ROI (return on investment), particularly on elective procedures, can be fantastic. Several articles developed for the group's ophthalmologists are expected to generate annual revenues of $54,000 for cosmetic procedures (removing crow's feet and bags under patients' eyes). Annual investment in newsletter services for these articles, meantime, is just $8,000. Indeed, the costs associated with the monthly newsletter are relatively minimal.

Having learned the customer-billing process in the early 1990s when the organization decided to redesign it, Padovani realized he could "piggyback" a marketing and communications resource onto the bill itself. The results have been stellar. It has proved an excellent way to cross-sell the organization's vast array of medical services and build customer relationships. Now Padovani is exploring ways to make the newsletter available monthly to *all* interested parties (including the patients of competing health care providers).

A service-industry firm usually has many opportunities to interact with its customers. Indeed, the best firms have always emphasized courtesy, understanding, and genuine "service," in the old-fashioned sense of the word. But how does even the best service enterprise ensure that its customer-contact people can actually *remember* an individual customer and his or her preferences? These days, they can do it with computers. The interaction is still courteous, warm, and personal, but the human being behind it can now be equipped with a silicon-enhanced memory.

British Airways recently upgraded its customer relationship programs with a new system that seeks to deliver seamlessly integrated responses to the preferences of its MVCs at every physical location in its system, worldwide. But rather than initiating the process with a long and obnoxious survey asking their very best customers for information about seat preferences and the like, British Airways has implemented a system for *observing* its best customers and *remembering* their preferences.

The workhorse of this program is a PC now carried in the galley of its planes for the use of the onboard service professionals. This is the instrument in which customer preferences are updated, while flying at five hundred knots in a 747, or cruising sixty thousand feet over the Atlantic at Mach 2 in the Concorde. Of course, BA started with a staff already trained to serve customers courteously and attentively. But now these same servicepeople can take note of particular customer requests and, using their own judgment, elect to enter their observations into the computer. This will update the customer's profile for future interactions.

British Airways emphasizes that it's not the computer that's directing the crew, it's the crew that's directing the computer, in order to do better what they have already been trained to do, which is to provide great service. According to one British Airways executive:

> It's the crew that's on board the flight on that day, or running the airport on that day—they're the ones who make the decisions. The computer provides the information, but our people make the decisions. So, for example, if we have a nervous passenger, then a crew member might use the computer to record that "this passenger is nervous and here's what we did this time . . ." But we don't want the system to dictate that on every flight, twenty minutes into the flight, the senior on board holds this passenger's hand and says it'll be all right. Instead, on one flight it might be appropriate to take a nervous passenger up to the flight deck, show him the panorama of landscape and instru-

ments, let him talk to the flight crew, while another day it would be better just to ask in passing if everything is all right today. We want our people simply to use their judgment to adapt to the situation on *that* flight, but with an accurate knowledge of *that* customer's needs.

Interaction at the point of purchase can be costly, or it can be extremely cost-efficient. Maybe you should equip your staff with "customer-preference cards," preformatted with specific categories of needs and completed on an ad hoc basis whenever a customer requests something or makes a preference known. This is what the Ritz Carlton does. It then enters the information into the Covia online reservation system. Or maybe you place a PC in the middle of the service area, so that your customer-contact people can immediately input data themselves, the way British Airways is doing. Or perhaps your cashier stations can be upgraded so that they not only take cash and record inventory turns but also display and capture individual customer information. Or maybe all you do is use the billing statement to convey information that is more personally useful to each customer.

Regardless of how you do it, the one thing necessary to become a 1to1 enterprise is to recognize and take advantage of every existing opportunity to interact with your customers.

Because interaction is the first aspect of a 1to1 relationship strategy that will have any visibility to the customer, you have to ensure that it looks rational to the customer. Whether the customer interacts via the call center or in a conversation with a salesperson, whether the customer interacts with Division 1 or Division 2, your enterprise must appear rational and self-aware to the customer. You want to remember the customer as well as the customer remembers you, and you have to be able to coordinate your activities and behavior with respect to that single customer.

To meet these needs, customer management is going to be necessary at some level. In Chapter Nine, "Infrastructure," we'll talk about the kind of organizational structure that will be necessary if you want to hold someone in your enterprise accountable for customer retention and growth. The key implementation tool a customer manager has is interaction and dialogue.

Interaction Is a Crucible for Integrating the Enterprise

The implications of this last argument are significant. What will really happen, as you struggle simply to behave rationally with respect to the interactions you have with individual customers, is that you'll be forced to wrestle with and resolve many of the departmental conflicts and divisional rivalries that plague any complex organization. Interaction is behavior, and to coordinate your own enterprise's behavior you're going to have to resolve internal conflicts first.

This will come as no surprise at all to anyone from a large, multidivision company who has ever tried to enable a call center or a Web site to interact with and serve customers individually. Steve Smoot of Owens Corning summarizes some of his firm's learning:

> The problem is, when we approach our own people about the Internet and what we want to do with it, many still see it in its limited role as a marketing-communications tool, pure and simple. And when we think about the dynamic across business units, the interactive environment makes an organization's inner workings much more visible. We also don't have the luxury of time to wait until someone else figures it out. Building 1to1 interaction capabilities requires solutions in process and infrastructure that cut across typical business-unit and product-line organizations. Integrating the technology is science, [but] creating understanding and trust of these new approaches is *art*.

In other words, putting a Web site together, or a call center, or even trying to rationalize and automate a direct sales force will require at least some level of integration of your firm around common customer objectives and strategies. It's *not* just marketing communications. It's interacting with customers individually, and treating them differently as a result.

If you can *integrate* the knowledge that you acquire through dialogue with individual customers into your product and service offering, you are in a strong competitive position. You have created a strong relationship that is extremely difficult and costly to replace. You have enabled customers to invest something in the relationship—and you have given them a stake in your continuing success.

Interaction is not an end in itself—a tactic we employ now that technology makes it possible. It's not just to make the customer feel better, like some kind of simulated "caring." Through dialogue, we get the information that makes it possible for us to do or make something for our customer that nobody—no competitor—can do or make who does *not* have the information our dialogue with our customer gave us. Dialogue is at the heart of the Learning Relationship.

With dialogue, we *engage* the customer. We learn the customer's preferences and needs. The 1to1 enterprise turns this dialogue into trackable and usable information. If we combine this information with our own enterprise capabilities, the information becomes knowledge. Because nobody can act on what we know about a customer, no one else can serve this customer so well.

So customer knowledge translates directly into loyalty, since the customer will have to reinvent the relationship to get the equivalent product somewhere else. Research across industries demonstrates repeatedly that increased customer retention and loyalty translates into increased profits. Dialogue makes it easier for you to deliver the right product at the right time for that customer. Dialogue is profit.

Think of it this way:

Dialogue = Information
Information = Knowledge
Knowledge = Loyalty
Loyalty = Profit
Therefore . . .
Dialogue = Profit

Cross, Richard, and Janet Smith. *Customer Bonding: Pathway to Lasting Customer Loyalty* (NTC Business Books, 1994).
Cross and Smith show that excellent service, great advertising, powerful data-

bases, and low prices are not enough to capture the customer. They present a marketing system designed to deliver lasting customer loyalty. In their book, they identify the five "degrees" of customer bonding: awareness, identity, relationship, community, and advocacy. They look at everything from frequent-flier programs to co-branded credit cards to grassroots organizing.

Forrest, Edward, and Richard Mizerski, editors. *Interactive Marketing: The Future Present* (American Marketing Association; NTC Business Books, 1996).

This book includes powerful essays from some of the leading lights in the customer relationship management field. Contributors explore marketing strategies and tactics, media tactics and techniques, and data collection and analysis. Don Peppers and Martha Rogers contribute an essay called "One to One Media in the Interactive Future." Other pieces are contributed by Richard Cross and Janet Smith ("Customer Focused Strategies and Tactics"), Richard Hodgson ("Focusing on the Basics in the New Environments"), and Rob Jackson and Paul Wang ("The Convergence of Database Marketing and Interactive Media Networks").

Hoffman, Donna L., and Thomas P. Novak. "A New Marketing Paradigm for Electronic Commerce," *The Information Society, Special Issue on Electronic Commerce,* January/March 1996, pp. 43–54.

This important article discusses the World Wide Web's transformational impact on marketing. In order for marketing to be successful in the new medium, the authors assert, the marketing function must play an integral role in electronic commerce.

Schultz, Don E., Stanley I. Tannenbaum, and Robert Lauterborn. *Integrated Marketing Communications* (NTC Pub. Group, 1994).

Integrated Marketing Communications encourages executives to confront the failure of mass communication and advertising. Schultz, Tannenbaum, and Lauterborn promote customer-focused marketing and show marketers how to reach customers in a diverse, fragmented marketplace. They provide guidance on planning, coordinating, and managing these efforts.

Thissen, Carlene, and John Karolefski. *Target 2000: The Rising Tide of TechnoMarketing* (American Book Company, 1998).

The authors provide a very insightful and forward-looking perspective on how new technologies will transform retailing and the packaged-goods industry. Loaded with interesting case studies, this book examines the impact and potential of new technologies now being incorporated into retail and online shopping.

Wunderman, Lester. *Being Direct* (Random House, 1997).
This book describes Wunderman's personal evolution as he helped to lay the foundations of the now pervasive direct marketing industry and includes fascinating stories about his own company's pioneering work with clients such as American Express and the Columbia Record Club.

CHAPTER 5: INTERACT

Activity 5A

Interactivity Issues for Your Transition Team to Discuss

Target Completion Date: _____

1. Elevator Speech: Why is it important to interact with customers?

_____

_____

_____

2. Complete the following table:

Name all the ways you can think of that your organization can talk to a customer	Name all the ways you can think of that a customer can talk to your organization

Note: Don't be surprised if the list on the left is significantly longer than the list on the right. Part of your goal should be to even the score.

3. How could your organization turn customer interactions into data that would help you provide a product or service your competitor would not be capable of providing?

_____

_____

_____

Activity 5B

Checkpoint: Complaint Resolution

One of the most important—yet unrealized—opportunities in the strengthening of customer loyalty lies in complaint resolution. Such interactions are critical to how the customer will think of your organization and discuss it with others. It's also an opportunity to determine the needs that your organization might effectively meet, for this particular customer. Here are some key questions to answer:

Answer yes or no to the following questions. Repeat this activity one year after the initial date you complete it.

Target Completion Date: _____

	Now	One Year from Now
Does your company treat a complaint as an opportunity to develop a stronger relationship with the complaining customer?	○ Yes ○ No	○ Yes ○ No
Do you use a customer's complaint as an opportunity to learn more about your customer and his or her particular needs?	○ Yes ○ No	○ Yes ○ No
Is the experience and understanding—the customer knowledge—acquired in the process of handling a complaint effectively captured in the customer's record and made easily accessible to others who will work with the customer in the future?	○ Yes ○ No	○ Yes ○ No

Does your company treat the resolution of a complaint as an opportunity to cross-sell or up-sell products?	○ Yes ○ No		○ Yes ○ No	
Are your MVCs and MGCs recognized when they complain, and are they treated with appropriate additional care during the complaint-resolution process?	○ Yes ○ No		○ Yes ○ No	

Activity 5C

Interaction Task List

Target Completion Date: _____

Who Will Do It? (initials)	By When? (exact date)	Task	75% Done (✓)	100% Done (✓)
		Use Activities 5C, D, E, and F to do a systematic "interaction inventory" and quality check across your entire enterprise		
		Devise a strategy for interacting with customers during the time and through the channels they prefer		
		Place someone (a "customer manager") in charge of managing the dialogue you have with your MVCs and MGCs, to ensure that conversations pick up where they left off and that these customers perceive a company that knows and remembers them		
		Remove MVCs (and possibly MGCs) from your standard mailing lists and outbound telemarketing campaigns, placing responsibility for their dialogue in the hands of the customer managers mentioned above		

Create more dialogue opportunities:
- A complaint-discovery program
- Invoices and other routine contacts
- Newsletter
- Discussion groups on Web site
- Other ____

Create a formal privacy protection policy for your customers:
- Notify customers of your privacy policy
- Make sure everyone in your organization understands the privacy policy
- Enforce the policy
- Review your current procedures for acquiring and using customer data to ensure that they comply with your privacy policy (check the "default" settings at your Web site, for instance, and the mailing-list practices in your direct marketing department)

Business-to-Business Interaction Tasks

Create a program for continual contact with customers on "first name" lists referenced in the "Business-to-Business Customer-Identification Task List," Activity 3D

Capture all interactions in contact management software

Ensure that your company is equipped to capture interactions at all customer-contact points (e.g., phone, Web, in person, etc.)

Determine whether your interactive media are available to customers when *they* want to interact

Decide what types of information should be available to the customer and how to make it available in real time

Ensure that information about transaction histories and past interactions is available to sales reps and, when appropriate, partners, suppliers, and other customers

Interaction Inventory

Inventory your organizations' mechanisms for interaction and write them into the table below. Be as specific as possible. List all the mechanisms that now exist for communicating interactively with customers. It will help if you divide your list into two communication types, based on whether the interaction originates:

- To the customer from the enterprise (in real time and non-real time), or
- From the customer to the enterprise (in real time and non-real time)

Be sure to distinguish between inbound and outbound telemarketing efforts, for instance. Some examples are provided to get you started:

1. To the Customer from the Enterprise			
		Target Completion Date: _____	
Substance	Medium	Check if in real time (✓)	Assess Value to Customer
Examples			(1 to 5)
Special promotion offers	Postal mail		2
Collections/invoices	Postal mail		4
	Phone outbound	✓	5
Web-site promotions	E-mail	✓	3

Target Completion Date: _____

Substance	Medium	Check if in real time (✓)	Assess Value to Customer (1 to 5)
Complaints about service	Phone inbound	✓	5
Orders/purchases	Mail		5
	In person	✓	5
	Phone	✓	5
	Fax		5
Inquiries	Phone inbound	✓	3

Activity 5E

Customer Interaction Quality Checklist: Part One

No matter what the interaction type, some fundamental 1to1 strategies apply.

Start by looking at the list in Activity 5D, Part 1, "To the Customer from the Enterprise." For every line item in this list of interactions, answer the following questions:

Interaction Effectiveness

Target Completion Date: _____

Number	Question
1	Does it *leverage current customer knowledge* at the enterprise—that is, knowledge of individual differences and past interactions—in an unobtrusive, useful, and visible manner?

2	Does it *build further customer knowledge* for future use?
3	Does the interaction enable the acquisition of customer knowledge *only obtainable directly from the customer?*
4	Will the interaction *encourage further investment by the customer* in building a 1to1 relationship with the enterprise?
5	Will the *results of the interaction be captured and recorded* by the enterprise?
6	Does the enterprise *honor its privacy policy* to customers?

Interaction Efficiency

Number	Question
7	Is the interaction simple and short (don't ask all your questions at once—surveys are for mass marketers)?
8	Does this interaction pick up where the previous one left off, with each customer?
9	Does the enterprise use the most cost-efficient media vehicle for this interaction?
10	If the customer interacts with one division, is the knowledge of that interaction accessible throughout the enterprise?
11	Does the enterprise follow up after a major interaction (sale, big complaint, special event, etc.)?

Activity 5F

Customer Interaction Quality Checklist: Part Two

Now you need to assess the ways customers contact your company. This time start with the list in Part 2 of Activity 5D, "From the Customer to the Enterprise." For every line item in this list of interactions, answer the following questions:

Number	Question
1	Is the company readily accessible to customers for each issue they need help with?
2	Can you improve the handling of customer inquiries?
3	Should additional media be used to provide greater customer interaction or access?
4	Do your customers find it in their own interests to use the most cost-efficient forms of interactive media?
5	Will the results of the interaction be captured and recorded by the enterpise?
6	Does the enterprise honor its privacy policy in this interaction?
7	Does the enterprise track the individual "success rate" of this customer-initiated interaction (e.g., complaints handled satisfactorily, inquiries generating leads, brochures fulfilled on time, etc.)?
8	Is the interaction simple and short for the customer (in other words, can the customer get quickly to the issue of concern to him? Are the menus simple, are the choices easy?)
9	Can the customer pick up with this interaction where he left off with the previous one?
10	If the customer interacts with one division, will the knowledge of that interaction become accessible throughout the enterprise?
11	Will the enterprise follow up after a major interaction (sale, big complaint, special event, etc.)?

Interactive-Mechanism and Media Considerations

Now examine every possible mechanism for interacting with customers and review your options for improving the interaction, ensuring the highest quality at the lowest possible expense.

Target Completion Date: _____

Topic	Steps	Complete
Direct sales calls	■ Determine the frequency and substance of live sales calls ■ Determine what products or services and what percentage of total sales are sold this way ■ Establish a method for selecting and personally conducting customer visits on a priority basis	
E-mail and electronic data interchange (EDI)	■ Determine what proportion of customers, if any, wish to be connected electronically to the firm ■ Determine what transactions and interactions can be accomplished online and which are online already ■ Find out what types of electronic commerce can be accommodated by the firm, including invoicing, product specification, fulfillment and delivery scheduling, and others	
Facsimile messages (inbound and outbound)	■ Determine what link fax communication has with other media interactions, like print, direct mail, or phone (e.g., can a telemarketing rep "hot key" a fax message to a customer to fulfill a request for information?) ■ Decide whether to use outbound fax for dissemination of price schedules, product information, or anything else ■ Determine how inbound fax messages are received, routed, and managed by the company	

Mail (postal)	■ Establish the frequency of direct mail campaigns and the general tenor of these campaigns ■ Track which customers are the most frequent recipients of mail ■ Establish a method for testing campaigns ■ Decide whether to fulfill in-house or to outsource
Point of purchase	■ Determine what information from customers is captured at cash registers or checkout positions (if applicable) and/or at the points of product or service delivery to the customer ■ Find out if your organization uses or has access to any point-of-purchase kiosks or interactive terminals, and if so, determine what sort of customer interactions these terminals accommodate
Telephone (inbound and outbound)	■ Establish a method for scheduling, executing, and evaluating outbound calls ■ Establish a method for routing, handling, and evaluating inbound calls and for escalating calls from best customers ■ Decide whether the same reps do outbound as well as inbound calls
Web-site interaction	■ See how easy it is to ask your own company a question via its Web site ■ Determine what types of tools your organization will use to capture customer information and automatically transfer it to a database for future use ■ Explore ways of tracking activities on your site and thereby observing the behavior of your customers ■ Examine your options in terms of automating responses to frequently asked questions ■ Examine options for differentiating communications with your best customers so they are treated with special care

- Ensure that your customers can help themselves and get all necessary information directly from your Web site. Ask yourself how difficult it is for a customer to:
  - Update his own profile
  - Find up-to-date product and service information
  - Configure and order products or services directly
  - Locate the nearest dealer or service point
  - Check the status of an order
  - Talk to other customers or users, perhaps with similar profiles or similar needs and problems

Customize Your Product or Service

HOW TO DO <u>EXACTLY</u> WHAT YOUR CUSTOMER WANTS

Identify   Differentiate   Interact   *Customize*

IMPLEMENTATION STEP 4: Act on what you've learned. Use your knowledge about individual customers to customize the way you treat them.

From the customer's perspective, interacting directly with an enterprise may be the first visible sign that the enterprise is taking a one-to-one approach, but from the enterprise's perspective the key step is the fourth one, *customize*.

Without some change in the enterprise's actual behavior toward a single, individual customer, what's the point of even calling it a "one-to-one" relationship? If the customer tells you something about how he or she wants to be treated and you *don't* act on it, what kind of relationship is that?

If you change your behavior toward a single, individual customer you are, in fact, customizing. Now, most businesses already do some type of customization, at least for some customers. Service companies—particularly companies that sell expensive or complex business services—tend to customize the delivery of their services as a matter of routine. Every customer needs to be served in a different way, and a service firm is not hampered by the constraints of a fixed assembly line.

But even manufacturing firms often customize the way they treat their customers. Companies that sell high-priced products to business customers will customize the services that accompany these products and will often customize the actual physical products as well, because the economics make sense. When an industrial customer buys a $700,000 piece of factory equipment, chances are the seller will configure that equipment to the buyer's specifications, at least to some extent. Businesses that don't sell complex and expensive products per se will often customize some aspect of the way they treat their very best, most valuable customers. If you have a single customer accounting for 15 percent of your business, you're likely to bend over backward accommodating that specific customer's needs.

In most cases, customization is reserved for detailed services, high-priced products, or most valuable customers for a valid and undeniable reason: because customization, as a process, is *expensive* for a business to undertake.

But one of the central ideas of 1to1 marketing is that you have to be able to change your behavior toward a customer based on that particular customer's needs. You have to be willing to customize.

The necessity for customization, however, raises issues of cost. How can a company possibly adopt a 1to1 marketing approach without driving expenses through the roof?

The answer is *mass* customization. The whole field of mass customization has been richly explored and developed over the last few years, including a considerable amount of writing we've done on the topic ourselves, and this book is not the place to review the literature.

Nevertheless, you need to know a little bit about how mass customization works before attempting to integrate your knowledge of an individual customer into the way you treat that customer.

Many firms initially embrace the discipline of mass customization as a means of reducing their manufacturing costs. By building a single product to a customer's order, as opposed to manufacturing it in advance, your inventory costs will decline, and often the time to market required for new, innovative products will decline as well. These benefits are more significant in some industries than in others, but the idea is straightforward. Dell Computer, for instance, has recently stolen a march on competitors by building to order. When Intel reduces the price on a chip, making it possible to reduce the cost of a PC hard drive, Dell is able to take immediate advantage by simply incorporating the new chip price into the next PCs being configured for particular customers. Competing manufacturers, on the other hand, must retroactively reduce the price for all their hard drives already loaded into their channel pipelines—pipelines that might include six to nine weeks or more of inventory at any one time.

So if your business already delivers customized products or services—even high-end products customized for high-end customers—you can use mass customization to reduce your costs.

The actual mechanics of mass customization are much simpler than most people realize. A mass customizer does not really *customize* anything at all. What a mass customizer does is preproduce dozens, or hundreds, of "modules" for the product. Then, based on an individual customer's needs, the company configures the right modules together to yield thousands, or even millions, of possible product configurations. In the same way that Levi's is able to produce 5,700 different jeans options for its Original Spin jeans simply by combining 227 waist/hip sizes with 25 leg sizes, NMFF's customized newsletter is individually configured in more than 50,000 versions by combining a few dozen individual articles. So when you think about *how* to change your enterprise's behavior to meet the needs of an individual customer, think "modularization."

Nor should your behavior changes be limited to changes in your physical product or your core service. There are *many* aspects of your overall product or service that can be tailored to an individual customer's need, from invoicing to packaging, automatic inventory replenishment to application notes. When considering the opportunities for customization, be sure to look at "off-line" manufacturing and fulfillment operations that might be better suited to short-run, "versions of one" production. Could you be more responsive to customers' needs by reverting to manual procedures? Should you establish a special service group, empowered to break the rules applied to most customer requests?

Once you do embrace the mass customization idea and begin to figure out how to modularize, it will pay to know all the various component elements your product or service can be combined with, connected to, reduced from, or built onto. Think about the *related* services or products you could offer, either by producing them yourself or by creating strategic alliances with other firms or simply with other business units in your own enterprise.

To take a simple example, an ordinary grocery commodity like milk can take on an entirely different character, with a different type of consumer appeal, when it is chocolate- or strawberry-flavored. And these physical product variations are eclipsed when the carton is placed at a customer's front door, fresh and cold, before breakfast each morning. Home delivery changes the product's dimension, yet is unrelated to the physical product itself. Add another dimension by predicting the household's consumption rate, by flavor, and debiting the family MasterCard, and it's likely that, over time, Pepsi sales in the household will drop as the family drinks more milk. You might also be able to improve their diets with other refrigerated dairy products you deliver, such as orange juice, yogurt, and eggs. Or you could deliver Pepsi as well.

If you consider the wide range of customization options beyond the physical product itself, customization often will be easier to deliver on. There are, in fact, many ways an enterprise can tailor the way it behaves with respect to an individual customer, other than customizing a physical product:

- *Bundling*: Try selling two or more products together. These can be related products or accessories (sweat socks with sneakers, monitors with computers, insurance with automobiles, or hamsters with cages). Or bundle consumable or replenishable supplies with a product (disks with computers, gas with automobiles, pet food with hamsters). Or consider offering certain high-volume customers a greater quantity than everyone else gets—a dozen bars of soap, two dozen golf balls, or half a truckload of product rather than a single pallet.

- *Configuration*: Without changing the physical product itself, perhaps you could preconfigure a system to your client's specs. Computer and office machine makers are noted for this. Phones are arriving with preset speed dials, preconfigured feature sets, and company directories already installed in the appropriate slots under the handset. Acumin Corporation, for example, develops an individualized daily vitamin prescription based on an extensive health questionnaire and an analysis of a single strand of the customer's hair. The firm preconfigures a daily assortment, often including a dozen pills or more, in a small plastic bag.

- *Packaging*: How many variations of packaging make sense for the consumer, and are there specific relationships or linkages between consumer types and packaging types? Do seniors want smaller, lighter packages with instructions in larger type? Do professionals seek different product information than consumers? Which customers would prefer multipacks and which would prefer minipacks?

- *Delivery and logistics*: Is the product delivered on your customer's schedule or yours? Does the product arrive exactly where it's needed or at the general location? Do delivery options vary based on customer value, with free shipping provided, perhaps, for MVCs and MGCs? At what point might a customer qualify for on-site inventory or perhaps a dedicated enterprise representative on-site at the customer's facility? Even the U.S. Post Office has mastered the concept of the on-site service rep, providing postal inspectors at the nation's largest magazine-printing plants to speed catalogues and publications directly to our mailboxes and help manage the postal needs of the very largest customers.

- *Ancillary services*: Does the new car come with quarterly detailing, biweekly wash-and-wax, or automatic pickup and delivery when it's time for maintenance? Are these options even offered? Extended warranties are a great mechanism for enhancing the core product, and a warranty can easily be customized based on intended use, whether measured in copies-per-month, hours-per-day, or miles-per-year. Ancillary services provided by strategic alliance partners are often best sold as part of the initial transaction in order to seamlessly address the customer's needs. Don't offer annual shampooing of that new luxury living-room carpet unless the seller can do the paperwork for the buyer, include the cost in the overall price, finance the purchase, and assure the quality.

- *Service enhancements*: Time-sensitive businesses and firms that buy mission-critical products or services for their operations appreciate the option of enhanced or special services. So make these services available to such customers on a "one stop" basis, even if you have to rely on other organizations, your strategic partners, to deliver them. Laptop makers quickly embraced the "next-day overhaul," at a premium price, which promises major or minor laptop repairs in less than twenty-four hours. Several firms have established large repair depots at the FedEx hub in Memphis. Repair crews work all night to have the PC on the next day's early-morning flight home. In most cases, these services are delivered only at an additional fee, but the availability and convenience of the service offers tremendous value to some customers. And there is no reason you couldn't *waive* the fee altogether for very-high-value MVCs or MGCs.

- *Invoicing*: Are invoices sent at the convenience of the customer or at your own convenience? Are they developed in the optimum, most desirable format for a customer or for ease of issuance by your accounting department? Could you provide the invoice digitally or over the Web? Could you provide flexible details, set up to help a customer distribute its own costs? Do you facilitate all types of EDI with your customers? Do you anticipate cash discounts? Do your bills offer favorable processes and terms to the customer? Is the customer aware of these options and their value, and reminded regularly in case needs change?

- *Payment terms:* Terms can vary widely to suit individual needs and preferences, without making the finance department grumble. Some buyers prefer smaller payments and longer terms, while others seek to forestall payment and will gladly pay the price. Increase the flexibility of payment schemes and methods you can accept, working over time to enable full customization in this relatively easy area of flexibility.

- *Preauthorization:* Working with the customer's management team, some marketers enforce preset authorizations and limits and customize the corporate approval system, in essence, to meet the different needs of different customers. Vice presidents are allowed to order leather desk sets and unlimited paper supplies from an executive version of the office supply catalogue, while secretaries perhaps find themselves limited to $100 per month or Lucite only.

- *Streamlining services:* Does the new "ship to" address of a longtime customer really need all that paperwork, or can you assume the creditworthiness and reliability of the firm? Can you streamline your accounting and credit-granting systems to make it easier for long-standing customers, MVCs, and MGCs? Why not empower your staff to reduce paperwork and processing time for customers meeting a certain set of criteria, preapproving them wherever possible?

As we pointed out in Chapter Four, the more different your customers are in terms of what they *need,* the more likely it is they'll find a tailored solution of some kind to be attractive. Customization is highly related to the customer differentiation analysis you've already completed. Obviously, the more broadly you define your customer's need—beyond the core product or service delivered by your business unit—the more likely it is that a custom solution will be able to ensure the customer's loyalty.

So when you're considering how to tailor your behavior to the needs of an individual customer, think carefully about all the possible aspects of your product or service that can be customized. Think also about the mechanics of mass customization. You can do it manually for a while, as a test of the concept, but in most businesses you're eventually going to have to modularize and automate the process in order to make it cost-efficient.

The sales and marketing departments at your firm, all by themselves, can easily increase the level of interaction with your customers, either by developing a frequency marketing program, or by customizing a newsletter, or maybe by placing interactive kiosks in your stores. But in order to create a true 1to1 relationship with a particular customer, the back end of your firm (the production and service-delivery parts) will have to come through based on what the front end (the sales, marketing, or customer service parts) have learned about this particular customer. This is "functional integration." At a functionally integrated firm the functions are coordinated so that each individual customer is addressed in a seamless fashion.

You could think of this as a form of "hand-eye coordination" for your business. Your production hands have to be coordinated with your marketing eyes.

The difficulty of planning and managing this kind of integration is why 1to1 marketing is not about just marketing. Marketing is only the beginning step in unlocking the business potential of the true 1to1 enterprise. Customization involves many more of the enterprise's functions than sales and marketing.

One way to illustrate the potential benefit of the 1to1 marketing idea, while also showing the degree of functional integration required, is to consider the example of the GameTime Playground Company. GameTime has used a sophisticated computer-aided-design system to integrate half a dozen corporate departments, rendering the walls between them invisible to customers and seeing its own market share rapidly rise.

Playgrounds are like the proverbial camels, known in the old joke as "horses designed by committee." Nearly every GameTime customer is actually a collection of customers—the PTA committee, the Parks and Recreation Board, a school administrator, maybe a generous group of Kiwanians or Elks. No matter which customer GameTime salespeople visit, they're always greeted by a variety of opinions. Each member of the playground committee has a slightly different vision for the playground: different accessories, colors, locations—everything from the number of swings to the color and location of the sliding board. And while each sale is fairly sizable—generally $15,000 to $30,000 and often twice that amount—repeated revisions to the sketch, parts list, and pricing can slow the process dramatically, increasing the cost of competing and allowing room for a quick competitor to step in.

To speed the planning and decision-making processes, GameTime developed a laptop-based computer aided design, or CAD, system that has helped it achieve dramatic market-share gains almost overnight. On the surface it seems no more complicated than a sophisticated design tool, but the tool is just an interface, and GameTime achieves the most benefit for its customers beneath the surface of this interface. The overall process allows GameTime to mass customize a nearly infinite variety of playground configurations simply by combining a few dozen different modules, which fit together according to preset constraints and rules.

While its competitors are arranging for overnight deliveries of drawings, changes, and documents to the plant for revisions, the GameTime sales rep can change every conceivable element of the playground on the spot, while the meeting is under way. "Want the teeter-totter in green, in the opposite corner? No problem." "Need to shave $5,000 off the total budget? Let's remove the tables for now."

To achieve this level of seamlessness for a customer, GameTime has had to integrate more than just its information systems. Departments have to work closely and automatically together, sharing customer-specific information at every point in the production and service-delivery process.

■ *Compliance*: GameTime wants to assure that when little Mary zooms off the slide she lands safely in the appropriate pile of wood chips, foam balls, or rubber mats. GameTime relies on representative expertise to ensure safety and compliance.

- *Production and design:* Some schools want yellow jungle gyms with blue slides between the red swings, while others prefer green tunnels next to their teal teeter-totters. The CAD system knows what parts don't go with other parts, and what configuration makes sense for the overall design of the playground as a system.
- *Finance:* Credit-granting, accounts receivable, terms, and collection are all accessible in real time.
- *Pricing:* The exact, total price of all components must also be incorporated, in real time, taking into account any special contract terms or payment discounts.
- *Product management:* GameTime still needs to market both its newer and older products, creating special combinations and deal pricing to move the slowest-moving components or increase its profit on bestselling items.
- *Sales:* The entire sales function now becomes consultative and collaborative, because the sales rep is actually reaching into the interior of GameTime's operation to guide every step of the design-and-development process. Better sales reps use their experience and the system's flexibility to make creative suggestions on the fly, often as a meeting is under way, to demonstrate GameTime's flexibility when compared to that of its competitors.
- *Shipping and inventory:* Most GameTime products are made to order rather than inventoried; however, GameTime is working on creating complete inventory records for parts and components, which would be available online for frequent updating to help the sales representative provide precise delivery dates or substitute in-stock items for back orders to speed the project.

What's important about the GameTime example is that it clearly illustrates how a simple, logical interface for the customer will actually be the result of a considerable amount of functional integration and detail within the enterprise itself. In order to deliver its product this way for any customers, GameTime had to create the capability for delivering it this way for every customer.

But such is not always the case. In a service business especially, where there will always be a good deal of human-to-human interaction and the service offering itself is a good deal softer and more flexible than a manufactured product, it is often possible to create a highly integrated environment for certain customers, without having to do it for everyone. The British Airways system of onboard customer-preference tracking is an excellent example. As one British Airways executive explained, the system has enabled the company to address its Most Valuable Customers appropriately, serving their needs in often simple but important ways:

> One of our customers was concerned about water. Now, you think water is perhaps one of the most basic concerns that a customer might have in a flight. And there are lots of ways to deliver water to a customer. You can walk up and down the aisle and have the customer ask you for water; you can wait for the customer to ask for water using the call button; you can let the customer go to the galley to get water; or maybe there could be a tap in the galley. Our standard first-class and business-class cabins each have a bottle of water right there so you can simply get up and help yourself at any time. But one of our most frequent fliers mentioned to a BA manager that she didn't want to have to get up for water, and that the crew didn't seem to be there when she wanted it. She just wanted to have water, always available. So we asked if what she wanted was a bottle or two of water, made available before flight. She said, "That's exactly what I want." Now, it's not part of our standard product to give every one of our business-class passengers their own bottled water. But that was what *she* wanted. And the next time she flew with us, she was amazed that as she sat down in *her* seat, we presented her with two small bottles of water. We make sure that whenever she flies she has two bottles of water for her own individual use. Now, this may seem a strange story, that such a little thing like water could mean so much. It only costs us ten or twenty cents for that water, but those particular pennies are exactly what keeps that particular customer's loyalty.

In this marvelous story of very straightforward, highly personalized customer service, there is an important lesson. The 1to1 enterprise certainly has to equip itself with the best technology available, but it's the relationship that matters, and the technology comes second. In a service organization, the primary vehicle for improving the relationship you have with a customer is not just a computer but the carbon-based life form who next comes into contact with that customer. It's your *people* who have to take the initiative to record a customer's preferences and then tailor the enterprise's future behavior to those preferences. People really do make the difference, and if you arm them with computerized information and interactive tools, they'll be able to make even more of a difference.

This particular British Airways story also illustrates another important consideration in tailoring your behavior to an individual customer. Sometimes it makes sense to let the customer know you're tailoring your service precisely to the customer's individual needs, and sometimes it doesn't. In the case of a single business-class passenger who is obviously the only one in the cabin receiving her very own bottles of water prior to takeoff, the service has been visibly personalized, and it would be pointless not to admit it.

But this isn't always true. Guestnet's Pat Kennedy says the primary goal for his client hotels would be to ensure that "when the loyal guest arrives on the property everything is in place, based on what we know about that guest's preferences. It's immaterial whether the guest knows this represents customization—in fact it's probably better for the hotel if the guest simply thinks *everyone* gets the extra robe in the closet or the golfing information on the table. We just want the guest's needs fulfilled seamlessly."

And NMFF's Padovani points out that in health care, the issues are very sensitive. "To protect patient confidentiality we *don't* put any name or personal identifying information on our newsletter at all. What you get from us is just identified as news from the physicians of the Northwestern Medical Faculty Foundation—news you can use. The other side of it is, if we put your name on the newsletter we decrease the likelihood you'll pass it along, even to a friend who might have a very similar medical situation. The information has become too personal."

When you change your behavior to accommodate an individual customer's needs, with either a customized product or a tailored service of some kind, the benefit is *not* that you have the ability to customize. Your customer isn't going to care about that at all. The benefit is that you will be able to meet *that* customer's needs in a very particular and individual way. When that customer decides whether to remain loyal to you, he will only be interested in whether you meet *his* needs. But if you do that, and not just for this customer, but for another, then another and another—pretty soon you'll have an extremely loyal customer base, built one customer at a time.

Left-Hand/Right-Hand Coordination

Most large firms offering multiple products and services are organized into different business units to simplify the management task. In almost all cases the business units themselves are split out primarily by specific product or service. In this way the division can function as if it were a stand-alone business, with its own inputs and outputs, its own set of customers, and its own profit accountability.

A global firm also separates business units based on geography, but in most cases the geographical boundary is less important to the overall enterprise than the product or service boundary. That is, a consumer-goods firm might have one division for soaps and detergents and another division for health-and-beauty aids. There could be separate companies managing operations in North America, Europe, and Australia, but probably the soap division's own activities in each geographic area will be fairly well coordinated, with shared manufacturing resources and even shared advertising campaigns.

At a large enterprise, any stand-alone business unit could undertake to create its own set of 1to1 relationships with its own set of customers, ranking customers by their value, differentiating them by their needs, interacting with them via the business unit's Web site or call center, and in the end treating its different customers differently. This is functional integration.

Over time, however, the 1to1 business unit will find its objective shifting to a more and more customer-centered point of view. Rather than constantly trying to find more customers for its products, the business unit will be trying to find more products for the customers whose needs it knows about. This is a natural shift in perspective as the unit tries to adapt its behavior to a better and better understanding of each customer's individual needs.

Under the circumstances, it's only natural that the different business units of a single enterprise should become increasingly connected and collaborative. If their products are related and if customer bases overlap, they will, over time, become more interested in coordinating business activities to meet their joint customer's needs as seamlessly as possible.

This is divisional integration. If functional integration is hand-eye coordination, then divisional integration is left-hand/right-hand coordination.

Stated simply, Division A and Division B both need to know whenever they're dealing with the *same* customer, and to the extent possible they need to coordinate their independent activities with respect to that customer. This does not necessarily mean that these two divisions have to join forces and interact with the customer uniformly. The customer may not want that, or it might be meaningless to the customer if you try to coordinate your activities. The customer could be highly decentralized, with different buying units making independent decisions with respect to the products you sell. It does mean, however, that as each division takes a broader and broader view of customer needs, it will help if the division has access to more knowledge about the customer.

Where divisional integration makes the most sense is when an enterprise's different products or services can be configured into a complete, integrated solution for a customer. Owens Corning discovered that much more often than not its end-user customers who interact in its online services or contact its call center don't expect the firm simply to satisfy a single product-based need from one of the business units. In order to satisfy the demand for integrated-building solutions—a demand that became more obvious with the firm's rapid growth in interaction with its end-user customers—the company had to integrate its individual division operations more closely. It also added services to better enable its customers to configure and specify its products, as well as professionally market the value of higher-performance construction and remodeling to the ultimate consumer. In doing this, Owens Corning continues to increase its average share of customer within this customer base.

As a business unit begins to look at its customers from the standpoint of satisfying a greater and greater share of each customer's needs, it will become increasingly clear that the enterprise must be divisionally integrated. At Hewlett-Packard, the business entity that manufactures and sells printers is separate from the one that manufactures and sells toner cartridges. The technologies and production processes involved, the distribution channels, the pricing dynamics—all suggest that the enterprise is wise to separate responsibility for these two products into two different, independently accountable business units. But the customer who buys a printer is the same one who buys the toner-cartridge replacements for it. To the customer, the products are not at all dissimilar. They are instead two interdependent, intimately related components of a single solution, and neither product is useful to the customer without the other.

As Hewlett-Packard evolves into more and more of a customer-driven, 1to1 enterprise, its various business units each will begin focusing less on products per se and more on individual customer needs. When this happens, the business entity that sells printers will begin exploring how better to meet its customers' needs for toner-cartridge replacements, with the result that the firm will be pushed toward divisional integration.

On the other hand, divisional integration isn't as necessary if business units sell products that are unrelated from the customer's point of view. The customers who buy oscilloscopes from Hewlett-Packard's Test and Measurements Organization are much less likely to link these scopes to the laser printers sold by a different business unit at HP. But even though the customer might not see a relationship between the two different products, it would still be an advantage to HP's printer-selling business unit if it knew the identities and needs of the bench engineers who are buying the oscilloscopes, and vice versa.

Obviously, different business units at an enterprise might produce a range of related and unrelated products. Below are three different types of product groupings, based on the degree to which the products are likely to be related, *either in the customer's mind or in the production process:* integrated-solution products, needs-related products, and production-related products. If your enterprise is comprised of different business units making different types of products or services, chances are most of them fall into one of these three categories.

Integrated-solution products. Products or services that are used by identical or very similar sets of customers, and are nearly always used together to solve a single problem or to meet a single need, even though they may be produced by different business units, such as:

- Computer printers and toner cartridges
- Razors and blades
- Fertilizer and bug spray
- Wallpaper and paper-hanging tools
- Hardware and software
- Home mortgages and property insurance
- Air travel and hotel stays
- Automobiles and oil changes
- Yellow Pages ads and print-ad creative services

If your product or service is part of a customer's *integrated solution,* a vital part of your customer relationship strategy will be delivering on other elements of that solution, whether they come from other business units within your enterprise or from strategic partners and alliances outside your enterprise. Moreover, the strongest possible type of relationship will be built around helping the customer to *configure and manage* the components of such an integrated solution. Instead of selling just computer printers, you could also sell toner cartridges and printing paper to a customer, or you could manage the customer's printer network, maintaining the machinery and automatically delivering the right volume of supplies at the right times. You could service all the customer's digital imaging, electronically archiving and managing documents and pictures for the customer.

Needs-related products. Products or services that have some link to each other, at least for some customers, but are not always configured together.

- Computer printers and digital cameras
- Adhesives and abrasives
- Petrochemicals and plastic-extrusion equipment
- Home mortgages and car loans
- Air travel and telephone calling cards
- Automobiles and car rentals
- Yellow Pages ads and direct mail campaigns

If your product or service is part of a set of *needs-related products,* coordinating your activities with the other components of that set isn't so vital but still highly advantageous. If your competitor does it first, you'll be at a significant disadvantage. By creating alliances with other enterprises that sell related products, you should be able to improve your relationship with your own customers. Alliances allow you to broker the knowledge you have of your customers' needs to other firms, in effect increasing your share of customer without having to open up a new line of business. In addition to carrying a customer on your airline from New York to Paris, why not sell the customer a prepaid telephone card to use in the pay phones? A customer who enjoyed driving one of Hertz's Ford Taurus automobiles might also consider owning one for himself. In addition to selling a business customer on a Yellow Pages ad, why not help with a direct mail campaign to build store traffic?

Production-related products. Products or services that have very little link to each other from the perspective of meeting a customer's need, but are often produced by a single, large enterprise.

- Computer printers and oscilloscopes
- Sandpaper and Post-it notes
- Home mortgages and car-dealer lease-financing packages

- Air travel and package-delivery services
- Automobiles and large trucks
- Yellow Pages ads and trade-show directories

If your product or service is part of a set of *production-related products,* the principal advantage you would get by integrating your operation with the business units that sell these other products is the sharing of customer information unrelated to the products themselves. An oscilloscope customer who is extremely price-sensitive is also likely to be price-sensitive when it comes to buying computer printers.

Regardless of how the products are related that are produced by your different divisions or business units, working with another business unit is never a simple task. Trying to offer customers a combined or integrated set of products can be extremely complex, primarily because most organizations today are set up to measure product-specific performance. Measuring customer-specific performance is okay, as long as you don't try to measure it across divisional boundaries. When you do, you encounter obstacles and organizational barriers.

Both the functional integration necessary to deliver on particular needs for particular customers and the divisional integration required to take an increasingly customer-oriented view of your business cross a large number of organizational boundaries. At most organizations the only way to succeed, in the long term, is to have the CEO's active participation or endorsement. As 3M's Bruce Hamilton, in charge of customer focused marketing, relates:

It becomes a whole conglomeration of things. We've even had instances now where business units feel that when they're representing another division maybe the service levels on that other division's product aren't at the level their own customer expects. There's always that concern: Are you taking care of *our* customers as well as you're taking care of *your* customers? So we're constantly challenging, and we make information available to our upper management to allow them to challenge, when necessary, the business units that don't seem to be keeping their eye on the "customer" ball. At 3M, this initiative is one of the key activities that our chairman continues to keep his eye on. A key goal he's set for us is to become more customer-focused and to increase our share of customer, and we measure our specific successes against that goal.

Extending Your Enterprise

Ultimately, when you begin building a 1to1 enterprise, you won't be satisfied having a single product or service for your customers, nor will you be happy about the fact that other firms interact with your customers without you. Every time you see a firm that makes a product or delivers a service related to yours, you'll want to create a link to that service or product, so you can bring your customer a better, more complete solution—so you can improve your share of customer.

You might learn that your customer needs something you just don't make—something that none of the other divisions in your enterprise have the capacity to make either. This is often the case with capital-goods manufacturers and service industries. A computer maker doesn't necessarily sell the software that runs on its box. An insurance firm won't always provide estate planning. The tax attorney doesn't offer accounting services.

Creating strategic alliances with other firms can help increase your share of customer, and many 1to1 enterprises find themselves creating these alliances in order to have the capability to create better, more individualized relationships with their customers. There are advantages and disadvantages to dealing with an alliance partner, so before you do, you might want to consider these questions:

- Will a single-source option provide a benefit to a meaningful number of your own MVCs and MGCs?
- Can you introduce your alliance partner's products without losing control of your own customer relationship and customer management function?
- Can you confidently market your partner's product or service and warrant customer satisfaction with it?
- Can you provide a combination of core and alliance products in a manner that is transparent to your customer?

- Will your own company benefit or suffer as a result of the loyalty (or lack of loyalty) of your alliance partner's customers?

In addition to seeking links to other enterprises outside your own, you will also want to forge stronger links down through your demand chain—bringing your channel members into closer alignment with the goals and strategies you have for individual customers, and even bringing the customers themselves into the operation. Now more than ever, creating collaborative links with your channel members and your customers is essential to maintaining their loyalty and protecting your margin. This is because the same interactive information technology that allows you to forge these links ever more cost-efficiently also allows your customers to acquire competitive information faster and more accurately, and to use that information to pit suppliers like you against other suppliers.

From your own customers' standpoint, using the Web to bid you out against other suppliers has become an increasingly attractive option, undercutting the close and collaborative relationships many suppliers have developed with big companies over the past decade. New technologies such as "extranets" are leading some firms to restructure their arrangements with suppliers altogether. In the early 1990s, many companies, such as Boeing and Wal-Mart, implemented proprietary, electronic data interchange (EDI) systems to streamline their supply processes. This tended to bring companies and their suppliers closer together. Even though EDI was usually implemented at the buyer's initiative and not the seller's, the result was that a seller and buyer were drawn more closely together, for the benefit of both.

Indeed, this technology raised barriers to entry and encouraged companies to limit suppliers to a select few. However, secure and reliable extranets, which can be accessed and used with simple Web software, now enable your business customers to reach out to a greater number of suppliers, and this poses a big threat to your relationships with them. America's Big Three auto companies, for instance, are hoping to save billions through their Web-based Automotive Network Exchange—a system that allows them to easily solicit bids for everything from complex components to customized design work.

For the 1to1 enterprise, the solution is to create an even more collaborative, solution-oriented relationship with each individual customer. Basing the interactions in this relationship on the Web makes a great deal of sense. The Cisco Web site that enables customers to configure their own systems also allows Cisco's reseller partners, like Alcatel, NCR, and DEC, to configure their own customers' systems using Cisco's products.

Great Plains Software (GPS), based in Fargo, North Dakota, provides Windows-NT based financial-management solutions to midsized companies. If a company needs a multistate payroll-accounting system up and running on a Microsoft SQL Server, chances are good that the right software product will have Great Plains' name on it. All of the firm's software is sold through channel partners, who for the most part are value-added resellers who consult with companies in various accounting and financial fields, and also install and maintain financial software.

To become more of a 1to1 enterprise itself, it was essential for GPS to turn its channel members into more profitable, more loyal customers, and to do this the firm launched a focused initiative, known as CORE (Center for Organizational Excellence). CORE's purpose is to give Great Plains' channel partners the knowledge, skills, and tools necessary to compete and win.

On one level, CORE provides a Web-based, interactive system that delivers information to channel partners about their own customers, including products registered and modules purchased, addresses/phone numbers, and even access to Great Plains' support-log records for the customer. It also enables channel partners to input and access information about their own organizations, such as sales figures, addresses/phone numbers, and customer-satisfaction scores.

But CORE offers much more than information sharing and tracking. It is designed as a comprehensive, integrated solution for channel members' own business problems. Imagine being a GPS reseller and having access to a Web-based tool that helps you develop a project plan customized to the needs of your own client. The tool incorporates the insights, methods, and best practices that have been learned by others in your particular area of expertise, but it also enables you to manage project knowledge specific to your individual client. You work with the client to define the scope and length of your engagement, and both parties become increasingly confident as the project plan is developed. This tool, which is called "Implementation Manager," was recently introduced by Great Plains as part of the CORE strategy. By accessing Great Plains' CORE knowledge base, you will be able to run your business more profitably and professionally. You'll have electronic access to everything from a checklist for running an accounts payable compliance meeting to a sophisticated reference guide that clearly maps out just how and when your project plan will be implemented.

The CORE initiative represents a dramatic shift away from the conventional, one-way distribution model, in which reseller and distributor "programs" are the norm, to a collaborative model focused on continually engaging all partners and ensuring their success. "Success in our business used to revolve around having the best products and services," says Don Nelson, general manager of CORE. "Now it's critical to also have the best channel."

Through CORE, Great Plains is accomplishing three important things for its resellers. It is extending the competencies and capabilities of its channel partners not only by making customer-specific information immediately available but also by providing technical training, including Web-based resources that allow learners to access knowledge on demand. It is building up the long-term capacity of its partners by helping them recruit, train, and place skilled professionals. And GPS is helping its partners achieve organizational excellence by providing management consulting services and keeping them up to date on best practices throughout the GPS partner network.

What Great Plains is doing on its own behalf is truly remarkable. It is extending its own enterprise, through a network of more than seventeen hundred independent channel partners, far beyond what it could have hoped to accomplish simply by making the best possible accounting software in its category. By reaching down into its demand chain to provide an integrated solution, rather than just a good product, Great Plains hopes to gain not only a greater share of each channel partner's business, but also a greater share of *their* clients' business.

Making 1to1 Marketing Really Work

Lots of companies think they're doing 1to1 marketing because they know their customers' mailing addresses and they track each customer's individual purchases. They might know how to interact with their customers individually, but they don't really tailor their product or service for each individual customer. While they give better service or lower prices to their MVCs, the fact is they give the *same* better service and lower prices to *all* MVCs.

But to gain the real advantage of 1to1 marketing you have to go beyond tracking your customers and interacting with them individually. You have to be willing to *act* on what you learn, with respect to each customer's individual needs. If you use your knowledge of an individual customer to tailor the way your firm treats that particular customer, you can earn the customer's loyalty even though your competitors are pursuing the same strategy. If every time the customer buys from you it becomes easier than it was the last time, *for that customer,* then with just a few exchanges or interactions you will have created a Learning Relationship and made the customer loyal. And the way you make it "easier" for the customer each time is by using an additional bit of knowledge about that particular customer's individual needs to customize the way you treat that customer a little more, every time another purchase is made.

As we've just learned, however, this is much easier said than done.

Recommended Reads

Bhote, Keki R. *Beyond Customer Satisfaction to Customer Loyalty: The Key to Greater Profitability* (AMACOM, 1996).
Bhote, a former Motorola executive who specializes in quality and productivity improvement, offers a powerful and persuasive discussion of the limitations of customer satisfaction. He identifies four stages of a firm's evolution toward enduring customer loyalty and offers practical advice on auditing the enterprise's efforts in this direction.

Davis, Stan. *Future Perfect* (Addison-Wesley Pub., 1987).
This classic book outlines some of the key business and technological trends now shaping the economy. Insightful and interesting, Davis has foreseen everything from the growing importance of interactivity to individualized production. He coins the term "mass customization" in this book.

Davis, Stan. *2020 Vision: Transform Your Business Today to Succeed in Tomorrow's Economy* (Simon & Schuster, 1991).
In this foresighted book, Davis explores some of the smart technologies, processes, and business designs that companies have adopted in recent years. It's a thought-provoking book, loaded with interesting examples and cases, that has only become more relevant with time.

Gilmore, James H., and B. Joseph Pine II. "The Four Faces of Mass Customization," *Harvard Business Review,* January/February 1997, pp. 91–101.
The authors outline the mass-customization process in clear and concise terms here. They discuss four distinctive approaches to mass customization: *collaborative, adaptive, cosmetic* and *transparent.*

Pine, B. Joseph II, and James H. Gilmore. *The Experience Economy: Work Is Theatre and Every Business a Stage* (Harvard Business School Press, 1999).
In this compelling new book, Pine and Gilmore argue that the economy has moved into a new phase—one that revolves around staging experiences as opposed to simply selling products and services. They cite Disney, Planet Hollywood, and the Las Vegas casinos as pioneers in this economic transition. Experience providers, the authors contend, will develop coherent themes, leave lasting impressions, eliminate "negative cues," sell memorabilia (to remind the "guest" of the experience), and actively engage all senses.

Pine, B. Joseph II. *Mass Customization: The New Frontier in Business Competition* (Harvard Business School Press, 1992).
As mass-customization guru Joseph Pine demonstrates in this powerful book, the era of mass production is quickly coming to an end. In its place will emerge an era of cost-effective personalization on a grand scale. Citing examples such as Motorola and McGraw-Hill, Pine explains that mass customization combines the personalized benefits of the preindustrial craft economy and the low

costs associated with mass production—often resulting in an overall cost *reduction,* when compared to standardized mass production.

Van Asseldonk, Ton. *Mass Individualization,* (TVA Management, 1998).
This far-reaching book looks at some of the theoretical foundations of the new networked world. With case studies from companies all over the globe, it examines the changing nature of the enterprise, supply chains, and markets as the demand for 1to1 relationships grows.

CHAPTER 6: CUSTOMIZE

Activity 6A

Customization Issues for Your Transition Team to Discuss

Target Completion Date: _____

1. Elevator Speech: Why are enterprises implementing mass customization? (Hint: Your answer should include Learning Relationships and cost reduction.)

_____

_____

_____

_____

_____

_____

2. What are the organizational issues involved in generating more customization?

_____

_____

_____

_____

_____

_____

3. A broad range of individual customer needs were introduced in Activity 4G, "Guidelines for Needs Differentiation." What are the customizable elements of that expanded need set?

_____

_____

_____

_____

_____

Activity 6B

Checkpoint: Do Our Customization Initiatives Meet These Criteria?

Answer yes or no to the following statements. Repeat this activity one year after the initial date you complete it.

Target Completion Date: _____

Statement	Now	One Year from Now
We use the information we already have.	○Yes ○No	○Yes ○No
Our customization is concrete and meaningful (i.e., it isn't simply a cosmetic change such as adding "Dear Mr. Smith" to the beginning of a letter that is otherwise impersonal).	○Yes ○No	○Yes ○No
We have a methodology for gathering information.	○Yes ○No	○Yes ○No
Our customization initiative does not assume that every customer is technology enabled (i.e., our interface is not limited to computer or fax-machine users).	○Yes ○No	○Yes ○No

We make sure that the right customer information is delivered to all the places within the organization where it's going to be used.		○Yes ○No		○Yes ○No	
We measure customer satisfaction.		○Yes ○No		○Yes ○No	

Customization Task List

Target Completion Date: _____

Who Will Do It?	By When?	Init. and Date	Task	75% Done (✓)	100% Done (✓)
			Determine the best opportunity for customization of: ■ Product ■ Product configuration ■ Product-service bundling ■ Packaging		
			Determine the best opportunity for customization of: ■ Service ■ Delivery and logistics ■ Renewable services ■ Ancillary services ■ Service enhancements		
			Determine the best opportunity for customization of financials: ■ Invoicing ■ Payment processing ■ Payment terms ■ Streamlining services ■ Preauthorization		
			Identify strategic alliance opportunities		
			If applicable, initiate a strategic alliance (see Activity 6D)		

Customize internal capabilities by bringing together data, operations, and service across all functions and product lines for each customer including:

- Accounting
- Advertising and promotions
- Collections
- Manufacturing
- Engineering
- Research and development
- Customer service
- Pricing
- Sales
- Product management
- Delivery and logistics
- Information systems
- Quality assurance
- Shipping

Determine all-in cost of servicing customer

Make customization a part of your organization's culture and bring everyone on board (see Chapter Nine, "Infrastructure")

Strategic-Alliance Criteria

Consider the following questions and issues in developing a strategic-alliance plan:

Target Completion Date: _____

Question	Check those that apply to our business unit (✓)	Check those that apply to our enterprise (✓)
Will the single-source option provide a benefit to a meaningful number of MVCs or MGCs?		
Can the company introduce the alliance partner's products without losing control of the customer relationship and the customer-management function?		
Can the enterprise confidently market the alliance partner's product or service and warrant customer satisfaction with it?		
Can the combination of core and alliance products be provided in a manner that is transparent to the customer?		
Is the alliance's customer base loyal to it? (i.e., will your combined effort benefit from the loyalty of your alliance's customers?)		

Activity 6E

Establish the Goal of Customization

Target Completion Date: _____

Consider the following benefits to customization:

- Develop and remember ongoing information-based relationships with *individual* customers
- Uncover additional sales and retention opportunities with individuals
- Increase customer loyalty
- Increase Lifetime Value
- Stay cost-efficient; maximize profitability
- Identify highest-value customers
- Increase customer satisfaction
- Increase share of customer
- Increase dialogue and make it easier

Activity 6F

Using Individual Customer Information: The 1to1 Customization Think Tank

Target Completion Date: _____

What would you do for each customer if you had all the information you could possibly get? If you work through the exercise of brainstorming these possibilities, and then listing the information you would actually need for each application, you will get a handle on the information you will need to implement 1to1.

Whether you gather around a worktable in your back room or take this exercise off-site for a day, we have some hints for getting the most from the work we are about to ask of you:

1. *Do it together.* No one will implement 1to1 alone. Enlist each other's support and brainpower as you draw up the plan. A group of ten to fifteen seems to work best.
2. *Get everyone on the same page.* Make sure everyone who participates already understands 1to1 and customer management.

3. *Choose your participants carefully.* Weigh the political obligations heavily. You don't want to antagonize those whose support you will later need for implementation. On the other hand, you want only the best and brightest here. Visionaries. Break-the-box thinkers. In this group you should include at least one longtimer who's knowledgeable about many of the practical issues facing the organization, one to four people from the MIS (IS, IT) area who are technical experts, and, of course, marketing people. Some effective think tanks have also included an ad-agency representative and/or top management players.

4. *Take it offline and put your feet up.* Turn off the phones, eliminate distractions, send the message that this is *very* important, and allow everyone to push the limits of "business casual." We encourage brainstorming in your socks.

5. *Divide into groups of three or four and avoid homogeneity.* Mix up marketers, communicators, IT types, and others. After each task, introduce new blood to each group by moving one person counterclockwise around the room. Move the person in each group:

   - Wearing the brightest color
   - Who is a marketer sitting nearest to the door
   - Who is tallest (shortest)
   - Who has the most buttons

6. *Don't think about technical or cost barriers.* Reality will come soon enough.

7. *Take at least one full day to work through this think tank.* Our goal is to help you make some serious decisions here. Take a few minutes. You will need at least one additional full day of at least one participant's time (and probably a subcommittee of two or three) to sort and report the findings.

8. *Stick to your schedule. Keep lunches and breaks brief.*

9. *Brainstorm 1to1 applications for your enterprise.* Don't be afraid to explore big changes that will require massive organizational-transformation efforts. But also spend time looking at more immediate actions you can take, especially ones that will strengthen your organization's relationship with its most valuable customers.

In an ideal world, you will also have someone write the gist of each idea on an 8½"-by-11" or larger paper or cardboard that can be attached to a wall. Once all the applications are up, your group can prioritize by moving the items around. If that isn't feasible, just list the applications on an easel or dry-erase board and number them 1–*n*.

Capture as much of the discussion as you can. You will be surprised later at how difficult it is to remember the exuberant details when you begin working your way through "Sort and Report."

Activity 6G

Sort and Report

Target Completion Date: _____

If the Think Tank is successful, you will have a pile of good customization ideas at the end of the day. Here's how to start turning them into money:

1. Edit the ideas. Often this will mean rewriting feverish scribbles, and many times consolidating several very similar ideas.
2. Sort them out by topic. This may require reassigning topics and groupings.
3. In each set, develop a priority ranking.
4. Determine action items. Turn your ideas and insights into purposeful activities that will get your organization moving toward the 1to1 future you have envisioned.

The goal of the Think Tank is to set up the basics for the 1to1 implementation planners, and to give everyone else an immediate to-do list. Once you have prioritized your applications, it will be the assignment of one or a few participants to work through each application and make a list of what information will be needed—*really*—to put the application into action. Some information on the master list will be ungettable, but the rest of the information will provide you with a blueprint for the data you need to understand and serve each customer—to *treat different customers differently.*

Chapter Seven

The One-to-One Gap Analysis

PERFORM YOUR OWN "GAP ANALYSIS" AND SEE HOW FAR YOU HAVE TO GO

The first task in turning your organization into a one-to-one enterprise is to assess your current situation. How far along are you, and how far do you have yet to go? What particular issues should you be working on first? Where are you in relation to your competitors?

This chapter consists entirely of three self-assessment activities:

- Quick Start Self-Assessment (Activity 7A)
- 1to1 Gap Tool (Activity 7B)
- Strategy Mapping (Activities 7C and 7D)

These activities are self-explanatory. After finishing them you'll have a clearer picture of just how your business is positioned, with respect to being able to execute 1to1 customer relationship programs, and how much work there is to do.

Jackson, Harry K., Jr., and Normand L. Frigon. *Achieving the Competitive
   Edge: A Practical Guide to World Class Competition* (John Wiley & Sons,
   1996).
Jackson and Frigon provide an approach to enhancing competitiveness using
business-process/management models and pull them together in ways that are
easy to implement. They explore everything from values and leadership to
product development and quality controls.

Kaplan, Robert S., and David P. Norton. *The Balanced Scorecard: Translating
   Strategy into Action* (Harvard Business School Press, 1996).
This book offers readers a valuable framework for determining how to allocate
their time most effectively and resources to enhance performance. While it includes valuable financial measures, it also offers new measures for value creation that address customer relationships, process improvement, and employee
development. Kaplan and Norton include detailed case studies on Chemical
Bank, Mobil, and United Way of Southeastern New England.

Luftman, Jerry N. *Competing in the Information Age: Strategic Alignment in
   Practice* (Oxford University Press, 1996).
Relying on insights and strategies from IBM's consulting group, Luftman
shows how to align business and system strategies with organizational and IT
infrastructures. The book includes an array of excellent contributions touching
on everything from culture to IT to benchmarking.

Whiteley, Richard, and Diane Hessan. *Customer Centered Growth: Five Proven
   Strategies for Building Competitive Advantage* (Addison-Wesley Pub.,
   1996).
The authors demonstrate how many companies have successfully put customer relationships at the center of their operations. They also provide a sixty-
page toolkit for self-assessment and strategy planning.

Activity 7A

A Quick Start Self-Assessment

How to Use the Self-Assessment Tools in Activities 7A and 7B

The best way to use these two self-assessment tools is to administer them to a number of people in your firm or associated with your firm and then compare results. The principal groups whose evaluations would be beneficial are:

a. The individual members of your 1to1 transition team
b. Senior management
c. Middle management and field managers
d. Channel members, if applicable
e. Line employees who interact directly with customers (call-service reps, sales and service-people, even retail clerks)
f. Customers

It's likely that the responses to these questions will vary widely among these groups. But they should be valued in inverse proportion to their position in the corporate pecking order: Customers' opinions are most important, followed by those of the line-staff people who interact with customers every single day, and so forth.

There's no secret to evaluating the results you get with these gap-analysis tools. The answers are pretty self-explanatory. The real learning will come from comparing the answers given to the questions by different constituencies, in different locations and functions, facing different agendas and issues.

Activity 7A is a Quick Start, brief self-assessment tool, while Activity 7B is a more detailed, richer tool. You can decide how best to deploy these questionnaires, but our recommendation would be to use 7A to ensure that you get a breadth of coverage, while relying on 7B to capture a more detailed, useful analysis of how your enterprise sees itself both culturally and organizationally.

Target Completion Date: _____

For each of the four questions below, circle the answers that most closely correspond to the situation at your firm. Circle *all* the answers that apply, even if you choose more than one answer per question.

1. How well can your firm IDENTIFY its end-user customers?

a. We don't really know who our end-user customers are or how much business they give us.

b. We have some end-user customer identities in various files and databases around the firm, but we're not sure what proportion of customers this really represents.

c. Some of the business units at our firm know many of their customers' individual identities, but not all of the units do. Our business units don't have a central database of customer identities, and we don't share much customer information with one another.

d. We sell to businesses or organizations, and while we know the identities of all or most of these organizations, we don't really know who most of the individual players are at each business.

e. We know who most of our customers are individually, but we don't know much about their relations with one another. If a customer refers another customer to us, we don't track this in our database. If a customer moves from one location to another, our database might show this as a customer defection followed by a customer acquisition, with little or no link between these two events.

f. We know most of our customers individually, and we can track them from place to place, division to division, or store to store.

2. Can your firm DIFFERENTIATE its customers, based on their values to you and their needs from you?

a. Since we don't have much, if any, customer-identity information, we are unable to differentiate our customers individually, either by their value to us or by their needs from us.

b. We have no real knowledge of how to rank our customers by their long-term value to us, individually.

c. We have an idea about how to calculate our customers' individual long-term values to the firm, but we don't really have access to enough data to generate a reliable ranking of our customers, individually, based on this calculation.

d. We have identified a number of different needs-based segments of our MVCs, but we don't have a reliable way of mapping any particular individual customer into the right segment.

e. We know how to rank most of our customers individually by value, and we can also identify, at least for most of our MVCs and higher-value customers, what needs-based segment is most appropriate for each customer.

3. How well do you INTERACT with your customers?

a. We have no practical mechanism to interact with our customers individually.

b. We interact with some of our MVCs and higher-value customers through personal sales calls and other contacts, but we don't systematically capture a record of these interactions through sales force automation or contact management systems. We rely instead on the initiative and memories of our account directors, salespeople, or others to manage these customer interactions.

c. We interact with most of our MVCs and higher-value customers through personal sales calls and other contacts, and we maintain fairly good records of these interactions and contacts in an automated system or customer database.

d. We have some direct interaction via mail, phone, or online media with a small proportion of our customers, but we don't coordinate these interactions across media.

e. We are in interactive contact via mail, phone, or online media with all or a substantial number of our customers, and we coordinate the dialogue we have with any single customer across these different media.

4. How well does your firm CUSTOMIZE, using what it knows about its customers to mass-customize products and services?

a. We provide standard products and services and tailor few, if any, aspects of our behavior to the needs of an individual customer.

b. We offer a range of options for our customers so they can choose specific product features for themselves, but we don't track or remember which features each customer chooses.

c. In the case of our MVCs anyway, we sometimes customize our peripheral services—contract terms, billing formats, delivery modes, palletization and packaging, service options, and so forth—and we keep track of each MVC's preferences.

d. We have modularized at least a few aspects of our core product and/or our peripheral services and by configuring these modules in different ways we can produce a variety of product-service combinations, fairly cost-efficiently. For a substantial number of our customers we track and remember which customers choose which options, so when a customer repeats with us we can automatically configure our product to that individual customer's previously stated preferences.

e. We have modularized many aspects of our core product and/or our peripheral services and we can cost-efficiently render a wide variety of product-service configurations. Rather than asking customers to sort through all these options themselves, we interact with most or all of them to help them specify their needs. Then we map each customer into a particular needs-based category, we propose a particular product configuration for that customer, and we remember it the next time we deal with that customer.

Activity 7B

1to1 Gap Tool

There are several questions listed below. For each one, read the summary statement and each of the answers. Then select the one statement that most closely reflects your opinion of the company as you view it personally today—*not* as you think it should or might be someday.

Target Completion Date: _____

1. Processes

This category assesses the importance placed on using customer-centric business processes. It is important to understand the degree to which the business processes reflect the needs and relationships of individual customers. It is also helpful to know the level of commitment the company has to ongoing change to better satisfy customer needs.

Managing continuous change

A: Our company does not consider quality-management practices

B: We would like to have formal quality-management initiatives

C: We have some methods in place to ensure quality-management initiatives

D: We have a formal quality-management organization

Processes for customer-centric interactions

A: We do not concentrate on building our business practices with a customer focus

B: We have some understanding of the link between customers and our business processes

C: We understand most of the interactions between customers and our business processes

D: We have full understanding of all the possible interactions between customers and our business processes

2. Technology

This category centers on the customer orientation of the technologies used by the company. IT architecture and system access demonstrate a company's centricity from a technology perspective.

Customer considered when selecting and implementing technology

A: Our IT department is rather autonomous and in charge of technology acquisition

B: We encourage that customer needs, not just internal needs, be considered when selecting technology

C: We use some degree of customer validation when selecting technology

D: We require that all technology selections be validated by a customer-focus process

Characteristic: Providing technology that helps employees help our customers

A: Our company is not particularly advanced when it comes to technology

B: We encourage the use of technology that helps our daily customer interaction

C: We provide technology in many areas to assist daily customer interactions

D: We provide the most effective available technology to all employees who have customer interactions

3. Knowledge Strategy

This category addresses the perceived emphasis the company places on using customer-specific information as a competitive advantage. The customer-centric firm has strategic plans for using customer information in ways that quickly impart knowledge about the customer to its staff. Customer knowledge consists of current, detailed information about an individual taken in the context of the company's accumulated experience with that customer.

Maintaining a customer-information strategy

A: We handle customer information poorly

B: We encourage collection and use of customer information to gain customer knowledge

C: We have programs to collect and use information and knowledge about select customers

D: We continually enhance our strategy to collect and use customer knowledge

Customer information combined with experiences to generate customer knowledge

A: We have poorly developed and inadequate processes for combining customer information with our own experience and knowledge

B: We encourage using processes and systems that support collection of both customer information and experiences about some customers

C: We have implemented systems and processes that collect and combine information and experiences about selected customers

D: We have rigorous processes to combine information and experiences about each customer

4. Partnerships

This area concentrates on the company's commitment to developing and maintaining business partnerships that are strategic to increasing customer satisfaction, expanding share of customer, and ensuring customer loyalty. Ideal customer-centricity implies that the company is willing to develop a partnership that is strategic or, in fact, essential to improving the overall relationship with each of its customers.

Selecting customer-focused partners

A: We pay little or no attention to whether the partners we select are customer-centric

B: We try to select partners that are customer-centric

C: We evaluate strategic partners based on their customer-centricity

D: We evaluate all potential partners based on their customer-centricity

Understanding the relationships among customers and partners

A: We have little or no understanding of the relationship between and among our customers and our partners

B: We try to understand the relationship between and among our customers and our partners

C: We understand the relationship between and among our customers and our partners

D: We understand and use the relationship between our customers and our partners

5. Customer Relationships

This category seeks to understand the emphasis the company places on its relationship with each customer. This implies that the company is interested in activities, information, and employee conduct that will sustain a long-term relationship with each customer rather than just day-to-day transactions. The customer-centric enterprise positions customer-specific knowledge as a corporate asset for use in constantly improving the relationship. Customer interactions are conducted with the emphasis on satisfaction, growing share of customer, and promoting long-term customer loyalty.

Customer valuation

A: We do not attempt to differentiate between customers

B: We attempt to differentiate between customers

C: We have methods in place to collect and use information from customer interactions to differentiate each customer and evaluate the importance to our business of that relationship

D: We have a continuously updated customer knowledge base that is strategic to each customer and provides all the critical business information about the relationship

Understanding the end-to-end customer experience and improving it

A: We pay little or no attention to the end-to-end customer experience

B: We know all the points where customers come into contact with the business and manage them to satisfy customers

C: We conduct frequent surveys with selected customers and take action on their feedback to make improvements

D: We have a continuous dialogue with each customer and use well-developed methods to improve our relationship

Measuring and reacting to customer expectations

A: We make no effort to understand our customers' expectations

B: We have some idea of our customers' expectations and use them in building relationships

C: We periodically solicit input from customers regarding expectations and take actions to improve the relationship where possible

D: We work together with our customers as a team to ensure that customer expectations are met or exceeded

Understanding and anticipating customer behavior

A: We pay little or no attention to customer behavior

B: We understand customer trends and buying patterns and consider these when making critical decisions

C: We collect customer information regarding preferences and other behaviors and use that information in our business planning

D: We maintain a customer profile and use it as part of our process for dealing with those customers

6. Culture

This category seeks to understand to what degree customer focus is reflected in staff behavior and conduct. Culture is one of the most significant indicators of customer centricity. It is important to learn if the staff inherently considers the customer in all that it does. Continuously adapting to changes in the customer relationship or using employee rewards to drive customer-centered behavior are examples of the customer-centric firm.

Empowering employees to make decisions in favor of the customer

A: We encourage employees to strictly follow procedures and policies developed by top managers

B: We encourage employees to make independent decisions within management set guidelines

C: We strongly encourage employees to make decisions that positively affect customer satisfaction

D: We require every employee to take whatever action is appropriate for the ultimate satisfaction of the customer

Linking employee rewards with customer-centric behavior

A: We make no link between employee reward and their treatment of customers

B: We use ad hoc methods to reward customer-centric behavior

C: We make customer-centric behavior part of performance-appraisal criteria

D: We make customer-centric behavior a significant part of performance-appraisal criteria

The customer is the driving force of our organization

A: We attach little significance to the views and opinions of customers

B: We place some importance on understanding customer impact on the business

C: We place importance on understanding the impact on the business of a selected group of customers

D: We place vital importance on understanding each customer's impact on the business

7. Products and Services

This category derives the perceived customer influence reflected in the products and services provided. We want to qualify the extent to which the company solicits and then leverages customer relationships and input when planning, developing, or enhancing products and services.

Designing goods and services to meet customer needs

A: We pay little or no attention to customer needs when we design our products and services

B: We make some attempt to develop products and services to meet customer needs

C: We use input from selected groups to assist with development of products and services

D: We design products and services to meet individual customer needs

Building individualized marketing programs

A: We build all marketing programs to reach a mass market for products and services

B: We build all marketing programs to fit perceived niche-market need for products and services

C: We build some marketing programs specific to each customer need for products and services

D: We build all marketing programs specific to each customer need for products and services

8. External Focus

This category addresses a company's awareness of other companies' approaches to customer relationship building. It is a gauge of how effectively your company is exploring trends in the field of customer relationship management and learning from the innovations of other companies.

Knowing other companies' approaches to customer-centricity

A: We pay no attention to customer-centered strategies in other industries or our own

B: We know what companies are customer-centric regardless of the industry

C: We know how our competition approaches customer-centricity

D: We know the "best in class" approaches to customer-centricity

Activity 7C

Strategy Mapping for Your Business

Should you be emphasizing interactivity or customization as a first step? Should you first expand the number of services and products offered to your customers, or integrate your customer relationships across different business units? These are questions of priority, and to answer them requires some clear thinking about the nature of your customer base and your firm's current capabilities.

In Chapter Three of our book *Enterprise One to One: Tools for Competing in the Interactive Age,* we describe a strategy map that can be drawn to help plot a company's "migration" toward 1to1 marketing. The strategy map depends on two basic factors—the differentiability of your customer base and your enterprise's capability to tailor its production and interact with its customers. If you haven't read *Enterprise One to One* lately, now would be a good time to reread Chapter Three, which you can find at http://www.1to1.com, because these are complicated issues.

Once you are familiar with the principles involved, you can use this exercise to help guide your thinking, in terms of plotting the right strategy for your own firm—the strategy likely to yield the fastest, most successful results.

The first two questions in this exercise are based on the fact that customers have different needs from a firm and represent different values to a firm. Depending on *how* different a firm's customers are in these two areas, the "natural" competitive strategy of a firm might be mass marketing, niche or target marketing, database marketing, or 1to1 marketing. By mapping your customer base according to how differentiable it is, you can begin to make plans for "migrating" toward doing business as a 1to1 enterprise.

To complete this exercise, take the following steps:

1. Focus on one business unit at a time, and for each unit, partition its customer base into constituent elements (business customers versus consumers, or large enterprise customers versus small and medium enterprise customers, etc.). For help with this step, see "Partition your customer base" in Chapter Four (pages 63–64).
2. For Questions A through D below, mark the *first* statement of the five choices in each question that is correct for the business and customer base you are considering.
3. We will use the answers from these questions to plot a "Migration Strategy" for your firm, on the Strategy Map in Activity 7D.

Target Completion Date: _____

A. How different are your customers in terms of their value to you?
  1. Fifty percent or more of our long-term profit is contributed by the top 2 percent or less of our customers.
  2. Fifty percent of our profit comes from about the top 5 percent of our customers.
  3. Fifty percent of our profit comes from about the top 10 percent of our customers.

4. Fifty percent of our profit comes from about the top 20 percent of our customers

5. The top 20 percent of our customers generate less than 50 percent of our profit.

B. How different are your customers in terms of what they need from you?

1. Virtually every customer we have wants a unique size, color, style, or configuration of the product or service we sell.

2. Our customers want widely different things from our product or service, using what we make in a variety of different ways or for different purposes.

3. Customers want different things from our product or service, but it is possible to group these customer needs into a few fairly well defined aggregates.

4. Customers tend to consume our product or service for the same or similar reasons, although they differ somewhat in things like cost-sensitivity and demand for quality.

5. Our customers tend to want the same exact thing, delivered in a standard, dependably consistent way, across the board.

C. How capable is your business, in terms of identifying and interacting with its customers individually?

1. We know the identities of all or virtually all our customers. We interact with them regularly, cost-efficiently, and with a rich interface (probably electronic).

2. We know the identities of most or all of our customers. We interact with them regularly, but not so cost-efficiently. The interface could be better.

3. We know the identities of most or all our customers, but we do not really interact with them very regularly. Interaction is not very cost-efficient either.

4. We know the identities of only a minority of our customers. We interact with those we know to the extent possible, but the interface is less than desirable.

5. We know the identities of very few, if any, customers, and we don't really interact with them at all.

D. How capable is your business, in terms of tailoring its behavior to the needs of small groups of customers or even individual customers?

1. We can cost-efficiently make products or render services to individual customer specifications, which are given to us with a rich design interface.

2. We may be able to make products or deliver services to order, but not so cost-efficiently. The design interface may be less than desirable and it is an expensive process for us.

3. We don't make things to order, but we offer a reasonable assortment of products and services

to our customers, to meet a variety of customer needs, and we occasionally tailor the services surrounding our core product.

4. We produce a small variety of products and services, letting customers choose the ones right for them, and we don't tailor any services either.

5. We produce only one or a few fairly standardized products or services, often perceived as commodity-like by our customers.

Activity 7D

Strategy Mapping

Target Completion Date: _____

Now we'll use the answers from Activity 7C to plot a migration strategy for your firm, showing you what types of 1to1 strategies to implement first, in order to move as quickly and efficiently as possible toward becoming a 1to1 enterprise.

Using the answers you circled in Activity 7C, place your customer base on the Strategy Map below by designating a "C" (for customers) in the appropriate square, corresponding to the statements you circled in answer to Questions A and B in Activity 7C.

Now place an "E" (for enterprise) in the appropriate square that corresponds to your own enterprise's capabilities for interacting with and customizing for customers. This will correspond to the statements you circled in answer to Questions C and D in Activity 7C.

Most organizations will discover that the customer base is a lot closer to 1to1 than the enter-

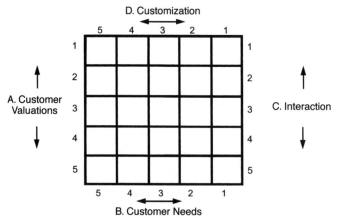

prise's capabilities are. So the top priority for migration will be decommoditization, increased interactivity, or tailoring and collaboration.

But some organizations may find that their own capabilities are ahead of their customers in the move toward the upper-right-hand—the 1to1—corner of this strategy map. If that's the case for you, your priority now is to discover why: Are your customers really similar in value and/or need? Or do you need better ways to see and track their differences? If, in fact, there are shallow skews in valuation, then your next step is to examine ways you can generate those differences—ways you can give your best customers a chance to stand out and be recognized.

Given both the position of your entity's customer base and the position of your capabilities for communications and production flexibility, list a number of *migration strategies* for moving the business toward becoming more of a 1to1 enterprise.

Migration of Enterprise Capabilities

To the right: Increasing the amount of customization

_____

_____

Upward: Increasing the level of interactivity

_____

_____

Migration of Customer Base

To the right: Expanding the customer's need set

_____

_____

Upward: Aggregating customers, across divisions or through time

_____

_____

To get help with your migration strategies, go to the 1to1 Web site. In fact, you may prefer to do this exercise on "Your Checkpoint Tool," an electronic exercise prepared for us by Executive Perspectives and located at http://www.1to1.com/tools/ct/default.pl.

Chapter Eight

Information Systems

IT: EVER-FASTER RATES OF CHANGE OFFER PITFALLS AND OPPORTUNITIES

This isn't your dad's database marketing anymore.

—Steve Blank, cofounder and VP-Marketing, Epiphany Inc.

In the same way that the faucet on your sink provides a steady stream of running water, your Web browser now offers you a steady flow of usable business data. Thanks to the Web, in fact, everyone with a PC, a browser, and a modem is empowered to become a one-to-one marketer. The rapidly declining price and dramatically increasing speed and power of microprocessors opens the playing field to anyone who can afford to plunk down a few thousand dollars for off-the-shelf hardware and software.

Certainly, a critical factor in the 1to1 revolution has been the emergence of sturdy, reliable information technology solutions that aren't based on DOS or proprietary mainframe operating systems. Affordable, off-the-shelf operating systems such as NT and Unix have essentially democratized the IT continuum, shifting power from the "geek" elite to the end user.

Here's what a typical industrial-strength system used to look like:

Proprietary database
Proprietary operating system
Proprietary mainframe

Compare it to the "democratized" system of today:

Oracle, SQL or IBM DB/2 database
UNIX or NT operating system
Intel-based PC or other readily available platform

The old model easily cost upward of $500,000—sometimes ten times that amount—to build and install. And heaven help you if the vendor went out of business. The new model can be assembled and installed for $50,000 or less. And you can buy the parts practically anywhere.

Just a year or two ago the massive scalable-data warehouses, often involving twenty or more terabytes of data, were essentially available only as proprietary systems from NCR Corporation, but NCR now offers these data warehouses in an NT environment.

For you, the 1to1 marketer, these changes have immediate consequences:

- You now have many, many more potential competitors.
- Those with newer (faster/cheaper/more flexible) IT have a marked advantage over those with older (slower/more expensive/more rigid) IT.

For example, the ability to access customer lists instantaneously from anywhere—a field sales office in Martinique, a customer service center in Ireland, the corporate HQ, or a sales rep on a wireless PC modem on

U.S. 1 in Miami—already has altered the competitive equation. In this new environment, traditional database marketing just doesn't make the cut. If you don't have a system that can leverage the flow of information at your fingertips, you're going to be left behind—if it hasn't happened already.

Planning

So how do you maintain the competitive 1to1 edge in a universe in which every player can drink from a flowing river of high-value information? And how do you stay ahead when the rate of change *of the rate of change* is so fast that the technology you buy is obsolete by the time you get it up and running?

Part of the answer is obvious: Don't try to do it all at once. Step back, define your vision, and ask yourself, "What are the three or four most important pieces of data I need to see on my screen right now to make this 1to1 initiative work?"

Once you've done that, you're ready to begin examining the data you've already squirreled away in your various legacy systems. You've got to take a good, hard look at what you've got and ask yourself:

- Is the data I need available to me now, or do I have to look elsewhere—inside or outside the company—to assemble it?
- If the data is available, what's the best way to extract it?
- If the data is not available, who can help me assemble it?

Remember, there's a strong possibility that the data stored in your legacy systems will require vigorous massaging before it's ready to be moved from your old database. Not too long ago, Wall Street dealt harshly with Oxford Health Plans immediately after the company revealed that a series of computer "glitches" had caused it to lose track of vital claims and billing information, resulting in the company's first unprofitable quarter. The rapidly growing managed-care company hadn't fully anticipated the challenges of a large-scale data conversion during an upgrade of its information system.

Unfortunately, the company's announcement coincided with an across-the-board drop on Wall Street, and Oxford lost more than half its market cap in a few hours of furious trading. *Fortune* magazine aptly called the debacle "one of history's most sensational destructions of shareholder wealth in a single day."

With the Oxford example in mind, it's easy to agree that ignoring or even underestimating the potential difficulties of the data-conversion phase would be foolhardy. Consider these examples of common data-conversion problems:

- Data that is considered a transaction by one system might be considered a balance in another.
- Not all the divisions or groups in your company may have installed software upgrades at the same time, so data-input fields might not match up at all.
- Not all systems put date and time stamps on transactions, which means the time frame for individual events often must be reconstructed.
- Despite the most glowing promises from the most impressive vendors, not everything works as advertised the first time.

Your CIO or IT chief probably can think of four or five additional glitches waiting to happen that are unique to your situation. So at the risk of overemphasizing the point, it's imperative to budget enough time, money, and human resources to accomplish the data-conversion phase smoothly and successfully, and to have adequate fail-safe mechanisms in place. The extra effort will be worth it. If you have any doubts, ask Steve Wiggins, Oxford's founder. He personally lost $125 million the day his company's stock went south.

Implementation

After you've prioritized your data needs and dealt with the conversion issues, you can start thinking about implementation. If you're going to develop a database system internally, make sure your IT people are on board, experienced, empowered, and fully invested in the project's success.

If you decide to outsource your database project, look for a seasoned vendor with experience and "bench strength" who will take the time to understand your exact needs. Stay away from anyone offering a generalized solution, which might be easier to conceptualize and install but won't get you where you want to go.

Remember, the first step is to define your vision. What are the end user's needs? After you've done that, you can communicate those needs with confidence and precision. Companies such as Cambridge Technology Partners and Epiphany have built their reputations on their ability to give customers exactly what they need—in the shortest possible time.

"It's called 'rapid application deployment,'" says Steve Blank, Epiphany's cofounder and vice president. "The system is up and running in forty days. It gives your managers enough data to get them going."

From that point on, the system evolves as quickly as you need it to evolve. Eventually your database begins to resemble a data mart—you've been custom-building it, brick by brick, to fulfill your specific 1to1 needs.

Building the Infrastructure

Let's set the technical issues aside for a while so we can talk about designing and managing an information infrastructure that is "1to1 friendly." What characteristics of a database and information system are most supportive of a continuous cycle of improving your enterprise's 1to1 initiatives?

Ultimately, understanding how to put a database together (or upgrade one) will involve a wide range of issues with respect to the type of data you'll want, the people you want to access it, and so forth. Activity 8C is a checklist of "Building the Database Architecture."

But there are a number of general principles you might want to think about in structuring your database.

Working with legacy systems. The word "legacy" itself is an extremely charitable term. Rich grandparents leave legacies, perhaps, but the system many firms are saddled with more often resembles an ancestral curse. Airlines, for example, were paralyzed for years in their efforts to move frequent flier data to the gate, where most interactions happen. Why? Hundreds of miles of twisted-pair copper wire woven through the ceilings of airports around the world would move only limited amounts of data toward the gate at reasonable speed. Although there's no short-cut for dealing with a legacy system, taking the time to understand how your old system works—and at what speed—will spare you many late-night headaches as you begin the process of migrating data to your new system.

Keep it current, or don't keep it. Sometimes simply keeping your customer information as clean as it ought to be can be a daunting task. Many catalogue merchants and direct mailers still find it cheaper just to continue mailing catalogues to the deceased and duplicate names than it is to identify those customers and update their lists. Address hygiene is an industry unto itself. De-duping, address verification, and merge-purging are among the fundamental disciplines that help a marketer avoid sending two or more solicitations to the same household.

The technology of de-duping and so-called list hygiene is more complicated than many realize. So seek professional help. The process can be expensive, but you should think of it as "table stakes" for becoming a 1to1 marketer. If you don't know the customer's correct name, or spell it right, or recognize that he or she has a spouse, your credibility in attempting a serious 1to1 relationship is hampered significantly before it starts. If you need encouragement, you can take comfort in the fact that list-hygiene expenses will likely be repaid several times over by the increased efficiencies of reaching only the right people in the first place.

Remember, spelling counts. Most large consumer-marketing firms with databases of millions of transactions have computer-assisted mechanisms for ensuring data accuracy. In addition to the check digits that prevent the entry of a transposed credit-card number or airline-ticket number, for example, a good data entry system will compare street addresses to zip codes and even automatically suggest that a "Mary" first name should be combined with a "Ms." salutation.

Respect and protect. Develop a culture at your firm that respects the value of your customer database and protects it from contamination. Everyone at your company who inputs data in any way should know how important it is to maintain accurate and current information. You may want to consider a "last stop" quality-assurance step—one or a few people at your firm who do nothing but review each day's data inputs from the entire firm, checking for obvious errors or inconsistencies.

It didn't happen if it isn't in the system. Many databases are used to record transactions, but not to record the interactions with customers who don't generate transactions. A customer could call with an inquiry, for instance, and when a brochure is shipped out, the transaction would get recorded. But if no brochure gets shipped, and no other "action" was taken by the firm, then the fact that the customer called with the inquiry in the first place might not be captured at all. Your job is to ensure that if a customer is going to be a part of your 1to1 initiative, then *all* of that customer's interactions—not just most of them, not just "where possible," but literally *all* of them—are promptly recorded in your database somewhere, somehow. Note that not all customers may be included in the initiative, and for those customers you can take shortcuts. There's no need to keep detailed records on onetime, occasional, or small-volume buyers with little if any growth potential.

Make customer information easily accessible. Everyone in the enterprise, even in the smallest offices, must have ready, handy access to the information relevant to his or her own customer interactions. They have to be able to query the system and retrieve the information they need, as simply as possible. Data should be summarized and presented in such a way as to make it easy to understand the customer, prevent misinterpretation within the firm, and give your management the ability to provide direction to users. Gold customers receive a 10-percent discount. If a customer has already called for service twice in the last ninety days, the next service is free. Present the enterprise's essential customer information in a simple, quickly read format.

Different keystrokes for different folks. Making customer information accessible everywhere does not necessarily mean it should be accessible in the same way to everyone in the company. While the depth of data actually recorded on a particular customer may vary (based on the customer's value, or purchase frequency, or product usage), not all users need—or want—to see the whole nine yards. Your actual goal should be to provide *less* data, rather than more data, to each user. Think of it as providing "just enough" data to enable a user to understand what action is appropriate. This helps provide confidentiality and data security, while rendering the data easier to use and interpret.

CASE STUDY IN CREATING AN ENTERPRISE CUSTOMER-INFORMATION SYSTEM

Note: *This case study is as close as we can get to reality—so close that the company involved will not allow us to use its name. The solution to their problems was a software-and-database package from Epiphany Software, a firm with whom our own company has a strong client relationship.*

If you've ever wrestled with the problems caused by insufficient information, poor data access, and impenetrable bottlenecks holding up your marketing inquiries, you'll definitely appreciate this story. Epiphany's solution is based on the simplest kind of browserlike, point-and-click interface. It represents the genuine future of customer-information management.

The database marketing group for this $2.3 billion financial services company has numerous Ph.D.'s and some of the best and brightest in their industry. They use the most advanced statistical and database marketing tools. Vendors think of this group as the ultimate reference account.

Given their expertise and experience, how does a group like this spend its time? Until recently, the team was mostly occupied filling routine information requests from marketing and field-sales managers. "We were spending seventy percent of our time doing standard reports and pulling lists," explains the vice president of database and relationship marketing. "We were answering the same questions week after week."

An Information Bottleneck

That wasn't the way it was supposed to be. "My charter was to get a handle on customer retention, cross-sell, up-sell, and build profitability," says the VP. "Ultimately my group should focus on optimizing the lifetime value of our customers—which is a key to succeeding as our industry becomes more commoditized and competitive. Yet we were spending little time working on the big picture."

Nor were sales and marketing users getting what they wanted. Reports took weeks to generate. For every new set of questions, a new report had to be written. "To our divisional marketing groups, who are responsible for product and brand management, our department looked like a bottleneck," says the VP.

The problem was not one of insufficient data—the company had a wealth of information on all of its five million customer accounts collected in a hundred-gigabyte mainframe-based data warehouse. Rather, it was a question of access: how to put query and access capabilities directly in the hands of end users so they could answer their own questions in a timely way.

Digging Out

A leading OLAP (online application processing) application seemed promising at first but was abandoned when the company discovered just how difficult it was to change. "It required programming in a proprietary language, and that was expensive," says the database-marketing VP.

A custom, internally developed application came closer to solving the problem. Dubbed Quickcount, the application enabled marketing users to do simple counting functions and answer basic queries such as "How many active customers do we have with investments greater than $500,000 who have traded on the Web in the last twelve months?" But users couldn't drill down or answer more complex questions, and they couldn't export the data to their Excel spreadsheets for further analysis. Moreover, Quickcount was a stand-alone program that had to be loaded monthly and individually maintained on every desktop, making for a heavy administration burden. After six months, it was time to look further.

At this point, the company turned to two Epiphany products for a solution to its marketing database problems—the Clarity information access application, coupled with its EpiCenter packaged data mart. Clarity's Web-based point-and-click querying interface is straightforward enough not to require training and can be used anytime and anywhere—like the Web itself. EpiCenter features an adaptive architecture to automate many of the most complex aspects of data-mart construction and operation, such as schema generation and modification, aggregation, and extraction of data from enterprise systems and external sources.

Information on Demand

Both these applications can be installed literally in weeks, rather than months or years. Surprisingly soon, the company brought up its own EpiCenter data mart, with Clarity configured to handle customer information. Information in the data mart includes demographic (PRIZM code), transaction, and account data, and is automatically imported from the mainframe database. Epiphany's system also performs complex transformations and filtering operations, such as:

- Filtering to include only pertinent account information
- Creating household data from account-level information
- Separating retail from nonretail accounts
- Identifying "lead account" in each household from which to draw household-level information
- Identifying "Web only" accounts
- Reporting on trades, revenue, balances, customer segment, channels, and account types

Now more than two hundred users in divisional marketing and corporate development no longer need to access the mainframe or depend on database analysts coding complex inquiries in order to answer basic questions about their customers, such as:

- How many households traded on the Web and also through a call center in the last twelve months?
- How many IRA accounts are there with balances of $100,000 or more?
- How many customers with assets over $1 million transferred their accounts to other financial institutions in the last six months?

Getting answers to questions like these is now as simple as pointing and clicking, and marketing managers with business expertise but little technical expertise can drill right down to study customer activity by segment, geography, revenues, demographic profile, and many other variables.

The system's security features allow the firm to control exactly who uses it, what specific data each different user is allowed to access, and which functions that user can apply. For example, the company permits marketing staff at branch offices to view account data for their own regions only.

Now users are getting not canned reports but fully flexible responses specific to their individual needs. Data on a wide variety of measurements, attributes, and services can be accessed, filtered, summarized, explored in detail, and exported to spreadsheets—with no training required. And because Clarity requires only a standard Web browser—not even Java is needed—users can access the system from any machine inside or outside the company. One marketing manager even logged in through a satellite phone link while flying to Tokyo.

The company's finance department has taken an interest in the data mart and is now working to add profit-and-loss data to the system, which will be accomplished with a second extractor, automatically importing the data from the company's comprehensive Oracle financial database. "Finally, we'll be able to see profit and loss by individual household," says the VP.

Five Steps to a 1to1 Marketing Database

Step One: Remember Basic Principles. Whether you sell to businesses or to consumers, the primary mission of a 1to1 database is to allow you to *identify* and *differentiate* your customers. Thus, many of the same basic questions you asked yourself when you went through Chapters Three and Four are the same questions you'll need to answer when planning your database.

- How many consumers are already known to your firm individually?
- How much is known about each one?
- What is the range of information on different customers? (For each information field, what percentage of your customers' answers is on file?)

- How many databases and locations contain that information?
- How much more information will your new 1to1 applications require the enterprise to acquire, organize, and archive?

Step Two: Inventory the Horsepower You Already Own. If you have an actual customer database now in place, obviously you should spend some time figuring out just what you have, where it came from, and how good it really is. So before launching a major overhaul, develop at least a top-line insight into the database's history, its limitations, any unique or unusual attributes, and the internal rationale that drove creation of the existing database in the first place. Activity 8B, "Understanding the Capabilities and Limitations of the Customer Database," lists the people at your own organization you might talk to and some of the questions you should ask them.

Most companies that don't have customer databases are still likely to have at least some customer data stored electronically, in some department or other. Customer data is probably used in accounting, warranty service, advertising or sales promotion, and credit, for instance. The best customer databases already available to you are often found in your call center, if you have one. Call center systems often have surprising expandability hiding on the server, and because the information system at a call center is a "mission critical" function, it will already come with enough capacity, redundancy, and resilience to be 99 percent reliable.

There are several benefits to upgrading an existing system if you can, rather than installing an entirely new one. For one thing, the data-conversion phase might prove less problematic. In addition, the IT folks who work on the upgrade will be more knowledgeable and comfortable, having worked with the earlier system, and the staffers who use the upgraded system will have less to "unlearn."

But if an existing system is to be used as the hub of a 1to1 database, it must be "expandable" in two ways: (1) It must be able to accommodate more customer records, and probably more data fields for these customer records, and (2) the architecture of the system must accommodate additional users, plus the attendant increase in "hits" to the server, without degrading current users' service or speed.

Step Three: Evaluate the Quality of Your Current Data. Customers are not static entities. People are constantly moving, getting married or divorced, having babies, sending kids to college, changing jobs or job titles, changing their minds, and changing their product loyalties. The more complex the information, the more likely it is to be outdated.

One way to evaluate the quality of your customer data is to conduct a random-sample data audit, focusing on a cross-section of the firm's better customers. Take an in-depth look at all the available data about a significant sample of customers and project the accuracy rates across the entire MVC database. For a summary of one "quick and dirty" method of doing this, refer to Activity 8D.

"Spring cleaning" is one option for improving the quality of your customer data, if you find it lacking, and you can do this just as easily in July or December as in April. Get a senior corporate executive to declare what is usually a one-day emergency, to "rescue" the customer database: "ALL HANDS ON DECK. Nobody will do anything on Thursday, July 12, *except* review each customer record he or she is responsible for, check it for missing or inaccurate data, and, when necessary, contact customers or other departments to assure the accuracy of our customer information." Make someone responsible for each customer record, assigning records alphabetically, by industry type, by sales territory, or using whatever allocation system works. For best results, create a carnival atmosphere: a "jeans day" with free pizza lunches, prizes for most updated records, music allowed. Save work time by doing it all on a Saturday, but don't quote us if you do.

Step Four: Who, What, When, Where, Why, and How? Determine how often, how easily, by whom, and for what purpose your firm's customer database is to be accessed. Start with a clear understanding of the overall nature of the current database, including how different users access customer-specific data, and why. Pay particular attention to each of your customer "touch points"—customer interaction occasions. Watch for differences in how employees with the same job use the database. Why does one customer-service rep place comments in every customer record while another rarely uses that field? Discrepancies like this often indicate weaknesses in the database or in how it's presented to its users.

Step Five: Where to from Here? Deciding on an action plan can be the hardest task of all. As you push toward increasingly sophisticated types of 1to1 marketing, expect to encounter the following effects:

- More people will want more access to customer information.
- Everyone will want more data, on more customers.
- People will find better ways to use the data, study it, and recut it.
- Therefore, more demands will be made of the database and the people supporting it.
- Making certain the data is properly maintained will become a challenge for the simple reason that developing something is more fun than maintaining it.

Address these critical issues carefully, thoughtfully, and openly with your IT, finance, marketing, service, and support people. Resist the temptation to settle for shortcuts or cheap fixes. Don't bully people in the process of driving for a decision, but work for a sincerely committed consensus. Remember: You are about to make a critical decision on the heart that beats at the center of your company. Do you want the cheapest cardiac surgeon? Or the one who's available tomorrow?

In overhauling, upgrading, or installing a database you have two basic ways to go: Do it yourself or have someone else do it.

Doing it yourself does not necessarily mean you have to start from scratch, mapping out your specifications and hiring the programmers. Instead, you can buy and install one of an increasing array of "shrink-wrapped" solutions, customizing it to your own needs as appropriate. ACT, Access, *GoldMine,* Maximizer, Sharkware, and dozens of similar products can be found on the shelves of Computer City or Staples. Some are easily networkable, for the multistation business with remote salespeople. For the larger, more complex business, off-the-shelf customer database applications are available from companies like Clarify,

Epiphany, Rubric, ATG, and Pivotal. Our own forty-person firm has used *GoldMine,* which does a fine job with our thirty thousand-plus client records. Following our own advice, however, and because of the size of our database, we are now migrating toward a more powerful, more customizable system that's almost—but not quite—off-the-shelf. Pivotal Relationship builds a wealth of features, functionality, and 1to1 relationship management potential atop a basic contact manager. And while it is not quite shrink-wrapped, the pain and cost of installation and initial setup pale when compared to its 1to1 benefits, including:

- The ability to coordinate actions among many departments within a company, stimulating one-off and programmatic customer interactions and follow-ups;
- Powerful customer and internal messaging "agents" that respond to or report on customer actions, inquiries, or requests, and
- Seamless integration of all forms of customer communication, from e-mail to Web or telephone interaction, to face-to-face, fax-to-fax, and others.

A totally different approach is to get someone else to do it for you, either by outsourcing your database to a service bureau, or by striking a "rent-to-own" agreement with a service bureau or software-consulting firm. Outsourcing offers some immediate advantages, including:

- Immediate start-up
- Access to database expertise in your own industry
- Latest technology
- Monthly invoices in place of upfront capital investment
- Access to value-added services (data mining, modeling, printing, NCOA, etc.)
- Insurance against a lone expert's abrupt departure

Some database management firms provide a rent-to-own option, in which the company contracts, up-front, to turn over all the data files, software code, operating manuals, and operational knowledge to the enterprise. This is usually offered on a fee-based buyout basis, after a prescribed minimum time period that allows the vendor to recoup its costs of sales and start-up, which are often substantial.

But, as with everything, there are disadvantages to the outsourcing approach, including:

- Higher all-in cost (because every activity, query, change, or add-on is billed)
- Less direct control
- Less flexibility on hardware and software (so look for service bureaus that use "open systems" and can readily exchange data with other systems)

The key philosophical issue in making an outsourcing decision has to do with whether you trust an outsider with your customer data at all. It's one thing to outsource a payroll system, perhaps, but many would argue it's another thing entirely to outsource the customer database.

There is a third, clearly popular middle ground between do-it-yourself and outsourcing. This "in-between" solution is to hire an integrator to build the solution, train people to use it, and help manage the transition from the old system to the new. The integrator also offers advice, guidance, and ongoing support and enhancements as the project goes forward. The integrator works alongside your IT people in all phases of the implementation process, assisting your staff as they install the new system and bring it up to speed.

Activity 8E is a checklist of questions to think about in selecting a database vendor, and Activity 8F is a list of things to consider when putting together the request for proposal.

While you're putting yourself through the paces, remember that information technology is the heart of 1to1 marketing. Build this heart with care, treat it well, and it will take you far.

Cortada, James W. *Best Practices in Information Technology: How Corporations Get the Most Value from Exploiting Their Digital Investments* (Prentice Hall, 1997).

Cortada provides a set of best practices for helping the IT executive to deliver greater value, explaining how companies might use concepts and models such as the Balanced Scorecard to ensure that they are investing effectively in IT.

Gilder, George. *Microcosm: The Quantum Revolution in Economics and Technology* (Simon & Schuster, 1989).

With remarkable foresight, Gilder has predicted many of the key technological and economic trends that have unfolded in this decade. In *Microcosm*, he explores the entrepreneurial opportunities created by the silicon chip.

Hughes, Arthur Middleton. *The Complete Database Marketer: Second-Generation Strategies and Techniques for Tapping the Power of Your Customer Database* (Irwin Professional Pub., 1996).

This book is a comprehensive and valuable resource for professionals in the customer-relationship-management field. One central aspect of 1to1 success is a powerful database capability, and the necessary foundations of a database marketing effort are all discussed here. Hughes addresses such issues as how to develop a method of interacting with your customer, how to determine who your preferred customers are, and how to develop a customer profile.

Recommended Reads

Activity 8A

Information System Issues for Your Transition Team to Discuss

Target Completion Date: _____

1. Elevator Speech: What are your organization's formal and informal goals for using the customer database?

_____

_____

_____

2. Who established those goals, and who measures success within the organization?

_____

_____

_____

3. Which departmental budget pays the cost of fueling and maintaining the customer database?

_____

_____

_____

4. What programs now rely on the customer database for their success? Which executives oversee the programs?

_____

_____

_____

5. Who at your organization must access the customer database or use output from it to execute or administer these programs?

_____

_____

_____

Activity 8B

Understanding the Capabilities and Limitations of the Existing Customer Database

In this activity and the one that follows, you may need to pull in some other people from your organization in order to answer the questions that will help you to fully assess your existing customer-database technology. Consider including the following people:

- MIS director or CIO
- Line manager in charge of maintaining the customer database
- Key managers of customer information use:
   Marketing managers and analysts
   Marketing research director
   Sales managers
   Call center managers
- Hands-on users (often the best sources of operational information): Use a random sample of the front-line customer-facing staff at each "touch point," where the company interacts with its customers. Focus these questions on the actual, day-to-day operation and use of customer data. Very often the answers uncovered here will be the most helpful.

Target Completion Date: _____

DATA AND INTEGRITY ISSUES

- How many unduplicated customers are included in the database?
- What proportion of the firm's overall customer base can be found in the current customer database?
   How is this estimate derived?
   What research, if any, has verified this?
   What efforts have been undertaken in the past to increase this proportion?
- How "clean" is the database?

How many customers are counted twice or more?
What sorts of customer transactions are not efficiently captured?
What proportion of customers in the database are classified "inactive"?
How often is the database sanitized or proofed?
Who at the firm is responsible for data hygiene?
- What customer descriptive data is included in the database?
  Demographics, psychographics, firm-ographics
  Transactional categorizations or summary customer data
  Strategic customer value (growth potential, per customer)
  What outside data is overlaid on the customer database?
- How is new or updated information input into the database now?
  Who has authority to enter new information?
  What internal and external systems automatically feed information into it?
  Who oversees and supervises the processes?

ACCESS AND USE ISSUES

- What sorts of customer transactions and interactions are captured regularly in the database?
  Purchases, refunds, warranty claims, invoicing disputes
  Inquiries, unresolved complaints
  Referrals of or from other customers
  Strategic value data
  Customization details or product-service specifications
- Who accesses and uses the customer database?
  Which departments, and which personnel in each?
  Which divisions or locations?
  Which telemarketing or call center contractors?
  Direct marketing agencies, fulfillment centers, or other outside service contractors?
- What programs depend on the customer database for their success?
  Handling customer inquiries, complaints, and orders
  Invoicing and accounting
  Marketing reports and research
  Tactical promotions
  Database marketing initiatives
  Loyalty clubs, frequency marketing programs
  Customer satisfaction measurements
  Sales incentive programs

- How is the database accessed, and how often?
  Via real time or batch report mode?
  Monthly, weekly, daily, hourly, continuously?
  Intranet access available?
  Security measures in place?
- If more than one division, selling to different but overlapping customer bases, is involved, then:
  How do customer records from one database compare to those of the others?
  Can a single customer be tracked through all the databases?
  Is customer behavior in one division reflected in the records of all?

Activity 8C

Building the Database Architecture

Target Completion Date: _____

PURPOSE

- What is the primary purpose of the database?
- What do you want to do with your data that you cannot do today?
- Will the database be used to drive direct-mail campaigns? Telemarketing?
- Will Internet-derived data be involved?
- Will you be combining information on different products and services, or from multiple divisions, into a single customer record?

SIZE

- How many customers will be in your database?
- How much data will be retained for each customer?
- How many prospects, if any, will you keep in your database?

ACTIVITY

- What volume of transactions do you want to include in the database?
- About how many records will be changing daily? Weekly? Monthly?
- How often will the database need to be updated to support your planned marketing use?
- Do any of your applications require real-time database access such as customer service?

INDIVIDUAL CUSTOMER DATA

- Will you require more than one address per customer?

- Will you want to collect and associate names of business colleagues, spouses and children, references, or others with the primary customer? (In other words, will you need "householding"?)

- Do you need to combine the records of each affiliate into a single record?

- Do you need demographic data on each customer? If so, what data elements?

- What dialogue data elements will you need to record for each customer?

- Will you be collecting attitudinal data on each customer? If so, what data elements?

- Will you be purchasing data from third-party sources to add to your customer records? If so, what data elements?

- Will you build portfolios by ethnic surname?

FINANCIAL HISTORY

- For what period of time do you want to maintain purchase history?

- Is method of payment important to maintain?

- Will you be keeping credit information on customers?

- Do you need credit-scoring data from third parties?

INFORMATION SOURCES

- What are all the sources of information that will be recorded in the database?

- Do all data sources generate consistent information fields, or are there differences between sources?

CONTACT RECORDS

- Will you maintain a complete history of each contact you have with a customer? With prospects?

- Will you be tracking responses to each promotion effort?

HYGIENE

- How often and from what sources will you collect change-of-address information?

- How often will you want to "clean" your records?

SELECTING RECORDS

- Will you maintain a file of names and addresses that you want to make sure you don't ever contact (suppression file)?
- How frequently will selections or extractions be made from the database?
- About how many names and what elements will be extracted each time?
- Who in your company needs direct access to the database to run queries and counts for planning and marketing campaigns?

REPORTING AND ANALYSIS

- What marketing decisions do you want to use the database for? (Examples include campaign planning, site planning, merchandising, partnering.) What customer-based information do you need to make those marketing decisions?
- What operational decisions are made based on customer information?
- What specific information is required for those decisions?
- What information will be required at regular intervals—real time, daily, weekly, etc.?
- What questions do you think you may have about customer buying habits? About the relationship between buying habits and demographic information?
- Will you want to use your data to predict behaviors of individual customers and prospects?
- Will you want to use transaction history or any other data elements to eliminate customers or prospects from selected promotions?
- Will you want to use third-party data-mining tools to analyze your data or will it be built into the functionality of the database?
- Should I use a data mart, or a data-warehouse approach?
- How does the solution integrate sales-force automation, customer service, and marketing automation?
- Is the solution I'm building a stand-alone application, or can it be used for future applications that involve my customers? (Obviously the second is preferable.)
- What type of online analytical capability is included in the solution?

LIST RENTAL

- Do you make your list or data available for rental or exchange? If so, how will orders be fulfilled?

STATISTICAL SERVICES

- Do you need assistance with statistical analysis of your data?

- How will you want to view the data? By account? By household? By individual? All of these?
- Who within your company requires access to the database? Shall access be limited or controlled in any way?
- How will employees input data? At what customer contact points?
- Do you need access to all of your individual customer detail, or are summaries of previous transactions satisfactory? For example, are totals of previous purchases satisfactory, or will you need a complete, detailed history?
- How much time will be spent accessing reports or information online?
- Will the data you access reside on a server or will it be at your site?

Activity 8D

"Quick and Dirty" Assessment of Customer-Database Accuracy

Target Completion Date: _____

1. Determine what database information you want to evaluate. Some data points you might want to check for accuracy include:

   - Customer name, address, ship-to, salutation
   - Phone number, alternative and fax numbers
   - E-mail address
   - Account number and/or credit card information
   - Purchase events, including dates, amounts, and items
   - Service record, inquiries, warranty issues, or complaints

2. Plan your data-validation method. If this means contacting selected customers by phone, create an interview sheet for callers to follow.
3. Pick a statistically representative sample of names from the existing database, and then manually evaluate this sample for accuracy.
   - If more than one database is to be sampled, select no fewer than 200 random names from each. A quantity of 200 names is more than sufficient to give you a quick idea of the general accuracy. For a more detailed picture, or to validate the accuracy of a large number of different variables (phone numbers, addresses, or recent purchases, for instance) use a larger sample.

- For every cross-tab planned, increase the sample by 200 names.
- Consult a statistician if more than 1,000 names will be selected.
- Consult a statistician to answer any question more complicated than "What percentage of our customer records are accurate in all respects?" If an alarming amount of inaccuracy is discovered, strive to determine which sources of data are most and least accurate, with respect to which particular facts. This process will involve cross-tabbing. One reasonably useful rule of thumb: Add another 200 records to a random sample for every "yes or no" question you're trying to answer.
- Note: It's not important to draw more names from a database with a larger population of customers in order to weight the sample. Instead, when the results are tabulated, adjust the "overall" results by applying the appropriate ratios.[1]

4. Select the records to be validated, and then print the information from these records on the interview forms, leaving space for the interviewer to write in correct information, where applicable. (If your company has a call center, the phone interviews could be conducted by call-center staff, and the "interview forms" could be screens designed for this purpose.)
5. Conduct the validation interviews. Interviewers should complete forms that can be quickly tabulated. Whenever a customer provides information that is inconsistent with the original record, the interviewer should not only note the inaccuracy but also capture the accurate information.
6. Compile the results and look for any interesting or unusual patterns. Unusual patterns could indicate the source of inaccurate data, or they could be the result of a nonrandom sample, or they could be statistical noise. In any case, patterns of data inaccuracy should be investigated separately, and could call for drawing additional sample records.

Note: When doing this kind of sampling it's important to ensure that the sample you draw is genuinely random, so it can be used as an actual statistical representation of the overall population of customers or data points. Randomness within a customer portfolio, such as "MVCs and MGCs," is perfectly acceptable. This sounds easier than it often is, particularly if your customer "database" is really several databases, located in different sections of your firm or maintained and used by different divisions or departments. Again, if you have doubts at all, seek professional help.

---

[1] Let's say you sample 200 names each from three different databases—600 names overall. Database A has 250,000 total names, Database B has 500,000 total names, and Database C has 1 million names. To get an approximate view of the *overall* accuracy of your three databases together, simply do a weighted average of the results of each 200-name sample. In this case, multiply the results obtained in Sample B by two, and the results of Sample C by four, then add all three sets of results together to calculate the overall approximation.

Activity 8E

Choosing a Database Vendor

Questions to ask as you are considering a database vendor:

Target Completion Date: _____

BACKGROUND

- How long has the firm been in business?
- Who are typical clients?
- Is the vendor financially stable and adequately staffed?
- Which services are outsourced or provided through affiliates or freelancers?
- What kinds of business challenges have their clients faced?
- Does the vendor specialize in a particular database size range?
- Does the vendor specialize in a certain industry?
- What equipment, software, and systems are used?

1TO1 ORIENTATION

- Do they understand 1to1 relationships and support your efforts to develop them with your customers? One of the biggest issues in working with a company to build a customer-centric information system is the ability to bridge the marketing/technology gap. Many companies have an excellent understanding of information systems technology. Few can bridge the business information gap.
- Is the firm experienced with customer-focused programs that the database must support?
- What level and kind of customer interactivity do I want the database to support? Telephone? Internet?
- How might I want to use database data online during customer interaction versus offline for forecasts and reporting?

ACCESS

- How do clients gain access to data?
- Can data be downloaded from the vendor's computers to the owner's?

HYGIENE SERVICES

- What are the vendor's credentials and resources for integrating databases from sources such as those you anticipate drawing on?
- Is merge/purge processing available? What are typical turnaround times?

SECURITY

- What measures are taken to safeguard files and data at each point of information transfer?

AVAILABLE SERVICES

- Which of the following data-based services are available?
  Data entry
  Integration (combining multiple sources of data into a central database)
  Householding
  Response analysis
  Data overlays
  Merge/purge
  Profiling
  Modeling (Online or off?)
  Scoring
  Mapping
- Which of the following value-added services are available?
  Marketing consulting
  Lettershop
  Printing
  Mailing
  Creative
  Telemarketing
  Call-center management or consulting
  Sales-force-automation consulting
  Point-of-sale integration of customer information
  Web-site creation and maintenance
  Reference information: newsletters, online resources, etc.

PRICING AND INVOICING

- How are services priced? By job? Year? Name? Adds/deletes?
- Are volume-pricing discounts available?

- What training is provided to the corporate staff?
- What support services are available and at what hours and cost?
- Is the firm a true twenty-four/seven operation?

*Thanks to Richard Cross and Alan Steele at Cross World Network for helping us to pinpoint the basics on choosing a database vendor.

Activity 8F

Developing a Database Vendor RFP

Here is a general outline you can use to develop your request for proposal (RFP). Use the answers to the questions you have gleaned from your own requirements-development process and from your shopping excursions to develop your RFP. The vendor's response will describe the firm's ability to meet your requirements.

Target Completion Date: _____

Your RFP Should Include

1. Basic description of the services required
2. Detailed description and explanation of services required
3. Description of the way work and information will flow between you and vendor
4. Detailing of support services required
5. Timeline
6. Cost elements
7. Backup materials

Factors to Consider in Evaluating RFPs You Receive

- Is the response professionally prepared?
- How well is the response suited to your stated needs?
- Are performance guarantees offered?
- How will your account be managed?
- Is there a dedicated support team, or will you be sharing an account manager?
- Can the vendor adapt to growth in your business?
- Are state-of-the-art options offered for electronic information access and delivery?
- No vendor selection process is complete without checking references.

Final Words of Advice

The following tips will help you develop successful vendor relationships:

- Limit the number of vendors you use to support your 1to1 marketing program. The larger the number of vendors, the more complex the management task. Also, responsibilities can become confused with many support organizations.
- Include performance clauses in your contract. There should be clear remedies for failure to perform at an agreed quality level or on time. Consider bonuses for project work performed ahead of schedule.
- Create a monitoring process that will ensure that work is done as agreed. This includes process capabilities, service quality, mail delivery, telemarketing quality, and program effectiveness.
- Monitor security issues through liberal seeding of your files and frequent visits. In addition, plant some fake names so you can be assured that data is never used in a way you didn't intend.
- Require prior approval of all subcontracting arrangements.

Finding a suitable database vendor is no easy task. We hope this section has helped you understand what you need to do to be successful at it. But, as you can see, the business is thick with jargon and technical issues that are often tough to get comfortable with. If you don't completely trust your own ability to wade through the selection process, you might want to call on some pros to help.

*Thanks to Richard Cross and Alan Steele of Cross World Network for their insights on developing an RFP for database vendors.

Activity 8G

Information-Systems Task List

Target Completion Date: _____

Who Will Do It? (init.)	By When? (date)	Task	75% Done (✓)	100% Done (✓)
		Define your customer(s). (See Activity 3C in Chapter Three, "Identify.")		
		Contact corporate marketing and other knowledgeable sources to find out what they know about each customer, and customer databases. In other words, figure out what we know already.		
		To the extent possible, pull together any existing data about your customers from wherever it resides in the company: other divisions, sales, records, etc. Don't break any laws.		
		Contact internal and/or external database consultants and data management specialists. Write a request for proposal for the database.		
		Pinpoint how and when new customer information enters the database, and which personnel or departments within the firm are responsible for enduring security.		
		Determine what events or processes result in new customer identities being entered.		
		Determine what events culminate in new transactional or other descriptive information being entered (e.g., sign-ups, direct sales calls,		

customer phone inquiries, promotional-card returns, marketing and sales promotions, etc.).

Determine what obstacles exist now which inhibit the capture of entry of a greater proportion of customer identities.

Determine what programs, tactics, or strategies exist today to increase the proportion of customers known, and the amount and detail of information known about them.

Determine how generally accurate the data is which is contained in the database, how/when it is edited, cleansed, or verified, if at all.

Determine who uses the database information, how often, and for what purpose.

Determine if the database is central to your organization's:
- sales, marketing, service, and support efforts
- policies, operations manuals, etc.

Determine who is responsible for updating data and how is this task emphasized company-wide.

Determine your organization's marketing goals and objectives for the database as well as any complaints about it or unrealized needs from it.

Determine how the database is used today.

Determine who within your organization makes the most requests for use of the database, or who has the most need for it and what details they need.

Determine what reports are/will be generated.

Determine how quickly custom reports or individual queries are provided to the database users.

Determine the rate at which new customers are added to the database and the source of that new data.

Determine what additional capabilities or data are immediately desirable for the database.

Determine what additional customer descriptions or transactions would be entered, if they were known or could be discovered (e.g., customer complaints made to a distributor, but not passed on to the firm).

Determine what obstacles to getting information exist, who is coping with these obstacles, if anyone, and how.

Chapter Nine

Infrastructure

HOW TO HIRE, TRAIN, ORGANIZE, AND COMPENSATE IN A ONE-TO-ONE ENTERPRISE

You say you want a revolution? Well, you know, the hard part isn't writing the chants and slogans. The real work is building a rock-solid infrastructure to replace the one you're dismantling. History is chock full of revolutions that failed to deliver on their basic promise: change for the better. So we're going to help you deliver.

In this chapter we talk about constructing the basic infrastructure needed to support your one-to-one enterprise. We'll start by taking a look at a few of the things you *don't* need to do:

1. Completely reengineer, overhaul, and make over your company's systems, culture, and products.
2. Set irrationally tight deadlines that will anger, frighten, and demoralize your employees.
3. Hire a "hatchet man" to oversee changes.

That was the quick "don't" list. Here is the quick "do" list:

1. Start small.
2. Expand gradually.

3. Hold people accountable for the right things.

4. Reward those who jump on the bandwagon.

By starting small, we simply mean don't try to do it all at once. In *Enterprise One to One* (pp. 372–377), we described this manageable transition process as setting up a "picket fence" based on customer valuation. First rank your customers by value. Then rope off the top few who account for a large percentage of your business—put them behind a picket fence. Start your 1to1 process with everything that touches these MVCs and MGCs. These customers come off the regular mass mailing lists, and they get excused from whatever telemarketing campaigns you might be executing. The customers behind the picket fence are now "under management," as in "customer management"—and we'll discuss the mechanics of this process in more detail in this chapter.

For the rest of your employees and your company operations—everything on the other side of the picket fence—things remain pretty much the same, at least for the moment. No big, abrupt changes. No wholesale overhaul. Slowly but surely, however, your plan is to move the picket fence out to include your next-most-valuable customers, and then the next most valuable after that, reallocating more and more of your mass media budget as you go along. As you build momentum, more of your employees will want to participate—directly or indirectly—in the customer management process. And since you will always have some customers who are simply not worth the effort of setting up a 1to1 relationship, you will always need some employees to keep doing what they're doing now. In addition, even in an advanced stage, you're still going to need the tools of mass marketing, for general awareness, brand campaigns, and product introductions.

If you begin with a pilot program that focuses on the company's most valuable customers, it shouldn't take long for you to generate tangible proof of the advantages of a 1to1 approach. And in the process, you will have acquired invaluable firsthand knowledge of how the concept works.

After you've made your case with the Most Valuable Customers, widen the program's focus to include the next most valuable level. Now you also can begin extending the program throughout the company, teaching and training as you go. Gradually, everyone in the company should become comfortable with the 1to1 approach.

Integral to this process will be your commitment to changing the compensation model. Compensation remains one of the best tools for fostering behavioral changes. At the same time, it remains one of the most serious impediments to change, because most compensation models reward behaviors that are product-oriented or process-oriented instead of customer-oriented.

Once you have the snowball rolling downhill, you'll need to start modifying the organizational structure. Although it's true that companies will always want people who can manage products and processes, you will also need people who can manage customers, if you plan to keep this snowball on course.

In this chapter we'll offer some specific suggestions for setting up and staffing the organization that you'll need to succeed.

By the way, you should expect and anticipate resistance. Remember, this is a revolution. There will be cultural barriers to overcome. These barriers come in many shapes and flavors, but here are four to watch out for:

1. People at or near the top who won't commit to change. ("Let's sit back and see what happens.")
2. Long-standing company policies that mandate identical treatment for all customers. ("I'm sorry, but that's our policy and I'm afraid we can't make any exceptions. If we treated you differently, we'd have to treat all our customers differently.")
3. Social climate that rewards and reinforces product-oriented behaviors. ("This car is a miracle of modern engineering. It's state-of-the-art technology!")
4. Paying more attention to competitors than to customers. ("That new Edsel has a push-button transmission! Why didn't we think of that?")

Start Small and Expand Gradually

Any company that's serious about 1to1 will eventually have to figure out how to hold someone—or some clearly labeled entity within the company—*accountable* for developing, nurturing, maintaining, and evaluating individual customer relationships.

Hewlett-Packard, for example, has integrated its outbound marketing and sales organizations. This action was necessary to clear a path for the company's future development, which will depend on unprecedented levels of cooperation and communication among its far-flung, decentralized businesses. HP, like other companies, is experimenting with new organizational structures designed to strengthen the company's ability to manage customers while integrating capabilities.

But these leaps into the future are not being made overnight. They are the result of many years of introspection and analysis—the culmination of a large number of incremental "baby steps" toward becoming a 1to1 enterprise. And the revolution at HP is by no means over. HP figures the process will continue for another five to ten years.

Engineering this type of change is no small feat. Remember that implementing a 1to1 program is an integrative task, requiring that customer-oriented activities be coordinated among a variety of different enterprise functions. But HP is a highly decentralized global corporation, perhaps one of the most decentralized in the world. For years, each of HP's seventy-six separate businesses had been encouraged to think, plan, and act as though it were an independent company. This far-flung empire engendered so much success that it became a model for corporate globalization. Like the character Ray Kinsella in *Field of Dreams*, HP relied on a sturdy, time-honored philosophy: Build it and they will come. In the case of HP, "it" was consistently superior products. Indeed, it's hard to criticize success when it's based on excellence. What, in fact, could be better?

But instead of resting on its laurels, HP took a long, hard look at its path to success and tried to gaze far enough into the future to see where that path was leading. Looking around the corner, they see a world in which product excellence alone will no longer be a decisive competitive edge.

In this new, richly interactive world, not only will HP have to continue making better products, it will have to be better than its competitors at relating to its customers and anticipating their needs. The new thinking will be "One step ahead of the customer and two steps ahead of the competition."

Making this work requires weaning the corporate culture away from product worship and guiding it toward a balance in which both customer growth and product excellence are rightfully prized.

Lane Michel, the Relationship Initiative Manager at HP, was an architect and cheerleader of the 1to1 program. According to Michel, staying focused on incremental gains helped the program win acceptance. "We try to avoid boiling the ocean," says Michel. "Then again, it's important to show immediate results. Those early successes earn you the right to take bigger steps."

One example of an incremental step is the customer-interaction program engineered by the Barcelona Division of HP's Consumer Products Group. The division wanted an ongoing dialogue with its HP DesignJet customers. So it developed a Web site, HP DesignJet Online, to serve as a user-friendly channel for interactive customer communication. The password-protected site offers DesignJet customers self-diagnostic tools, a quarterly newsletter, a user feedback section, new product notifications, and an upgrade program. The division is counting on the site to increase market share, reinforce customer loyalty, and provide a steady stream of timely market knowledge.

Another incremental but important step taken by HP was the development of an electronic customer registration system, along with a master set of questions and a database to store the information. The initiative was born from ideas and feedback generated across several of the company's groups and divisions. The new system largely replaces paper registration, which has proved a poor method for collecting usable customer data in most parts of the world.

Over time, these "baby steps" add up to great strides. As our *Fieldbook* goes to press, Hewlett-Packard has roughly one hundred such incremental 1to1 initiatives now under way at various locations around the world. Each is being tracked and monitored centrally, with information made available throughout the HP enterprise on the firm's intranet at a special relationship-marketing section. Keeping the process going requires champions and leaders of change. At HP, these leaders have titles such as relationship-marketing manager, customer-advocacy manager, and installed base loyalty manager.

That doesn't mean you have to adopt a new hierarchy of jobs and titles to become a 1to1 enterprise. What you absolutely need, however, is to be able to hold someone accountable for managing customers, and someone else for managing your enterprise's capabilities.

Let's take a closer look at the organizational issues involved in running a 1to1 enterprise.

Customer Management

Because interaction with a customer can take place at so many touch points, the 1to1 enterprise must not only be able to orchestrate the various interactive media, including front-line service personnel, it must also be able to coordinate a strategy for each customer. If a customer needs to borrow money, your bank is not going to get far by trying to sell investment opportunities. So coordinating various interactions, whether they occur via the call center or a cash machine or at a personal meeting with the branch manager, is not just a technological problem. It is a management issue.

We dedicated Chapter Six of *The One to One Future* to the idea that a 1to1 marketer should manage customer relationships, and not just products and brands (reread it now or access it at http://www.1to1.com). To do this it will be necessary to divide your customers into manageable groups, which we call "portfolios." A portfolio should be comprised of customers with generally similar needs, because this will make the customer manager's job easier. Ideally, the customer manager would be held accountable for increasing the LTVs of the customers in his or her portfolio. To do this, the customer manager's primary job is to set the strategy for each customer and to oversee the execution of that strategy by supervising all forms of addressable and interactive communication with these customers.

Chapter Four of *Enterprise One to One* was a case study of one large, customer-oriented firm—MCI—that did just this. It first identified its top retail customers. The company knew that its top 5 percent of customers were responsible for some 40 percent of its consumer-side business. Within this rank of MVCs, MCI analyzed calling patterns to identify three different needs-based groups. The company then assigned the groups to portfolio managers. With respect to the customers in their own portfolios, the portfolio managers had the authority to manage all mail and phone solicitations. They would be evaluated based on their ability to make their customers bigger and more loyal.

We used the MCI case study as a cautionary tale, however. In spite of significant and quantifiable financial gains, the program was killed soon after being implemented. The primary problem at MCI was that customer management simply crossed too many departmental boundaries, and top management at the firm failed to anticipate the degree of enterprise integration required.

In Italy, the regional bank Credito Emiliano offers another instructive example of a customer management program's being put into practice, but this example has a happier outcome. Credito Emiliano is based in Reggio Emilia, where it has 260 branches serving roughly 360,000 customers. Credito ranked its customers into three tiers based on their value, and differentiated the customers further into thirty portfolios, based on such customer needs as investment goals, aversion to risk, and so forth. The information the bank needed for this differentiation came from a combination of questionnaires, brief interviews with customers, and third-party data.

Each portfolio is now the responsibility of a "segment manager" at Credito's headquarters, who sets the objectives and strategy for dealing with the customers in his or her portfolio. The branch managers are the primary sales channel for interacting with the bank's customers, but their job is to follow the strategy and achieve the objectives set by the segment managers. So when a customer comes into a branch to discuss a banking matter, the branch manager calls up on his screen not only the customer's name, address, and account information but also the tier and portfolio to which this particular customer belongs, along with the objectives set for the customer and some suggested strategies to achieve these objectives, including products or services to be offered.

Even at large industrial firms, the issue of customer management boils down to a similar problem of setting objectives and plotting strategy for individual customers. The key difference for a business-to-business firm is that the customer expertise itself may be difficult to capture in a database. Understanding a particular customer's needs and the system configuration or the product and service specifications that derive from those needs might require a good deal more old-fashioned human brainpower.

This, in turn, means having some expertise not just in the physical, core products that get moved out the door, but in the "bundle" of surrounding services and even related products or services. Customer expertise does not necessarily stop at the enterprise's own border. If your organization places managers in charge of particular customers—professionals whose mission will be to satisfy a greater and greater share of their own customers' needs—what will happen is that these customer managers will naturally tend to expand the boundaries of the enterprise's operation, over time.

At 3M, customer focus required a new class of marketers entirely. Previously all the company's marketers were product experts. But, as 3M's Bruce Hamilton explains, the new class of marketing people are:

> . . . focusing on the needs and the processes of their customer. And these new marketers are the ones that are bundling products and technologies to take to their customers. They're the ones that are interfacing with the product marketers to say that the product that we're making available isn't quite what the customer wants. They want a certain type of feature, or a certain adjustment. And they have to understand the nature of all our value-adds. As an example, we need to know what type of terms the customer wants and what type of delivery. We need to know how we can best meet the customer's needs, beyond just the products we're supplying. Our marketers really are customer-focused, far beyond product, and they really are getting more involved in all the other value-adds.

Maybe you try to manage your relationships with only a few of your most valuable customers at first, the way MCI did. Or maybe you can allocate the whole customer base into different, individually managed portfolios. But whatever you do, the functions that need to be deployed include customer management and capabilities management. So let's take a closer look at how we would define these roles:

Customer Manager. This is the person who sets your firm's objective and strategy for each customer. The most efficient way to manage customers is first to group them into unduplicated portfolios. A single customer should never be assigned to more than one portfolio—otherwise, how would you know whom to hold accountable for that customer's continued loyalty and growth? In addition to ensuring that each of the customer relationships within his or her portfolio endures and grows, the Customer Manager must also see the organization from the customer's point of view and serve as a customer advocate. When necessary, the Customer Manager is the one who will probably take responsibility for breaking down internal barriers to make it possible for the organization to tailor its products and services—in order to make his or her customers more valuable to the firm.

The Customer Manager's primary tools consist of dialogue and interaction. In a 1to1 enterprise, someone has to ensure that the conversation you have with a particular customer is directed toward a goal that makes sense to the enterprise—*for that customer.* So the Customer Manager sets the objective, determines the strategy, and manages the dialogue. Dialogue management is a skill set vital to the success of the Customer Manager. A good portion of the Customer Manager's effort will consist of engaging his or her customers effectively, learning from them, and tracking the resulting data.

Dialogue management should not be confused with media management, which involves the operation of various interactive media tools, from call centers to Web sites, sales force automation systems, and point-of-purchase customer interfaces. A call center manager is essentially an interactive media manager, and his real clients are not the individual customers calling in, but the customer managers who represent the enterprise in dialogue with these customers. At a 1to1 enterprise the call center, Web site, or other interactive media platform is a vehicle through which a dialogue between a customer and the enterprise is played out. While the customer manager uses the dialogue to advance the firm's strategy, the media manager works to ensure that the interaction takes place cost-efficiently.

Capabilities Manager. In addition to managing customer relationships, someone at the 1to1 enterprise needs to be accountable for deploying the firm's capabilities—that is, the firm can pay close attention to managing its customers, but it must still produce things and render services. Joe Pine, author of *Mass Customization: The New Frontier in Business Competition,* calls this "capabilities management," which dovetails with customer management to ensure that your company's capabilities are deployed or developed for maximum effect. (Remember, in the 1to1 universe, the needs of the customers should determine the company's capabilities, not the other way around.) The Capabilities Manager is also responsible for managing partner relationships—strategic alliances—so the company can intelligently repackage and resell goods and services it doesn't produce on its own.

The point of this discussion is not that you have to have customer managers and capabilities managers, with exactly those job titles, in order to succeed. But if you want to concentrate on customer relationships, you will definitely have to execute those *functions* somehow. If you want to keep your customers longer and grow them bigger, then ask yourself *who* is responsible for this, and what authority does that person actually have to make things happen with respect to individual customers?

Hiring

Once you have established what your organization will look like, your next step will be hiring, assigning, or promoting the right people to manage it. Rule number one here is to find candidates who either already are 1to1 fanatics or show potential for becoming 1to1 fanatics. Because the truth is, if you're not ready to fall on your sword for 1to1, you probably don't belong in a 1to1 enterprise.

The Customer Manager should be hired from within. Why? Because the Customer Manager must be somebody who already knows the company and its myriad eccentricities inside out, forward, and backward. You need someone with proven networking skills and a keen understanding of the company culture. The Customer Manager must know where the roadblocks are likely to be and possess the skill, tenacity, and intelligence to slide past them or, when necessary, crash through them. The ideal candidate will be well known and highly respected throughout the company. This will stack the odds in his or her favor and make it more difficult for naysayers to sabotage the program. It will also ensure a wider field of potential allies as the program gains momentum.

The Customer Manager also needs some specific skills, such as computer proficiency and a certain fluency in the argot of high technology. That doesn't mean you have to hire a New Age digital guru; it means the ideal candidate must be familiar with the World Wide Web and comfortable surfing the Internet to keep up with developing trends.

The best candidates for the role of Capabilities Manager are likely to be former product managers. It must be someone who knows how to translate knowledge into products and services with value, someone who can apply technology effectively.

Your 1to1 enterprise also will need people with proven expertise in interactive media technology. This in-house expertise will ensure that your Web site, your call center, and other communications channels have the best and latest technology available to maintain, nurture, and develop learning relationships with your company's customers.

High-level positions won't be the only ones affected by changes in the hiring equation. The process will change at lower levels, too. In the traditional organization, the call center is judged primarily by its efficiency—how much does it cost to handle a call? Knowing that her compensation and job security depend largely on this one-dimensional metric leads the call center manager to hire the cheapest labor and devise the fastest training schedules. To this manager, the best operator is someone who never calls in sick. The notion of routing high-value customers to more highly skilled operators often runs counter to the perceived mission at a call center, which is to get the job done fast and cheaply.

The 1to1 manager, on the other hand, would understand that the call center's real job is to increase the value of every customer who calls. Her operators aren't just disembodied voices taking orders or listening politely to customer complaints—they are interactive minichannels in the 1to1 enterprise. The 1to1 manager judges her operators not by speed but by who gives the best "phone." The 1to1 manager makes sure her operators have the tools and training to fulfill their 1to1 mission. Ideally, the net result of each inbound call should be a measurable increase in customer value. In a 1to1 enterprise, the media manager will have an intuitive grasp of this concept and will pass this understanding along to her staff.

Another example: In the old days (three years ago), the Webmaster was someone who could write HTML and design a home page that looked reasonably pretty. In the 1to1 enterprise, the Webmaster will be judged on how well the entire Web site collects, tracks, and organizes the data generated by each hit and every transaction. A new generation of interactive-software solutions, such as Learn Sesame, makes it possible to profile visitors dynamically as they click along through your Web site—learning more and more specific things about a customer with every interaction. And sophisticated matching engines such as Net Perceptions' GroupLens now enable Web sites to offer personalized suggestions for new purchases through a process called collaborative filtering. When hiring a Webmaster, you should look for someone who understands and feels comfortable with these advanced types of software.

Culture and Training

For years your company's culture has rewarded behaviors that focused on products and processes. Measuring the results of programs based on generating product sales is quick and simple—so simple that Wall Street can reward a company for quarterly sales much more easily than it can analyze the long-term value of the firm's customer base. In publicly held companies, a proposal to spend millions of dollars on a new customer database that might not pay for itself for several years is likely to encounter stiff resistance from the board of directors. Privately held companies won't face this particular hurdle, but there will be other obstacles and challenges to implementing a 1to1 program.

So there's no getting around the fact that you'll have to change your culture as your company makes the transition from a traditional, product-only form of competition to more customer-centered, 1to1 marketing. To a large degree, the success of your efforts to evolve the company culture will depend on getting your people the training and education they need to:

1. Understand what 1to1 is all about,
2. Achieve a comfort level high enough to ensure sustained cooperation and loyalty, and
3. Do it instinctively and intuitively.

Eventually you'll want to get everyone in the company trained to the point where every decision they make is infused with 1to1 thinking. But who needs training first? Consider that you'll need three basic types of individuals to make the program bear fruit:

- Visionaries (to visualize the company's future)
- Promoters (to inspire and describe the big picture)
- Implementers (to get things done)

Taking this approach ensures adequate representation at all levels. It's important to remember that while cultural change doesn't require unanimity, it does need a certain critical mass before it will produce real results. Many companies benefit by approaching training efforts on three levels: *Lead, Follow,* and *Get Out of the Way.*

LEAD

Who: Executive leadership, such as senior vice presidents, executive vice presidents, directors, transition team leaders, customer managers.

Training time: 2–5 days (requires the most training, since this group will be doing the heavy lifting of implementation)

Training agenda:

- Identify, differentiate, interact, customize
- Wrestle with customer database issues
- Determine roles and responsibilities
- Reach consensus on implementation

- Structure the compensation plan appropriately
- Set up and allocate budgets
- Set up customer strategies and dialogue plans

FOLLOW

Who: Front-line employees, such as bank tellers, cash register clerks, and reservation takers.

Training time: 2–3 hours

Training agenda:

- Overview and explanation of 1to1 philosophy
- Explanation of new compensation plan that rewards front-line workers for building share of customer, collecting customer information, and growing customer value for the company
- Preliminary overview of the tools being made available (sales-force automation, call center screens, customer records, etc.)
- Specific marching orders
- Inspiration, coaching, and pep talk from executive leadership

GET OUT OF THE WAY

Who: Highest-level decision makers such as CEO, CIO, CFO.

Training time: 90 minutes (these are the people most likely to dig up the tulips to see if they're growing, so make sure they're on your side)

Training agenda:

- Overview of the basic principles of 1to1
- Review and discussion of the company's 1to1 mission
- Implications for the broader enterprise

Metrics of Success So now you've hired the right people, organized them and set up training for them. Next step is to figure out how to measure their success and compensate them appropriately.

In any business organization, you will get what you pay for. If you pay people the most and reward them the best for pushing products, you'll get product sales. If you reward your employees for identifying, differentiating, interacting, and customizing, you'll get strong Learning Relationships with your best customers. Ultimately, you want to develop farmers, not just hunter-gatherers. You want people to worry about cultivating long-term customer relationships, not just finding more customers wherever they can be found. In Chapter Eleven, "The One-to-One Sales Organization," for example, we'll discuss a couple of different ways to compensate salespeople more for acquiring the kinds of customers who will remain loyal and grow in value to the firm.

We don't have to tell you that most of the traditional metrics of a company's success—net profit, return on equity, sales volume—will continue to be important. But if you are focused on managing and measuring customer relationships, then metrics such as market share in a product category, and new customers acquired, may not be as important as they once were.

To get a handle on your own enterprise's success, you'll need to ask yourself questions such as these:

- What proportion of our firm's incentive compensation goes toward increasing customer value?
- Do we have the technology necessary to manage individual data within and between functions?
- How long does it take to coordinate customer-specific activities across functional boundaries? Between product divisions?
- How quickly and efficiently does information about customers flow through our organization?
- What percentage of our customers is "under management"? What is our goal for one year from now?
- What is the readiness of our organization to be customer friendly? How central is the customer to the actual culture of our enterprise?

Support the Revolution

Rome wasn't built in a day. It took a year of systematic experimentation by Thomas Edison to produce the first truly incandescent light bulb. It took more than a decade of continuous work by NASA to land an astronaut on the moon. Don't expect your company to change overnight. On the other hand, if you don't get behind the revolution *now*, it's going to pass you by. Companies that haven't made the effort and fought the battles to develop 1to1 skills will lose their customers to companies that have.

Hewlett-Packard didn't decide to become a 1to1 company on a whim. HP decided to become a 1to1 company after discovering that its customers didn't want to be treated as markets, segments, or niches. Do yours?

Recommended Reads

Best, Roger J. *Market-Based Management: Strategies for Growing Customer Value and Profitability* (Prentice Hall, 1997).
Best applies market principles to the processes of a corporation and demonstrates how resources can be more effectively channeled and customer relationships more effectively built. The book explores an array of marketing strategies that are thoroughly driven by the needs and demands of the market.

Crego, Edwin, and Peter Schiffrin. *Customer Centered Reengineering* (Irwin Professional Publishing, 1994).
Applying Business Processing Reengineering principles to the development of customer relationships, Crego and Schiffrin say readers should see customer relationships from the perspective of an ongoing process, and companies should take an outward-looking view of reengineering.

Dow, Roger, and Susan Cook. *Turned On: Eight Vital Insights to Energize Your People, Customers, and Profits* (HarperBusiness, 1996).
Top business coach Susan Cook and Marriott executive Roger Dow demonstrate how to generate vitality by allowing employees to think for themselves, take control of their jobs, make decisions, recognize problems, and find and implement solutions. Examples include Xerox, Motorola, Charles Schwab & Co., and Mary Kay.

Halal, William E. (editor), Raymond W. Smith (editor), and Cedric Crocker (editor). *The Infinite Resource: Creating and Leading the Knowledge Enterprise* (Jossey-Bass Business and Management Series, 1998).
The Infinite Resource is a splendid overview of trends contributing to the emergence of a knowledge economy, exploring changes within the enterprise as well as the broader economic and technological changes that management must address.

Hammer, Michael. *Beyond Reengineering: How the Process-Centered Organization Is Changing Our Work and Our Lives* (HarperBusiness, 1996).
Hammer argues that corporations are being transformed and hierarchies are being overturned by "process centering." Processes are becoming corporate assets, and as a result workers increasingly have broad, self-managed jobs.

Hiebeler, Robert, Thomas Kelly, and Charles Ketterman. *Best Practices: Building Your Business with Customer-Focused Solutions* (Simon & Schuster, 1998).
This book looks at some of the world's most profitable companies—such as FedEx and American Express—and examines their customer relationship building strategies. Hiebeler, Kelly, and Ketterman, who all are partners at the management consulting firm Arthur Andersen, present some of the key insights that they have gained about customer-focused companies.

Jaffe, Azriela L. *Honey, I Want to Start My Own Business: A Planning Guide for Couples* (HarperCollins, 1996).
Drawing on her own experiences as well as those of 130 other couples, Jaffe developed this powerful guide for power couples who are attempting to build their own businesses. In this book, she recognizes the opportunities for applying the principles of 1to1 marketing to make a small business grow and flourish.

Kouzes, James, Tom Peters, and Barry Posner. *Credibility: How Leaders Gain and Lose It, Why People Demand It* (Jossey-Bass Management, 1995).
In this book based on surveys, case studies, and interviews, the authors deliver an explanation of credibility's role in leadership and propose six key disciplines that strengthen a leader's ability to develop and cultivate credibility.

Peters, Tom. *Liberation Management: Necessary Disorganization for the Nanosecond Nineties* (Fawcett Books, 1994).

Peters forecasts the overthrow of staid, hierarchical companies and the emergence of entrepreneurial, networked, project-oriented firms. It's a great read, reminding us all of the tenuous nature of success and the importance of continual reinvention.

Prusak, Laurence, editor. *Knowledge in Organizations: Resources for the Knowledge-Based Economy* (Butterworth-Heinemann, 1997).
Prusak has provided an excellent compendium of articles addressing the leveraging of knowledge within enterprises. Contributions explore knowledge strategy, knowledge networks, and organizational memory.

CHAPTER 9: INFRASTRUCTURE

Activity 9A

Organizational Issues For Your Transition Team to Discuss

Target Completion Date: _____

1. Elevator Speech: Describe how your organization will change as you make the transition from a traditional way of doing business to a customer-centric approach.

_____

_____

_____

2. Who *wants* the changes we are talking about in this chapter?

_____

_____

_____

3. Who has to lead change within the organization for it to be implemented?

_____

_____

_____

4. How receptive is your organization to making changes?

_____

_____

_____

5. Go through your old organization chart. Everywhere that "product" appears in someone's title, re-place it with "customer." See if that helps you visualize new roles and responsibilities. (If you have product managers, don't you need customer managers? If you have product developers, shouldn't you have customer developers?)

_____

_____

_____

Activity 9B

Checkpoint: Traditional Versus 1to1 Metrics

For each of the questions below, provide an answer for your current organization, and for an "ideal" 1to1 enterprise, organized to identify, differentiate, interact with, and customize for its customers, one customer at a time.

Target Completion Date: _____

Questions	Current Organization	Ideal Organization
1. How do you evaluate the success of the overall enterprise?		
2. How do you evaluate your position relative to competitors in the marketplace?		

3. How do you assess the strengths and weaknesses of your company's strategy?

4. How do you evaluate individual tactical marketing campaigns and initiatives?

Activity 9C

Obstacles to Making Progress: A Brainstorming Competition

Target Completion Date: _____

1. Collect a bright group of managers at your firm from a variety of functions and business units. It is important that all of them be generally familiar with the principles involved in implementing a 1to1 marketing program. It would be best if they've all read at least the first eight chapters in the *Fieldbook*.

2. Divide into teams of no more than three to six people each, and head off into appropriate breakout rooms. This is a competition, and each team will be trying to outdo the others.

3. Each team, as a team, should give themselves fifteen minutes to write down as many reasons as they can think of to show why making the transition to becoming a 1to1 enterprise will be difficult, or won't work at all, for your organization. Quantity is as important as quality here. You want to uncover every last possible obstacle to making progress.

4. Meet again, as a group, and each group presents its list of obstacles. Organizational barriers, cultural barriers, lack of information, no funding, lack of senior management buy-in, an overly resistant sales force—these are the kinds of reasons that should be on everyone's list.

5. Award a prize to the group that came up with the longest list of obstacles. Give another prize to the group that came up with the single best statement of the most insurmountable obstacle.

6. Now collate and consolidate the lists from all the groups, and go over the obstacles one at a time to identify in each case the most cost-efficient, least burdensome way of overcoming it. Will it require a budget? Does the CEO need to weigh in? Do you need a different compensation structure?

7. The result will be an infrastructure "wish list" for your enterprise, and should be incorporated as a part of your transition-planning documentation.

Activity 9D

Organization and Metrics

Target Completion Date: _____

Allow one hour for this written exercise. Feel free to use additional sheets of paper, and to talk to other members of your transition team. At the end, discuss the exercise, but no one will be required to share their particular answers, nor will anyone read anyone else's answers without permission.

1. Choose a specific customer base, within either the end-user or the channel member constituency. If you focus on end users, choose large enterprises, or small businesses, or consumers, etc. If you choose channel members, choose distributors, or retailers, etc.

2. *Within* the customer base you have chosen, how might you rank customers into value tiers and differentiate them into needs-based groups? List some of the logical portfolio groupings for the customer base you have chosen:

_____

_____

_____

3. Assuming you were to set up a customer-management system structured into portfolios like this, how would you gauge the success of your customer managers? What *strategic metrics* do you need in place to do this?

_____

_____

_____

4. What short-term *interim metrics* would you put in place to gauge the progress of your business unit in terms of how it is working toward customer management and operating as a 1to1 enterprise?

_____

_____

_____

Activity 9E

Competitive Metrics: Benchmarking Checklist

Target Completion Date: _____

How to Benchmark	
Task	**Considerations**
Develop benchmarking plan	▪ Collect third-party data about industry best practices
Mini-benchmarking as a precursor and supplement	▪ Web site visits ▪ Phone calls ▪ Letter and e-mail exchanges
Competitive environment: What provoked this benchmarking initiative?	▪ Who was the catalyst and what was the primary reason?
What kind of budget do you have?	
What is the time constraint?	
How wide and deep do you want to go?	
Who goes from your firm to an on-site benchmarking visit?	
Whom do you want to see at the benchmarked firm?	
What sort of documentation do you want to bring back?	

Target Completion Date: _____

Whom to Benchmark	
Task	**Considerations**
Be sure you have the right business category (doesn't necessarily have to be *your* category, just a category that will provide useful lessons)	

You want to benchmark with other companies that:	■ Operate with a business model similar to yours
	■ Serve a customer base with characteristics similar to yours
	■ Face problems similar to yours
	■ Sell products or services like yours
Consider business size:	■ Dollar volume of sales
	■ Number of customers served
	■ Number of locations, work stations, outlets, call centers
Consider aspirational companies	■ "I wanna be like . . ."
Consider negative benchmarking, too	

Target Completion Date: _____

What to Find Out

Task	Considerations
What kind of learning do you hope to gain?	
Come up with a manageable number of key questions (for each benchmarking candidate)	Consider the following:
	■ Annual spending on technology
	■ Organizational changes
	■ Compensation issues
	■ Walk through customer touch points
	■ Processes
	■ Mistakes made/pitfalls encountered: How do you learn from them (failed initiatives?)
	■ Challenges: How you overcome them?
	■ Tracking dead ends: How do you measure your own progress?
	■ Leadership: Who are the champions and what are their strategies?
	■ Training: How did you spread the word?

What Do You Do with What You Learn?

Task	Considerations

How will you transfer/integrate knowledge of best practices into your enterprise?

You may want to institutionalize the practice of benchmarking.

- How often will you benchmark other firms?
- Can you follow up later with the same company?

Chapter Ten

Channel Management

EVALUATING CHANNEL MEMBERS IN THE ONE-TO-ONE ORGANIZATION

BUYER: Hey, I thought this product had an unlimited warranty. What's this bill for?

SELLER: Well, the factory might have warranted it if you hadn't dropped it. But I can't give you the computer back without $235, cash.

BUYER: Why didn't you fix the recall on the hard drive, at least, while you had it open?

SELLER: Oh, we don't do that here. That's a factory thing.

Channels. Autonomous. Independent. Often at odds with even the best, most well-intentioned, one-to-one manufacturer's programs. Channel policies conflict with factory programs, promises, and procedures so often that the relationship can easily be more adversarial than constructive. And despite their own best efforts, manufacturers in most industries can barely touch the tip of the iceberg when it comes to ensuring quality control with a global network of dealers or distributors.

Any channel member is clearly closer to end-user customers than any manufacturer, and—as a rule—the enterprise that is closest to the customer wins, particularly in the 1to1 environment. The closer an enterprise is to a customer, the better its ability to cultivate genuine 1to1 relationships—with greater impact on enduring customer value. The winner is often the one who communicates directly with the customer. Sometimes the retail consumers who buy CD players at Best Buy interact with the retailer's own customer service and sales organizations. Yet they still see the Sony logo and may opt for the Sony help line or Web site instead.

As a rule, customers don't care which channel they deal with, whether it's an authorized distributor, a gray-market reseller, a VAR (value-added reseller), an independent dealer, retail chain, warehouse distributor, street hawker, or pushcart. They talk to their channel contact of preference—and that preference often is defined by the channel contact's ability to deliver a 1to1 relationship of value to that customer, individually.

Today's consumer is far more informed and demanding, usually aware of the best prices and most competitive product specs. So they expect consistent policies, procedures, programs—and *relationships*—with the enterprise that manufactures the product or stands behind the service.

Conflicting channel relationships will endure, at least in most industries. Manufacturers want channel members to conform to a set of standards for selling, servicing, or repairing the product. Channel members claim ownership of the customer relationship and stress their own arm's-length relationship with "the factory." Things go from bad to worse when a manufacturer "goes direct," or works to develop 1to1 end-user relationships that imply service delivery, individual interaction, or customer memory. Usually it's the confused customer who loses—which means everyone loses.

But a manufacturer can use the same basic 1to1 principles that govern how to create profitable relationships with end-user customers to develop profitable relationships with channel members, too. There are some important differences, of course, between channel members and end-user customers, but in this chapter we're going to document step-by-step procedures for creating the tightest, most mutually beneficial relationships with channel members. We're writing the chapter from the perspective of the manufacturer, however, and not the channel member per se. If the nature of your business involves being part of someone else's channel, then you should be applying these same principles to your own customers, or to the channel members one step down on the demand chain from you.

As with the analysis in the previous chapters, the right way to proceed is first to be sure you understand exactly what type of customer base you're dealing with. Are your channel members completely independent dealers or retailers? Do they configure your product, install it, maintain it, or repair it? Or do they just hold it in inventory, consolidating your product supplies with many others? Do you have channel members who add value beyond your product, by consulting or providing other services for the product's users, or perhaps by bundling your product into a "system" along with equipment from others?

Identify Your Channel Members

Most businesses operate in multiple channels and channel types. So for each type of distribution channel, your first step is to identify all the channel members, individually. Of course, you already have all the particulars with respect to those channel members to whom you ship products directly, including billing information, loading-dock opening hours, inventory-control bar codes, and so forth. But what about the dealers or the independent retail stores who take product from these distributors? Are you certain you have identified all of the key channel members? And for all channel members, do you actually know the names and titles of the people at each firm who have a vote with respect to marketing, buying, and merchandising your product to their customers? The accounts payable people who send out the checks are hardly the right contacts.

Your channel members are nearly as different from one another as your end-user customers are. As with any other 1to1 assessment, differentiation begins by evaluating the whole range of value- and needs-driven factors (see Activity 10D).

Differentiate Your Channel Members

In addition to the more obvious variables, consider the clout or heft your enterprise holds in a channel. If you are the sales rep firm or distributor's largest, most profitable product line, for example, this differentiator may well overpower all others. Cigarette manufacturers hold immense sway over candy and tobacco wholesalers nationwide—at least for the short term. This kind of dominance, or clout, certainly affects the success potential of any 1to1 program, although it may be very big with respect to one channel partner and all but insignificant with respect to others. Demand for your product, a channel member's willingness to sacrifice margin for growth, and the number of competitors in a given arena—all are variations on value that are harder to calculate and subtler in their impact on an individual channel-partner relationship.

Each individual demand chain must be evaluated separately. Mass merchandisers, distributors, rack jobbers, and sales rep firms all can serve a single manufacturer, and often do. When ranking channel members by their value to you, be sure to evaluate each channel type separately, since so many of their individual variables will differ widely. Start with the obvious, simple parameters, such as a proxy variable based on last year's volume and margins. A "double-A" distributor provides high volume and profits, but not perhaps when compared with Wal-Mart and other direct accounts.

Share of customer is particularly important in the channel. Do your products account for 10 percent of a particular channel member's volume? Or 80 percent? If your firm begins interacting more frequently and individually with a given distributor, will any tangible benefits accrue? In the case of a small retail chain where your products already dominate the shelf space and the buyer is working night and day, you may see little upside from your marketing and communications efforts to improve your share of customer. Identifying these issues up-front and avoiding a one-size-fits-all approach is exactly what 1to1 marketing is about.

One inherent channel conflict is often troubling. It's the push-pull between a channel member's autonomy and independence and your firm's need to control how that channel member presents your product and services to "your" end-user customers. In general, the greater your share of customer for a particular channel member, the less conflict you'll have. The higher you can drive your share of customer, the more the channel member will likely collaborate to provide information to and about end users, and to turn your joint operation into an increasingly profitable venture for both of you. So besides ranking your channel members by their actual, ongoing, "run rate" value to your firm, you really need to spend some time trying to estimate what share of each member's business you really have.

Consider a simple "data scoring" model for weighting each partner in a channel. A candymaker ranking distributors might use the following system, for example:

Criteria	Points
More than $100,000 annual volume	3
We're one of the distributor's top five candy lines	2
We're on the cover of their monthly catalogue	1
They are our major distributor in the market	1
Willing to collaborate to strengthen the end user's loyalty	1
Creditworthy and pay bills on time	1

These scores should be adjusted based on what's important to your own enterprise. Whatever system you choose, its goal is to provide a "language" everyone in the enterprise can use to categorize customers—"All sevens get the special promotion," or "We ship sixes and up on the same day no matter what," or whatever rules can be developed to actualize this simplistic, value-based differentiation system.

If you have trouble ranking your channel members by their value, use the channel member's "importance" to you instead. If your channel members have exclusive territories, this measure might be more useful. Whatever ranking criteria you use should also factor into the channel member's own knowledge of and enthusiasm for creating relationships with end-user customers.

There are very few examples of success when it comes to integrating distribution channels into ambitious 1to1 customer relationship-management programs. Great Plains Software's efforts (see the discussion in Chapter Six) are notable for their originality and innovation. Using the Web to structure an "extended enterprise" capable of helping channel members sell a service-intensive software product to business customers is one idea. But it turns out that the biggest problem faced in implementing this system is not figuring out the right strategy or installing new technology. The biggest problem faced by Great Plains' managers is persuading their reseller partners that creating

1to1 relationships with customers makes good business sense in the first place. Spreading a revolutionary idea down through a network is challenging enough, even when the revolutionaries sign the subjects' paychecks. But when the subjects are independent businesspeople themselves, the best-laid plans of enlightened manufacturers often wind up on the warehouse floor.

If you were Great Plains, faced with this problem, how would *you* solve it? Launching a training and indoctrination program for your channel members would be important. But the way you approach it should include trying to estimate the degree to which different channel members "get it" or don't, and to concentrate your efforts first on empowering those who really understand the idea.

Great Plains calls all of its reseller channel members "partners." This is a label intended to convey a greater degree of collaboration and joint effort than exists in most similar channels. The word "partner" is probably a good measuring stick for you in your own business. Which of your channel members are most likely to be able to become true partners in launching and cultivating relationships with end users? The truth is, if you can't apply the word "partner" to a channel member, you might want to seriously consider the word "disintermediation" instead. In other words, if you can't develop powerful, collaborative relationships with your channel partners, it may be time to go direct to your customers and eliminate the channel altogether.

Differentiating by Needs

After assessing the channel partner's value, consider looking next at what the partner needs from your enterprise. Sometimes the channel partner markets or distributes your products out of habit or because "we've been doing it since 1954," but the partnership provides little value to the channel. At other times, your firm may be providing a "calling card" product line that makes little money but opens a lot of doors for the distributor. Understand why the channel member is doing business with your firm in the first place—and adapt your firm's behavior accordingly.

Needs-based differentiators vary dramatically. (Many are listed in Activity 10D.) Sometimes these needs have dramatic impact on your profitable service of the channel—as in a distributor who can't repair or properly install a product, for example, resulting in higher warranty and factory-service costs. Beer distributors are well known for taking on new products ad nauseam, since "the truck is going there anyway," and another brew might bring a few more dollars in profit per day. But the unsuspecting brewer gets very little preferential selling, even less merchandising and display activity, and zero hope of 1to1 relationship building from this kind of channel partner.

The computer channel might seem a lot like the beer business to many high-tech manufacturers. Resellers and distributors heap one new product atop another in hopes of "striking it rich" with the next Microsoft. But whether your firm sells computers or widgets, try to identify some telltale needs-based differentiators that can guide all customer-contact personnel in their interactions with a channel member. For example:

- *Competence providers:* These are true professional organizations that reliably support a product in every way, from providing information and diligently selling a product to performing superbly, almost as an arm of the manufacturer, in such areas as installation, help desk, and service and repair functions.
- *Lead trawlers:* These channel partners are best avoided where possible. They "carry" the product but do little else—unless, of course, a sales lead is generated by the manufacturer. These partners often play the law of averages and hope that, by dint of their size, they will receive enough inbound inquiries to warrant carrying the product. Don't count on partners like these to provide any meaningful support—or true distribution, for that matter.
- *Service providers:* These players can be important channel partners, even if they don't proactively sell or even stock the product. Ready access to high-quality service or installation in a market can be extremely helpful, although differentiating these types of channel partners one from another is often crucial. You can refer cus-

tomers for service and installation, but not necessarily when an aggressive sales presentation is called for.

Whatever your product or industry, identify the channel partner types that are of value to your firm in each of its activities. Recognize that it's often easier to recruit additional partners to support one aspect or another of your firm's total product and service delivery—and know what you're getting from each partner.

Review the task lists at the end of this chapter as you develop what is almost always an individualized channel strategy.

Interact with Your Channel Members

If Kellogg's and the food distributor both know the supermarket manager's birthday and spouse's name, can either one ultimately profit from this information in a measurable way before retirement? All too often we gather inappropriate or useless information because a data field exists for it in "the system." Collaborating with channel partners to isolate the best, most readily garnered but *usable* information is a vitally important step.

No matter what the medium, the interface or handoff from manufacturer to distributor and back again has got to work! If a customer has complained profusely to his or her company-based customer service rep, a clear 1to1 imperative is for that customer's distributor sales rep to learn about the problems and in near-real time, to follow up.

This poses particularly daunting problems for 1to1 marketers, including—among others:

- *Lack of confirmation:* The sending party is often uncertain about receipt, let alone follow-up, by the channel partner on the receiving end. Urgent messages are sometimes "lost in space," with the result that a company's much-touted "seamlessness" of service is quickly exposed as a false promise;
- *Lack of memory:* What's phoned or faxed sometimes doesn't make it into the database at either end, unless it's an order;
- *Lack of uniformity:* Seldom are two messages communicated the same way, in the same format, although orders are again often the

exception to this rule. Parties at either end of the dialogue often don't receive all the information necessary to deal with the specifics of a customer's situation.

Explore opportunities to facilitate direct, department-to-department communication—preferably electronic—between various departments of a manufacturing enterprise and its sales channel. By keeping salespeople out of the middle, yet informing them as needed, communications throughout the channel are smarter and faster. Maybe that's why scores of M.B.A.'s report to work at one of Procter & Gamble's largest field offices in Arkansas. It's down the street from P&G's top customer, Wal-Mart, where P&G employees from every discipline interface with their Wal-Mart counterparts. And it's no doubt a contributor to the gold rush for office space in this area.

Channel proximity need not be physical to be successful. Cisco's Web site (see Chapter Six) provides reseller-specific information, pricing, and contact data. Each of its major channel partners has its own Web-housed communications channel that sits astride the core Cisco Web site. BroadVision channel partners can interact, reach the firm's help desk, read about updates, and much more on the channel partner section of the firm's massive Web site. In both cases, manufacturers are working hard to make the link between manufacturer and channel partner a seamless one—nearly invisible to the customer, just as it should be.

Cisco partners are hard to differentiate from employees. Cisco partners are required to undertake a rigorous training program to become silver-, gold-, or platinum-certified. The channel member's efforts are rewarded with discounts, cooperative marketing, and lead-generation activities funded by Cisco. Resellers are encouraged to move up to higher levels of certification in order to compete more effectively with others in the channel.

Customize for Your Channel Members

Channel management requires the same approach as customer management. Each one is different and has different values and needs. Avoid basing your customization for channel members merely on size or distance from the customer. Both of these factors are solid first steps, but wherever possible you should customize your channel-member relationships to increase yours and the channel partner's mutual volume, which provides the most demonstrable proof of the 1to1 concept for partners on both sides of the desk.

Identifying mutual value opportunities: What customer-keeping and -growing activities can provide incremental profits to both the manufacturer and distributor? When your number-two distributor's top sales rep calls in to check on the details of an order, is he or she told to turn on the PC and use the million-dollar Web interface? Is the host company still snail-mailing everything it e-mails to every distributor every Friday? And can manufacturer executives end-run the system?

Creating Learning Relationships with channel members gradually: Moving a channel increasingly toward 1to1 marketing is going to be a gradual process, so you'll need to develop a multi-year, phased plan. But if you do develop this plan, *keep it to yourself,* at least for a while. Channel partners will accept increased demands on their time, their systems, and their attention paid to any given product line or supplier only as they see measurable progress.

You can use progress-tracking mechanisms such as quarterly or semiannual review sessions to demonstrate the specific impact of 1to1 program components. Based on agreement as to metrics and success against those measures, collaborate with individual channel partners—often at varying speeds—to continue expanding the integration of 1to1 techniques into the organization.

The following questions will help you determine some levers you can use to minimize channel problems and improve the service of end users:

- Is there some aspect of your product or service that the distributor configures or sets up—and can you help the distributor do this more efficiently?
- Can you take advantage of new "postponement" manufacturing processes to help your channel members participate in the actual configuration and manufacturing of your product? As Edward Feitzinger and Hau L. Lee argued in a *Harvard Business Review* article entitled "Mass Customization at Hewlett-Packard," by modu-

larizing the basic manufacturing process, a producer can postpone the final assembly of a product, offsetting slightly higher manufacturing costs with usually dramatically lower inventory-carrying costs. From a channel management perspective, one side benefit of this is that the channel partner has more of a product-configuration role to play than would otherwise be the case.

- Are service and support of your product done by the channel member (like the car dealer repairing the car), and if so, can you provide the channel member with the information tools to do the job better?
- Could you help the channel manage some *other* aspect of his business, like accounting, or payroll, or inventory control?

Conclusion

Start small. Don't be too ambitious, at least at first, so (a) you can gain small victories and build on them; and (b) you don't tip your hand about what else might be coming down the road.

You want to put the "partner" into "channel partner." Don't settle for a distribution chain that doesn't participate with you in creating stronger, more profitable relationships with the end-user customers who are at least as much yours as they are theirs.

BUYER: And the broken handle? Why didn't you fix that, for Pete's sake?
SELLER: Our computer was down, so the part didn't arrive. It wasn't in the warehouse, so we'll send you a postcard in a few weeks when it arrives and you can bring it in. We'll only need it for a few days.

Recommended Reads

Blackwell, Roger. *From Mind to Market: Reinventing the Retail Supply Chain* (HarperCollins Publishers, 1997).
Blackwell makes the case for a "radical reinvention of retail"—arguing that companies must more actively learn and address their customers' needs, and manage their "demand-chains" more effectively.

Feitzinger, Edward, and Hau L. Lee. "Mass Customization at Hewlett-Packard: The Power of Postponement," *Harvard Business Review,* January/February 1997, pp. 116–121.

This piece discusses the organizational-design principles that underlie successful mass customization. The article explains that companies must develop independent product and manufacturing modules as well as supply networks capable of cost-effectively and flexibly delivering the modules to the facilities performing the customization. It also explores postponement as a method for filtering products to customize needs more precisely.

Iyer, Vinoo. *Profitable Sales Partnerships: A Guide to Managing and Motivating Agents, Distributors, Importers, and Anyone Else Who Sells Your Product!* (Irwin Professional Pub., 1994).

With the lowering of trade restrictions and the expansion of global trade, opportunities are opening up for companies to expand abroad effectively. Vinoo offers checklists, advice, and evaluation tools for companies that are seeking out channel partners and distributors.

Tichy, Noel M., and Eli Cohen. *The Leadership Engine: How Winning Companies Build Leaders at Every Level* (HarperBusiness, 1997).

Tichy and Cohen ably tackle the challenges of organizational change, demonstrating how leadership can be cultivated at all levels. Basing their argument on consultations with such leading companies as PepsiCo, Royal Dutch/Shell, and Ford Motor Company, they contend that top leaders have a distinct point of view, which is codified and communicated throughout the enterprise.

Activity 10A

Channel Management Issues
for Your Transition Team to Discuss

Target Completion Date: _____

1. Elevator Speech: If your CEO asked you what your organization's biggest problems are with your channels, how would you answer him or her from a 1to1 perspective?

_____

_____

_____

2. What criteria are being used to determine which channel members can contribute the most to your organization?

_____

_____

_____

3. What criteria will you use to determine which channel members add the most value to *their* customers—your end users?

_____

_____

_____

Checkpoint: Channels

Target Completion Date: _____

Answer yes or no to the following questions. Repeat this activity one year after the initial date you complete it.

	Now	One Year from Now
Do you identify mutual value opportunities with your channel members?	oYes oNo	oYes oNo
Do you isolate sharable data of the greatest value?	oYes oNo	oYes oNo
Do you implement a seamless channel interface?	oYes oNo	oYes oNo
Do you know which of your channel members are truly "partners"?	oYes oNo	oYes oNo
Do you know which ones are more valuable or important?	oYes oNo	oYes oNo
Can you differentiate your channel members by what they need from you, individually?	oYes oNo	oYes oNo
Can your departments communicate directly with the counterpart departments at your channel partner firms?	oYes oNo	oYes oNo
Do your channel members add value to your product and/or services for your end user?	oYes oNo	oYes oNo

Channels: Identify/Interact Task List

Target Completion Date: _____

Who Will Do It? (init.)	By When? (date)	Activity	75% Done (✓)	100% Done (✓)

1. Determine the type of customer base you are dealing with:

<table>
<tr><td></td><td>Yes</td><td>No</td></tr>
<tr><td>■ Are your channel members completely independent dealers or retailers?</td><td>___</td><td>___</td></tr>
<tr><td>■ Do they configure your product, install, maintain, or repair it?</td><td>___</td><td>___</td></tr>
<tr><td>■ Do they hold your product in inventory with numerous others?</td><td>___</td><td>___</td></tr>
<tr><td>■ Do you have channel members who add value beyond your product?</td><td>___</td><td>___</td></tr>
</table>

Describe the types of channel customers with which your organization deals:

■ _____

■ _____

■ _____

■ _____

■ _____

2A. Try to list all, or at least your top ten, channel members:

Partner?
Check if yes

- _____ ____
- _____ ____
- _____ ____
- _____ ____
- _____ ____
- _____ ____
- _____ ____
- _____ ____
- _____ ____
- _____ ____

2B. Name your top secondary dealers or independent stores that take products from your primary distributors.

- _____ ____
- _____ ____
- _____ ____
- _____ ____
- _____ ____
- _____ ____
- _____ ____
- _____ ____
- _____ ____

2C. Which of the firms listed in 2A and 2B do you describe as true "partners" to your firm? Place a check mark in the blank to the right of each name in 2A and 2B.

3. Be sure you know the name and title of each person from each channel member in 2A and 2B who has a vote with regard to the marketing, buying, and merchandising for their customers.

4. Assess and define opportunities to facilitate direct, department-to-department communication between various departments of your manufacturing or service enterprise and your sales channel. These will probably be electronic.

Activity 10D
Differentiating Channel Partners

Target Completion Date: _____

Below are points to consider when differentiating your channel members both by need and by value or importance. Think of it as a worksheet for *each channel member.*

By Value/Importance	
Points to Consider	**Description**
What was the last year's volume and margin yielded to your organization? Total sales?	
What is the sale of your products versus their total sales (share of customer)?	
What is the profitability of the channel member?	■ What is the cost to service this channel member? ■ How many calls are made for support? ■ What kind of demands do they make?
How much of your product does this channel member sell (what percentage)?	
Do they sell profitable products/services or lower-margin options?	

Are they strategically important?	<ul><li>Are they growing fast?</li><li>Do they have relevant skills/expertise?</li><li>Are they developing programs/innovations you can share with other channel members?</li><li>Are they in a hot or important industry/niche?</li></ul>
Do they collaborate with you?	<ul><li>Do they participate in manufacturing-sponsored events?</li><li>Do they invite their customers?</li><li>Do they attend your training programs?</li><li>Do they respond to your offers?</li><li>Do they respond to your questions?</li><li>Do they provide you with important insights/feedback?</li><li>Do they tell you how to better serve their needs and those of their customers?</li><li>Do they provide you with end-user feedback/insights?</li></ul>

Creditworthiness: Does this channel member pay its bills on time?

Does this channel member keep your costs down (lower factory and warranty costs)?

By Needs

Issues:	<ul><li>Does this channel member need your help adding value beyond your product?</li><li>Does this channel member need your help with breaking bulk, configuration, installation, maintenance, and/or repair of your product?</li><li>What is your channel member's financial business model: Does it want growth or immediate results?</li></ul>

	■ How many competitors does this channel member have? How competitive is that particular market?
Communications	■ Does this channel member need more information or less? ■ Does this channel member need information in a different format? ■ Does this channel member allow you to choose when, why, and how you communicate with it?
Product	■ Does this channel member want/need to mass-customize the final assembly/delivery of its product? ■ Does this channel member want unique configurations? ■ Does this channel member want it to be "branded" under its name?
Customer Service	■ Does this channel member need help communicating with its customers? ■ Does this channel member need help providing product support to its customers? ■ Does this channel member need more product/service knowledge, or training for its staff and/or clients?
Pricing	■ Does this channel member need pricing based on usage? ■ Does this channel member need pricing based on the value of the customer?

Ten Problems to Solve in Building Learning Relationships with Channel Members

Below are ten potential obstacles to building Learning Relationships with your channel members and solutions to overcoming them. Read through the list with your transition team and cross off the problems that do not apply to you. Work through the remaining problems and solutions.

Target Completion Date: _____

Who Will Do It? (init.)	By When? (date)	Problem	Solution Tasks	75% Done (✓)	100% Done (✓)
		1. Channel fear of oversight by seller or channel managers	▪ Go through channel members one at a time. Based on what you know, determine what each one needs and whether it's in your best interest to partner ▪ Determine whether to revise distribution contracts to mandate participation		
		2. Lack of local-management interest in 1to1	▪ Demonstrate potential additional uses of newly gathered customer data in channel ▪ Present incremental, measurable profitability of program to channel enterprise ▪ Institute training in 1to1, or begin by sharing books and publications on 1to1		

3. Inability of partner to serve entire "mission"	■ Create localized teams of channel partners by pairing firms with complementary strengths
	■ Use quarterly or annual review process to reinforce needs for added 1to1 activities
4. Incompatible data systems	■ Consider a data-development project to be jointly undertaken with those partners currently data-incompatible. You spearhead the project
	■ Consider using browser-based software applications wherever possible
	■ Consider voice mail, fax broadcast, or use of other universal systems, such as Netscape browsers
	■ Consider bringing in an outside party
5. Lack of confirmation about receipt and follow-up by the channel member; lack of database memory for anything except orders	■ See "Channels: Identify/ Interact Task List" (Activity 10C)
6. Distributor policies forbidding customer-data sharing	■ Develop a written privacy protection pledge
	■ Contractual guarantees of data security

	■ Use third-party data or printing facility to keep each distributor's data private and sequestered, and notify each distributor about this firewall
7. Incompatible compensation systems	■ Develop incentives other than cash, including recognition programs, contests, and sweepstakes ■ Subsidize existing programs in channel to refocus interest in 1to1 programs
8. Channel members who create too much cost for you through increased warranty and servicing costs	■ Make specific suggestions to each of these high-cost channel members as to how to reduce the cost for your partnership ■ Reflect cost analysis in a contract revision
9. Competing programs from other manufacturers	■ Develop individualized communication about program and local successes within channel ■ Simplify ground rules or details of program ■ Increase in-channel promotion of program
10. Lack of owner interest	■ Discreetly solicit alternate partners in market ■ Reduce the scope of activity with this channel partner

Chapter Eleven

The One-to-One Sales Organization

NEW DIRECTIONS FOR SALES IN THE 1TO1 ENTERPRISE

The best salespeople firmly believe they are already expert one-to-one practitioners, and they often are. The most successful salespeople in almost any industry execute many of the strategies in this book almost by instinct. They differentiate customers based on proxy variables for Lifetime Value or long-term growth potential. They interact with their best customers frequently and internalize the learning. And they customize everything, from the sales presentation to the product delivery, based on observed or expressed customer preferences.

But most good salespeople hoard their information, seldom sharing it diligently throughout the enterprise they represent. Their record-keeping is often suspect, and their thinking will often skew toward the shorter-term, order-oriented activities that dovetail with their compensation. Salespeople are usually quite motivated to acquire customers, which can interfere with a company's customer-retention efforts and long-term business development plans. It isn't a simple thing to keep a good sales force motivated while still focusing the overall organization on creating and cultivating long-term customer relationships.

While good salespeople have always had personal, 1to1 relationships with their clients, organizations have not. They have been dependent on particular salespeople to maintain and build these relationships. The 1to1 enterprise, however, must play an integral role in the management of customer information and relationships. It must capitalize on the information that the sales force acquires and encourage salespeople to share it. It must be able to recognize a customer immediately and pick up where the last interaction left off. It must also be able to support the efforts of salespeople to develop more collaborative and effective ways of addressing the individual preferences and priorities of customers in the field.

In this chapter we're going to discuss how the fundamental principles of 1to1 marketing should affect and enable the enterprise's direct sales force. If you are trying to manage your transition to a 1to1 enterprise, the sales force will almost certainly lie at the very center of your organizational plans, as either an asset or an obstacle, or both. So along the way we'll consider such issues as sales-force automation and sales compensation structures.

As with every task, the key to understanding how a 1to1 program should be implemented is to rely on the four basic implementation steps to guide your thinking: identify, differentiate, interact, and customize.

Identify Your Customers

When you think about a sales rep identifying his or her customers, what does this really mean? Again, start with the basic definition of customer. We've already mentioned that in business-to-business selling, the identified "customer" might be the company itself, or the purchasing manager, or the end user, or even an influencer within the firm. But what about prospective customers? Don't many sales organizations spend a disproportionate amount of time with prospects? If the strengths of 1to1 marketing are customer retention and growth, how do you apply these ideas to customer acquisition?

Actually, it's very simple to apply 1to1 marketing to the customer-acquisition process in any business-to-business situation. In Chapter Four, when we ranked customers by value, we were able to identify three interesting types of customers—MVCs, MGCs, and BZs—each of which should be subject to a different set of objectives, calling for different strategies to be applied. MVCs are the Most Valuable Customers—the ones doing the most business with the firm at present. Since just a few MVCs can often account for the vast majority of any company's profit, the key objective is customer retention. At the other end of the spectrum were the BZs, or Below Zero customers, who cost more to serve than they are ever likely to return in profit. Here the key objective is divesting these customers or converting them to profitability. Often either objective can be met by imposing appropriate charges for all the services being rendered to these customers.

The MGCs, or Most Growable Customers, are those with very high strategic values relative to their actual, current values. These are the customers not yet living up to their full potential with your enterprise. They could clearly be worth much more to the business. Share of customer is defined as the ratio of a customer's actual to strategic value, and in general an MGC is a potentially substantial customer with whom you have an unacceptably low share of customer.

Especially in a business-to-business environment, where a direct sales force sells to organizational customers, use this methodology to suggest an interesting perspective for thinking about prospects:

A prospect is a customer with whom you have 0 percent share of customer.

Prospect development might occur when a noncustomer gives a business its first, small, experimental order or contract. Or it might occur when a long-established, highly profitable customer selects the firm for another new project. But the key objective for a salesperson at any company is almost certainly going to be customer growth, and using 1to1 principles can make customer growth into a more efficient and rewarding activity for any enterprise.

Identifying customers is the first step, but before that we have to define the word "customer" so as to include those 0 percent share of customer entities known more formally as "prospects." Sometimes the selling process is defined in terms of converting suspects into prospects and converting prospects into customers. Whatever the terminology, a good sales force should be focused on these suspects, prospects, and customers, trying to identify, track, interact with, and influence multiple individuals within each organization who play a role in the buying process.

In our own consulting business we sometimes hear from someone with a business-to-business marketing company that his firm is already practicing most of the principles we espouse as 1to1 marketing. The executive might say his typical salesperson meets individually with each customer, takes careful notice of the customer's comments and even body language when discussing a proposal. The rep knows the customer well enough to entertain customer and spouse at the opera or the ball park, as appropriate. What could be more 1to1 than that?

Actually, this describes a very good 1to1 relationship—for the salesperson. But the enterprise doesn't benefit directly from the relationship itself. The only benefit to the enterprise comes from employing the salesperson, thus enabling the organization to tap the rep's own personal store of customer knowledge. If the rep gets run over by a truck, or—more likely—takes a job with a competitor, then all the benefits of reading a customer's body language evaporate, along with the personal insights gained during dinner.

Sales Force Automation

For most sales organizations comprised of more than one or two sales reps, identifying and tracking customers will require some form of sales force automation. Sales force automation allows the enterprise to capture information about individual customers, rather than letting this valuable information waste away in the fading and imperfect memories of individual sales reps. Equipping a sales force with laptops or PCs is becoming easier, of course, as technology continues to become cheaper and more powerful. Today it is even possible to automate a sales force using a machine other than a PC, such as a "personal digital assistant," and in the future there will likely be many such alternatives that match the needs of even the most mobile sales organizations.

A colleague of ours once asked the managing director of a Netherlands-based distributor of office products why he decided to automate his sales force. "Simple," the manager said. "Now, when one of my salespeople gets to the end of a street, they don't flip a coin to decide whether to turn right or left." This manager's problem stemmed from an unusually high attrition rate within his sales force. Half the sales team had departed within just the previous six months. Since he had no automated account records, he had to rebuild relationships from scratch, sometimes over and over again with the same exact customers.

Automating and synchronizing a sales force involves designing and customizing an appropriate system, getting PCs or other electronic tools out to the sales reps, training them in the system's use, automating the sales contact procedure itself, and automating the communications, follow-up process, and rewards structure as well.

Here are some important issues to consider:

- Is the system as easy for neophytes to use as it is for trained veterans? Spot-checking and training are essential.
- Does the system provide actionable customer knowledge? Be sure the data you require of sales reps eventually results in a program of treating different customers differently—or else don't ask for it.
- Does the system keep the manual activities of writing, filing, analyzing, and reporting to the lowest possible level, minimizing cost and errors while still facilitating the capture of all useful customer data?
- Does data move efficiently *through* the system, whatever system you implement, so that service technicians, for example, learn promptly about problems disclosed to sales reps, or that sales reps learn immediately about customers placed on "credit hold." Not all data is urgent, so evaluate different data sets and their requisite speeds.
- Does the system allow salespeople to share information with each other? When making any contact with a prospect or customer, a sales rep should be reasonably sure of having a complete record of that particular customer's previous transactions and interactions, even with other sales representatives.

This last point represents one of the most important issues of all. Exchanging information within the enterprise is vital to the success of any

1to1 system. Every person at your company who has any contact with a customer must be able to tap the company's "institutional memory" in order to ensure that your relationship with that customer picks up where it left off. *Only* in this way can you develop genuine Learning Relationships with individual customers, making them more loyal to you over the long term, with all the financial benefits that customer loyalty entails. So whatever sales force automation tools or system you use, you have to both feed the institutional memory and make it easily accessible.

The benefit of having a sales force that is easily networked and coordinated is hard to overstate. When searching for a way to explain the tremendous growth and the exploding benefits of the Internet, Bob Metcalfe, inventor of Ethernet, founder of 3Com, and a technology pundit with the International Data Group, has been an influential person. George Gilder coined the term "Metcalfe's Law," in his book *Telecosm*, which states that the value of a network increases in proportion to the square of the number of users. A simple example might be the fax machine. If you have a fax machine in your home, but no one else has a fax machine, then your machine will have very little value to you. But the more people have them, the more value yours will have. Metcalfe's point was that the more people rely on the Internet, the more useful the Internet becomes, and because of the interconnectedness of everyone, its real utility grows exponentially, not just arithmetically.

The same exact principle—Metcalfe's Law—applies to connected networks of salespeople as well. If you have a sales force automation system used by just one or two sales reps, it has very little real utility, other than serving as an electronic filing system for them. But when you begin adding just a few sales reps into the mix, the usefulness of your networked, automated sales force soon explodes. Therefore, it's vitally important that you ensure that all your reps use the system. Feeding uniform, current information into the system is usually the biggest problem. Once enough reliable information is in it, you won't have to encourage reps to use it.

Or think about the process of hiring and training new salespeople. If you've ever been a sales rep, just imagine how a database rich with accurate knowledge of individual customers would have helped you step immediately into your new job.

The customer benefits as well from dealing with an automated sales force. Besides providing better access to information ranging from pricing schedules to delivery timetables, the key benefit for any individual customer is that she will no longer need to answer the same question twice—even if the salesperson leaves or gets reassigned. The new salesperson will know to call on Friday afternoons and not on Monday mornings, not to bulk-ship via TransTruck, and to provide at least sixty days' advance notice of price changes for this customer.

When you decide to automate, here are the checkpoints:

1. Start with the Information Technology group at your firm, and be sure your objectives and direction are compatible with their plans.

2. Inventory all the functions and processes in your current communications with the sales force to determine what *can* be automated. You'll also want to automate as much of their personal record-keeping as possible (scoping this out will take some time).

3. Create a template of the information fields you intend to track. (Obviously the sales force is a great resource for this list.) Be sure to track the information and interaction that will be the most useful to you in creating a Learning Relationship with the customer.

4. Look at your lead-generation and follow-up process. You should automate the lead-management process, using your sales force automation tool to evaluate leads, feed them into the sales force, and track them all the way to the close.

5. Assess skill levels and training needs. Some salespeople will need to be taught very basic computer skills, while others may have already automated their sales practices on their own. If you track your own sales reps' computer-skill levels, you can sometimes pair skilled reps with those who need help.

6. Begin actually rolling out the implementation only when some value can be made available to your sales force. Distributing leads is a great place to start. If salespeople get used to filling in fields that are associated with a new prospect, they will be more inclined to fill out the same information on existing accounts.

7. Shift your sales reporting from paper to an electronic format. You can make it optional at first, as long as the e-filers find it easier to complete their reports than the paper filers.

8. Ask your sales force for forecasts and tracking information on individual prospects. Require that they report regularly on each prospect's relative position in the selling cycle. Is a prospect a level-one account about to close, or a level-five competitive user who may be a more viable prospect two years from now?

9. Once it is implemented, make use of the system *absolutely mandatory,* no exceptions, beginning with the sales management team.

10. Offer continuing, ad hoc training and "upgrade" sessions for those sales reps who want to improve their ability to use the system.

A good place to begin the automation process is with the major- or national-account organization. These salespeople will likely be your most seasoned practitioners, and they are also the most important leadership group to enlist.

But even if your sales force is located in a retail-store environment, facing customers over cash registers rather than desks and office coffee tables, automation can pay big dividends. The trick is to find the right lever by which to encourage your salespeople to use the system.

The next step after sales automation will be creating and using an Internet-based tool for making more selling materials and information available on demand to the sales force, whether in the store or in the field. Once your sales reps are automating their account calls, they will be asking for online brochures, shipping information, pricing, proposal templates, presentations, and other information formerly available only in hard copy. A more efficient use of advertising collateral, all by itself, can pay a large portion of the bill for sales automation.

Any good salesperson is already going to be highly skilled at differentiating his or her prospects and customers. What you want, as a 1to1 marketer, is to capture these insights for everyone in the enterprise to use for the customer's continuing benefit. Your company's own transaction records probably will be the principle source of information for ranking customers by their actual value to the company. But what about customers' growth potential?

Evaluating a customer's growth potential is something you'll need your salespeople's help with. Not only will a salesperson have an idea or two about a customer's long-term plans, but with respect to short-term, immediate opportunities there's literally no substitute for a set of eyes and ears to pick up information in the customer's office. So another important role of the sales force automation system should be to accommodate different sales reps' subjective and observed estimates of a customer's immediate and long-term growth potential. Leave plenty of room for numbers in the system, for sure, but allow for judgments, too.

In addition, the sales rep will be constantly evaluating customers by their needs. Any good selling methodology proceeds from a needs-based analysis of the prospect, whether those needs are expressed in personal, psychological terms or in terms of product and service features and utility. So in addition to accommodating information about a customer's strategic value, the sales force automation system should also accommodate other, needs-based variables, perhaps even offering a selection of standard customer categorizations.

Customer descriptions and ratings, such as "apostle or irritant" or "product or politics," can provide valuable insights for later selling efforts. Keeping the system simple, consistent, and operational is equally crucial, so, to the extent possible, you should accommodate a wide range of "standardized" customer categorizations. Think of this as a mass-customized, or modularized, set of customer descriptions.

Wherever possible, consider adding additional qualitative descriptions that can be defined in a phrase and simply clicked on the screen

Differentiate Your Customers

rather than having to be entered in the "comments" field. A pull-down menu of stock phrases would be useful, such as:

- Eager to trade up
- Worried about budget
- Loyal to Acme Industries sales rep
- Good with referrals
- Wants turnkey, no-hassle solutions.

You Get What You Pay For

If you want to acquire, keep, and grow the Most Valuable Customers, that's what you should be paying for. One of the most critical challenges facing the 1to1 enterprise is the need to compensate salespeople and others for encouraging and ensuring customer loyalty. Most salespeople are compensated today in ways that make them virtually indifferent to customer loyalty. In some cases, new-customer-incentive programs perversely encourage them to benefit from customer churn, which enables them to resell a product or service to a relatively educated (and fickle) customer.

If customer loyalty and profitability are your real objectives, then you should be exploring compensation systems that reward sales reps (and others) on the basis of each individual customer's long-term profitability—or Lifetime Value. There are two basic ways to do this, with many variations:

1. *Targeted commissions.* Identify in advance certain types of customers who tend to be worth more than others—maybe they tend to be more loyal or to buy multiple product lines—and pay a higher up-front commission for acquiring this targeted type of customer. Consider lower commissions for "price" buyers or returning former customers, as well as other variable commission plans that emphasize the acquisition and retention of customers whose value is greatest to the enterprise overall, not just the salesperson.

2. *Gradual commissions.* Pay a lower commission on the acquisition of a customer. Instead, link compensation to the profitability of a customer over time. For example, instead of paying a $1,000 com-

mission merely for landing a customer, pay $700 for landing a new account and $200 per year for every year the customer continues to do business with you.

Obviously, to the extent possible, correlate the sales reward structure with individual customer profitability. Both of these ideas attempt to do that. The company paying a gradual commission might, for instance, pay the salesperson a straight percentage of the margin on products or services sold to a customer for the life of that customer's relationship with the firm. This would mean the sales rep has a direct interest in a customer's continued satisfaction with the firm. This alternative is usually better for firms selling a product or service that is consumed over time, or at least not consumed all at once. It is an old-fashioned concept. Before computers and call centers put most door-to-door salespeople out of work, many of them operated this way. Through the seventies, door-to-door life insurance salespeople were paid commissions based not only on new policies sold but also on their actual collections of premiums from their existing customers. A late payment meant a reduced commission check!

Consider intensifying this approach. Pay an *increasing* commission, based on a rep's ability to proactively enhance a customer's value and loyalty. If a rep signs a customer to a three-year contract, for instance, you could back-end-load an escalating commission rate—maybe 2 percent on transactions with that customer during the first six months, 4 percent during the next year, and 6 percent in the final eighteen months.

Or you could specifically establish a customer-profitability goal for the sales force and provide either a bonus for achieving it or a reduced commission rate for those missing the mark. *Midrange Computing* is a trade magazine published out of Carlsbad, California. This is how Ian Thompson, formerly the manager of education and training, describes *Midrange Computing*'s new sales compensation plan:

We are wresting with 1to1 strategies at this time, and the issue of compensation is central to our goal of better service for our customers. Our new program now specifically identifies our best customers, who we label as "Preferred Buyers." If a sales rep nurtures a customer along until their purchases elevate them to "Preferred Buyer" status, the rep receives an additional 3-percent commission on all purchases the customer makes.

Certainly one big advantage of paying gradual commissions is that it promotes not only customer loyalty but employee retention as well. In many fast-growing segments of the economy, retaining good people is increasingly difficult, and paying sales commissions gradually, in the form of an "annuity" on a client's continuing business, has the effect of making the sales rep more loyal.

That is, a gradual commission will make a certain type of sales rep loyal—one who is willing to cultivate client relationships. On the other hand, a gradual commission could actually drive off the more aggressive, instant-gratification rep, so before you move from a straight, acquisition-based sales commission to a more gradual payment, you'll need to brief your sales team and carefully explain the program, emphasizing the economic benefits *to them*. It might also help to phase in the program, rather than making a sudden change. Abrupt changes often can have a severe impact on short-term sales and sales-force retention as the "hunters" head for new hunting grounds—at the competition!

CACI Marketing Systems is a marketing research consultant and information provider. A client usually begins its relationship with only one product, or doing business in only one department. As the client grows or becomes more educated about and skilled at using CACI's information, CACI is able to sell additional products and introduce the client to other departments. To promote the sale of multi-year contracts, CACI used to compensate reps on multi-year deals with a higher commission, paid 100 percent up-front. But once the initial multi-year contract was signed, the rep had no reason to continue servicing the account. If a rep signed a multi-year deal with a client, collected a big commission check, and then left, no one at the firm had much interest in keeping that client happy because there was no money in it anymore. Eric Cohen, CACI's VP and managing director, describes his firm's efforts to structure a different sales-compensation plan:

We wanted to be careful and not drastically reduce our salespeople's commission plan in one year, so we embarked on a two-year program. In the first year, the sales reps receive commission on 70 percent of the net revenue on a three-year agreement, and will then receive 15 percent each subsequent year. The second year we changed this to 60 percent of net revenue in the first contract year and 20 percent each subsequent year. This encourages salespeople to ensure that their clients are pleased with our service. It also discourages a salesperson from placing a halfhearted sale and then leaving with a big commission check. To reap the rewards of their sales, salespeople must stay around to service and grow their accounts.

Separating "hunting" and "farming," the functions of customer acquisition and customer service, can be good for many organizations, although it has the potential for creating the appearance of a second-class role for the customer-service function. Hunting is glamorous, while farming is tedious. Hunters are lone wolves, fiercely independent and self-sufficient. Farmers are collaborative by nature, dependent on others. A professional-services firm might unflatteringly classify its executives as finders, minders, or grinders.

Rather than paying both types of commission, one to hunters and one to farmers, another heretical, 1to1-friendly alternative would be to stop paying commission. Particularly if your business depends for its livelihood on customer or client loyalty over the long term, or if there is a very heavy customer service element to the product you're selling, you might want to consider this approach. Rather than paying transaction-specific or customer-specific commissions or bonuses, provide employees incentive by using funds based on the aggregate performance of the organization. If average customer retention increases, or if the overall customer satisfaction index improves, everyone receives a reward.

The no-commission approach can be a useful way to clean up your sales compensation program if the commission plan has taught some salespeople how to "game the system." When the managing director at one UK motor finance company unilaterally decided that the salespeople at his firm would be paid a salary and bonus rather than commission in the next fiscal year, a number of them promptly resigned. The MD, however, was happy with this, because he calculated that many of those who left were the people who had learned the best way of "cheating" the old system, by booking orders one month, canceling them the next, and so forth. What replaced the commission system was a profit-sharing plan for everyone involved in delivering service to the customer—sales, administration, maintenance, and vehicle disposals.

Results were significant and immediate for this company, which reached its annual sales goals in the first six months of the no-commission year. The remaining salespeople stayed longer, the quality of customer information (and therefore the firm's application-processing efficiency) increased, customer satisfaction grew, better business was being written, and customer retention improved.

Interact with Your Customers

If you do a good job identifying and tracking your prospects and customers, along with all the various players within these organizations, and if your salespeople differentiate customers in ways that make sense to the overall company, the next step in implementing a 1to1 marketing program is *interaction*. Of course, both sales force automation and sales compensation will significantly affect the type and quality of interaction your salespeople engage in with customers. In the context of launching a 1to1 marketing program, planning the type of interaction your salespeople have with customers is vital.

If you've already begun implementing a 1to1 marketing program at your firm, chances are a few of your customers—the ones with more value and growth potential anyway—are now the responsibility of customer managers. The customer manager sets the objective and defines a strategy for interacting with these customers. The sales executive with primary responsibility for the account may or may not be designated as the customer manager (more about this later), but regardless of *who* actually interacts with the customer, for now what is important to note is that *any* interaction with a customer—including a sales call—should adhere to the customer manager's objective and strategy.

Planning the sales call itself has already been the subject of bookshelves' worth of excellent material, much of which is applicable in the 1to1 environment. How-to sales books stress the importance of preparing for the call, knowing the customer, studying any recent or prospective changes in the customer's business, and learning about the customer's experiences with the company's product line. In the ideal 1to1 enterprise, a salesperson will first review the specific objective and strategy set by the customer manager for that customer, then plan ahead by carefully identifying both the information likely to be useful to support the sales call *and* the elements of information to be sought from the customer during the interaction.

Support information:

- The customer's recent experiences and interactions with the enterprise
- Information about each individual on the specific customer team
- Relevant experiences and learning from similar customers

Information to be sought from the customer:

- Customer data that needs to be validated or updated
- Needs-based and value-based information to help further differentiate the customer
- Share-of-customer growth opportunities

One of your principal goals, when interacting with a customer, should be to learn things about the customer that enable your enterprise to tailor its behavior, locking the customer into an increasingly convenient relationship, making it easier and easier for that customer to do business with you. The more you learn about what the customer needs, the more potential you will have for adapting your firm's behavior.

Successful 1to1 programs demand fresh, current data, which means that every interaction should be feeding your customer database, through the sales force automation tool. So, following each sales call, you should expect a sales rep to spend some time feeding the system to update the enterprise's knowledge of the customer. Here are some important post-sales call issues to consider:

- How much time should reps spend on post-sale data entry?
- How can reps most readily move specific customer findings and requests to other departments for action, clearing their own desks for more sales work?
- What is the qualification and prioritization procedure for inquiries stemming from visits with existing prospects or customers?
- How is that prioritization communicated to others in the organization so that every request is not a five-alarm emergency?

The real problem here is likely to be one of culture and organizational resistance, more than technology. Salespeople are notoriously independent creatures. Of course, it will help if you have a system that is simple and convenient, but you're almost certainly going to need some powerful incentives and disincentives to ensure that it is used, especially in the beginning. Some ideas:

- Sales management should insist that all customer contacts be entered into records on a real-time basis. You can do this with a combination of rewards and penalties, but there is no substitute for a top-down *mandate* that customer files be updated after literally every single interactive contact.
- Audit the system regularly to assure compliance. Conduct spot checks, more frequently in the beginning, or with sales reps who are new to the system.
- Most databases allow for oversight on new records and updates. Appoint a "data steward" whose role includes checking or spot-checking all entries for timeliness and thoroughness, assuring standardized data entry, and overseeing data hygiene.
- Consider a contest for the best overall database, a reward system for complete customer files, or other similar mechanisms. Training can be helpful here, but it is no substitute for vigilance.
- Be prepared to revise the system as it is put into place and usage

of it begins throughout the sales force. Even with the best advance planning and system-specification process, you are still likely to have overlooked a shortcut here or there, so watch for them.

- On a quarterly basis, insist that all members of the sales organization review each of their customer records, or at least all MVC and MGC records, with an eye toward updating general or subjective information such as future opportunities, next steps, ratings, and the like. Consider making such activities part of regional or divisional sales meetings to demonstrate the system-wide nature of the activity.

Interacting with a customer is vital to creating and cultivating a relationship with that customer, but if you've installed a good system for coordinating the interactions of all your salespeople, you can leverage the interaction process itself to take maximum advantage of Metcalfe's Law.

In 1994, when Astra AB of Sweden and Merck & Co. launched Astra Merck Inc., the companies had a unique opportunity to design a marketing organization from the ground up. The joint venture incorporated a technically sophisticated customer database and sales force automation system into its operations from the very beginning.

Astra Merck's marketing system allows best practices to be shared across the enterprise, enabling the deployment of "virtual teams" to address the specific needs of individual customers, no matter where they are located geographically. This was a critical element in maintaining the competitive edge in a business that relies on skilled sales reps to remember the individual proclivities of particular physicians and adapt the sales message appropriately. Because pharmaceutical products are extremely complex and medical practitioners have widely diverse needs, Astra Merck's sales force faced a unique set of challenges.

Thanks to its sales automation technology, Astra Merck had the only field organization in the industry capable of producing preapproved promotional materials and patient information locally at any one of its customer units. The joint venture's sophisticated technology also enabled it to leverage its sales effort in ways that would have been impossible for a nonautomated sales force. One example of this was the use of "mirrored" sales calls. Astra Merck wasn't the only company to employ this technique, which effectively amplifies the efforts of a sales force. Here's how it works: Two Astra Merck sales reps would visit the same physician at different times, but with completely coordinated sales calls—sales calls that literally mirror each other, in terms of the background each rep has on the physician's own particular knowledge of and intellectual take on the company's products. Using mirrored sales calls, Astra Merck effectively doubled its exposure to and interactions with each physician.

Astra Merck has since become part of Astra Pharmaceuticals LP, but its pioneering use of automation amply demonstrates the power of customer interaction, especially when that interaction is coordinated at the enterprise level and used to leverage other interactions.

Customize for Your Customers

At a 1to1 enterprise, not only should customer information gained by a sales rep be used to leverage the way the sales force interacts with that customer, it should also be used to update the entire enterprise's treatment of that customer. Most sales reps will instinctively resist efforts to rein them in and more thoroughly integrate their activities with others in the enterprise. But implementing a 1to1 marketing program invariably pulls the sales rep closer in, with the enterprise demanding more of his or her "secret," intimate customer.

For most companies, either the sales organization "is" the company or it's just one of several channels of distribution. In the former case, sales reps assigned to particular accounts often take on the role of "customer manager" for their own accounts, quarterbacking the entire enterprise's effort to support the customer and deepen the customer relationship. Customer service and support, inside sales, product specialists, and others who "touch" the customer directly become subordinate to the sales exec who is serving as customer manager, setting the objective, and planning the strategy for the customer.

Alternatively, when the sales channel is central to the firm but the individual reps themselves are not assigned to specific customers, the customer-management function will reside outside the sales force, or it may be completely automated. Charles Schwab, for example, discourages the development of personal relationships between particular brokers and "their" customers. Except for the firm's largest clients, there are no relationship managers. Whoever picks up the phone also picks up the conversation, and the relationship with that customer, exactly where it left off the last time. In focus groups, Schwab customers report being comfortably untethered, because everything Schwab knows about them, individually, is digitized and readily available to whomever they talk to next at the firm. Schwab's powerful Oracle database, coupled with Siebel sales automation tools, allows the firm to set different priorities for different customers.

When sales is but one of several channels, it competes for leadership of the customer relationship with other candidates. Other functional areas within the firm, including management, inside sales, customer service, or field service, may each opt to lead a given customer relationship, often directly supplanting the sales relationship at a long-standing or dormant account, such as the satisfied owner of older capital equipment.

PLACING A PREMIUM ON PERSONALIZED PRESENTATIONS AT THE HARTFORD INSURANCE COMPANY

Few businesses practice "relationship selling" better than the highly competitive business of commercial insurance. At the Major Account level, 1to1 selling can make a significant difference in the heated competition for a million-dollar-plus annual premium. But very often the sale is made by an independent agent, not employed by the company, in conjunction with an account team from the company—and thus it's unwise for the company to dictate what's said in the presentation or how the information and the company are actually presented.

The Major Accounts unit of The Hartford's Commercial Lines insurance group has cracked the code on individualized sales presentations, driving its corporate message down through many of its account teams countrywide, while enhancing the individualization of each one of the rep's presentations. The Hartford created a customizable, personalizable sales-presentation system that blends the company's corporate message with as much customer-focused information as the sales rep cares to gather.

The Hartford's marketing director for Major Commercial Lines, Rich Bulat, developed a customizable slideware system for his major-account specialists with help from Media Designs Interactive, Inc., a New York–based innovator in personalized sales presentations. "We try to present our programs as a team," Bulat says, "with the agent, loss prevention, claims management and other experts all in the room. But when that can't happen, as is often the case, it allows any member of the team to present the entire package alone—giving stronger support to areas where the presenter is not an expert."

The system includes a "library" of corporate modules about The Hartford's services such as risk management, claims services, and the like. But it allows the rep to build a totally customized presentation from that point forward, including every aspect of the customer's insurance and individualized, creative solutions to keep costs down and optimize service and responsiveness. "In our business, price is the first step," Bulat says. "Once you've made the first cut, then you need to begin differentiating your service from your competition," he adds, and the system helps The Hartford do that—hundreds of thousands of times a year. The slideware system blends traditional PowerPoint slides generated by the rep with custom modules and audio/video clips featuring everything from claims administration to comments from the firm's CEO. According to Bulat, the CEO clip was used 88 percent of the time.

User reaction to the customized system has been—in three words—"give me more." A survey of presenters commissioned by Bulat after one year found that nearly 60 percent of major-account specialists had used the system, but wanted the ability to customize the presentation even further.

"We look at our system as a sales development tool that helps our reps think through the precise needs of their customers and tailor every aspect of the presentation to the customer's needs," says Bulat. It allows for customization while maintaining integrity of the corporate selling messages. And, he says, "in a very competitive year, some of our folks say this new 1to1 tool really helped them get some very competitive business."

A good relationship is whatever the customer says it is. To a customer, "sales" is often an extended enterprise that includes many more people than those few who have the word in their job titles. A customer should be able to deal with whomever they please at a company, confident that the contact is empowered to "make it happen" and that the customer's own individual interests will be both remembered and respected. This is possible only if a customer management function is being performed somewhere at the enterprise, either from within the sales force itself or outside it. Someone at your firm has to set a strategy for each customer relationship.

For a multidivision, multiproduct organization, selling various products to the same basic set of customers, or to significantly overlapping customer bases, deciding whether to have a unified sales force or to field a separate sales force for each division can be problematic, especially if the products are technically complex. On one hand, understanding the proper way to install or use the product will require a specialized level of technical competence, making it difficult for someone without the right expertise to talk intelligently about the product. It would be disastrous to put an unprepared sales rep in front of a customer who almost certainly will have a high degree of technical expertise in the firm's product. On the other hand, the same customer can be expected to buy products from different divisions at the firm, and from a cost-of-sales standpoint alone it will be very tempting to try to squeeze multiple products and product lines into each sales rep's arsenal.

Whether or not your multidivision firm operates separate direct sales forces, one thing the Astra Merck case clearly demonstrates is that, even for a technically complex product, where each product is represented by skilled specialists, there is still tremendous benefit in connecting the sales force so that *customer* knowledge can be shared across the enterprise.

In a 1to1 enterprise, as with any firm, the single most important instrument for building and deepening customer relationships is likely to be the direct sales force. However, the same self-sufficiency and independence of thought that are the sales force's biggest assets can easily become the biggest obstacles to launching a 1to1 marketing program, unless you carefully plan the automation of your sales processes, leveraging the strengths and the individual customer expertise of your salespeople.

The simple truth is, some of your company's best salespeople could probably have written this book themselves. They will know, instinctively, how to create deeper relationships with customers, how to prioritize their efforts based on each customer's current value and growth potential, and how to adapt the firm's behavior to meet the needs of individual customers. Your mission should be to empower them to do this for the benefit of the enterprise, connecting them tightly to an enterprise-information system and structuring the sales-compensation system so as to further the mission of creating long-term, profitable customer relationships, rather than settling for quick-hit, isolated transactions.

American Cyanamid's Agricultural division sells crop-protection products, mostly for weed and bug control. The Cyanamid customer is a farm operator—a smart, experienced, analytical producer who happens to wear denim and drive a tractor. Many of the American farms that still operate today are sophisticated, substantial business enterprises contemplating a calculated investment in crop protection. Farm operators are careful buyers who recognize that every decision can have significant benefits or consequences.

Cyanamid's sales reps are college-educated, aggressive, and customer-focused. The firm long ago began differentiating its customers and focusing each rep on the top one hundred growers in a territory—then proceeding to learn everything about those customers, up to and including the dog's name, best time to call or visit, favorite coffee shop or restaurant, where their children go to college, and several more serious business variables, including:

- The crop grown on each field and the tillage practice
- The crop protection, fertilizer, and seed brand and type used, by field (either Cyanamid's or competitors'), as well as the weeds and bugs they need to control
- Exact prior-year purchases of Cyanamid products, in gallons and dollars (collected through a point-of-purchase frequency-marketing program);
- Share-of-customer estimates
- The farmer's satisfaction with, and prior year per-acre crop yield for Cyanamid and—more important—its competition

Each spring and fall, the data is collected as crops are planted and crop protection products applied, or as the crops are harvested and the farmer totals up his or her results. Then, each summer and winter, the sales rep's time is put to work developing a specific, tactical action plan for each of the hundred MVCs in a territory.

The plan is simple—one page, one side, and extraordinarily tactical in nature. It includes straightforward action steps, which might include such things as:

- Work with local Cyanamid dealers to plan joint grower calls
- Bring an entomologist to see why results on the back forty were disappointing
- Encourage trial use of herbicide products to control weeds
- Understand results with and strong preference for competitor's products on soybeans
- Ask for introduction and lunch with customer and next-door neighbor who's overly loyal to competition

The plan is reviewed with sales management before implementation. Cyanamid's best sales plans include comments:

- Don't visit in December, they're gone to the Bahamas
- Ask about son John, on aircraft carrier in the Persian Gulf
- Watch out for big black dog
- Bring chocolate doughnuts

IBM GOLD SERVICE: CHANNEL? WHAT CHANNEL?

When a prospect calls IBM, it's hard to know whether one's speaking to ol' "Big Blue" herself or to one of her tens of thousands of channel partners. And "speaking" is something of a euphemism, since Web, fax, "bingo card" and voice-based leads are all funneled seamlessly to independent IBM channel partners while the firm's remaining salespeople "hunt elephants" with margins that can support "factory" salespeople.

One of the biggest challenges IBM and its competitors face is cost-effective growth of its largest, most important customers. In focus group after focus group, IBM found customers eager to consolidate purchasing, maintenance, and growth of their IT architecture. To deliver on a global basis, IBM needed technical, communications, and marketing architectures in place.

What IBM Gold Service took as its foundational strategy was to overhaul and reengineer the way it does business with its most important customers. IBM decided that the only way to make this work would be to invest in an infrastructure that would not only reengineer itself but create an architecture that would also bring evolutionary value to its largest corporate clients. Truly, if one could find a great example of a company's practicing what it preaches, it is here in IBM Gold Service. IBM's main thrust in its worldwide brand messaging has been e-business. IBM Gold Service is the internal infrastructure through which IBM is taking not only its message of e-business but its deployment of it as well.

IBM committed investment in an infrastructure that would provide secure intra- and extranet sites that could be accessed by anyone from anywhere that had the permission and security to actually purchase hardware, software, and services from IBM. Not only that, but IBM set about defining a truly 1to1 experience by tailoring each site to meet the needs of a variety of segments who would use the sites. So, at run time, based on the conditions and negotiated prices and configurations of the IBM offerings, users from, say, Motorola, would experience a completely different experience than, say, the users from Boeing. This, coupled with a dedicated telemarketing arm that complements the sites, gives IBM a powerful value proposition by offering procurement managers, office management, department managers, etc., an easy, effective way to do business.

On the other side, back at IBM, this model has helped those old fedora-wielding client teams by delivering quality intelligence and insight into the buying habits, number of visits, affinity for specific channels (Web-based versus telemarketing or mail). For example, since every visitor is tied to a specific PIN number, the IBM back end is able to keep the client teams up on new individuals' general usage statistics and, eventually, will be able to automate the stream of communication with visitors on behalf of the client teams. For example, in the event of a first visit, an automated e-mail will be sent on behalf of the client rep, thanking the visitor for coming and encouraging future communications by giving the rep's e-mail and phone number.

Recommended Reads	Khandpur, Navtej, Jasmine Wevers, Kay Khanpur, and Patricia Bruce. *Sales Force Automation Using Web Technologies* (John Wiley & Sons, 1997).

Khandpur, Navtej, Jasmine Wevers, Kay Khanpur, and Patricia Bruce. *Sales Force Automation Using Web Technologies* (John Wiley & Sons, 1997).
Khandpur, Wevers, and Khandpur offer a thorough review of technologies that are focused on enhancing selling on the Web. They also give IT executives and Webmasters helpful strategies for implementing these tools.

Mackay, Harvey. *Dig Your Well Before You're Thirsty* (Currency Doubleday, 1997).
The one who taught us how to "swim with the sharks" now offers a wise, witty, and breezily written book on a subject he definitely knows: personal networking. He believes that your underlying success is dependent not on talent or experience but, rather, your network of relationships. Drawing on his own relationships with people like Lou Holtz, Erma Bombeck, and Larry King, he explains how to build and maintain a network. Powerful suggestions for a sales team and everyone else.

Peppers, Don. *Life's a Pitch . . . Then You Buy* (Currency Doubleday, 1995).
This readable and entertaining collection of anecdotes is based on Don's personal experience trying to win new clients in the advertising business. Ideal for anyone selling in a b-to-b situation—new ways to prospect, new ideas for pitching, new methods for differentiating your company from your competitors.

Petersen, Glen S. *High-Impact Sales Force Automation: A Strategic Perspective* (Saint Lucie Press, 1997).
This book looks at the latest technologies and the opportunities for sales force automation that they afford. Petersen draws on his discussions with top solution providers to describe how companies can apply these tools to great effect.

Siebel, Thomas M., and Michael S. Malone. *Virtual Selling: Going Beyond the Automated Sales Force to Achieve Total Sales Quality* (Free Press, 1996).
From the Silicon Valley entrepreneur who created Siebel Systems, this book makes a powerful case for enhancing the salesperson's role by establishing a more collaborative relationship with the customer.

Wilson, Larry, and Hersch Wilson. *Stop Selling, Start Partnering: The New Thinking About Finding and Keeping Customers* (John Wiley & Sons, 1996).
This book discusses how the sales process has changed in recent years and offers a strategy for improving it through collaboration with the customer. The authors emphasize the importance of developing a relationship as opposed to just making the sale.

Activity 11A

Sales Issues for Your Transition Team to Discuss

Target Completion Date: _____

1. Elevator Speech: Explain to your CEO how a change in sales force compensation could affect your company's ability to make the transition to a 1to1 enterprise.

_____

_____

_____

2. Is your company's success linked to long-term customer loyalty and value? Do you compensate your sales force to build customer value and loyalty or to sell products and services?

_____

_____

_____

3. If customer loyalty is to be the objective, what compensation systems will you explore that will reward customers' long-term profitability or Lifetime Value? Before you answer this, your transition team may want to look at Activity 11D. Possible systems include:

   - A basic commission for landing the customer, plus additional commission for increasing the value of that customer
   - Rewarding the salesperson more for selling products to MVCs than selling the same product to less valuable customers
   - Group profit-sharing for all members of the team that increase customer value
   - Pay much higher base salaries and give merit raises based on performance, reducing or eliminating sales commission altogether
   - Pay higher commissions the more business a customer does (sliding scale)

_____

_____

_____

4. Whose support does your transition team need in order for your firm to automate the sales force?

_____

_____

_____

Activity 11B

Sales Checkpoint

Answer yes or no to the following questions. Repeat this activity one year after the initial date you complete it.

Target Completion Date: _____

	Now	One Year from Now
Our organization is dependent on an in-house or field sales force for its success	○Yes ○No	○Yes ○No
We compensate our sales force for building long-term customer loyalty and value	○Yes ○No	○Yes ○No
We have high-level support for customer value compensation	○Yes ○No	○Yes ○No
We have some form of sales force automation in place	○Yes ○No	○Yes ○No
Our sales force automation provides information about each individual customer to whomever is in contact with that customer, and is constantly and accurately updated	○Yes ○No	○Yes ○No

Activity 11C

Task List: How to Set Up Your One-to-One Sales Force

Target Completion Date: _____

Who Will Do It? (init.)	By When? (date)	Task	75% Done (✓)	100% Done (✓)
		Establish prerequisites: ■ Sound cost-accounting system ■ Some method of valuing customers fairly, if not with pinpoint accuracy (proxy variable) ■ Management the entire sales force has confidence in		
		Make your sales force willing to input customer data in the company-wide database by making that information valuable to them in the field		
		Use synchronized contact-management software that includes, among other things, a tickler system and sales call planning tools		
		Convince your sales force that 1to1 is a good idea: 1. Allow them plenty of opportunities to provide input early on		
		2. Make it clear that there is an opportunity for them to make more money in the long run ■ Better lead management ■ Better time management ■ Ability to make more money by spending time more wisely		

3. Reward sales force for getting and selling to MVCs versus less profitable customers who may represent easy sells

4. Special recognition for salespeople who demonstrate acceptance (plaque, employee of the month, etc.)

Activity 11D

Ten One-to-One Sales Force Compensation Ideas

Here are ten "thought starters" for sales force compensation.

Item	Description
1. Growing Lifetime Value	Use customer's lifetime value as a primary measure of success
2. Growing share of customer	Pay for a greater share of each customer's spending
3. Cross-selling	Compensate members of the sales force for cross-selling. Provide incentive by compensating salespeople in multiple divisions
4. Finding products for a customer	Cross-sell and build strategic alliances with other companies whose core competencies don't overlap
5. Reward for accuracy and depth of data about a customer entered by the salesperson	Make it possible for the company and the salesperson to jointly own the relationship by building in memory about a customer electronically
6. Increased retention	Reward the salesperson for keeping the customer longer than would be otherwise expected. Analyze and reward retention rates appropriately

7. Customer satisfaction	Consider both the immediate transaction and long-term ongoing trust and commitment. Practice "best interests" marketing
8. Referral bonuses	Compensate salespeople for getting referrals from customers
9. Commission on a sliding scale	Pay on monthly revenue and profit, with a sliding scale-up based on the tenure of the customer. The more the customer buys, and the longer the customer stays, the more a salesperson is compensated
10. Reward service and support people	Build in increased compensation for service and support people who maintain or increase customer value

Activity 11E

Twelve-Point Task List for Sales Force Automation

Target Completion Date: _____

Who Will Do It? (init.)	By When? (date)	Activity	75% Done (✓)	100% Done (✓)
		1. Work with the Information Technology group at your organization to confirm that your objectives and direction are compatible with their plans and capabilities		
		2. Inventory all the functions and processes in your current communications with the sales force to determine what can be automated		
		3. Create a template of the information fields you intend to track that will be most useful in developing Learning Relationships with customers		

4. Examine your lead-generation and follow-up process to determine how to automate lead management to evaluate leads and track them all the way to the close

5. Assess skill levels and training needs, and pair skilled representatives with those who need help

6. Implement only when some value can be made available to your sales force. Start by distributing leads

7. Shift your sales reporting from paper to an electronic format

8. Request forecasts and individual prospect-information tracking from the sales force and require that they report regularly on each prospect's relative position in the selling cycle

9. Once in place, make system use mandatory, beginning with the sales-management team

10. Offer continuous training and upgrade sessions for the sales representatives who want to improve their ability to use the system

11. Begin with your most seasoned practitioners and your MVCs

12. Create and use an intranet

Activity 11F

Getting the Sales Force to Provide Customer Data

Target Completion Date: _____

Objectives: Use Existing Information About Customers to Strengthen the Sales Process

This includes:

- Recent experiences

- Individual information

- Relevant experiences from similar customers

- Needs- and value-based information

- Share of customer

- Identification of others who influence a purchase or satisfaction

Activity: What Specific Data Will You Need?

Consider the kind of information that is likely to be useful on a sales call and make sure the information is linked across your organization so the salesperson has access to it. We'll start the list, but you may want to add some items for your own organization.

1. Review the customer's recent experiences and interactions with the enterprise

2. Collect and maintain information about each individual on the customer team

3. Apply community knowledge (i.e., relevant experiences and learning from similar customers)

4. Detect customer data that needs to be validated or updated

5. Determine needs- and value-based information to help further differentiate the customer

6. Examine share of customer growth opportunities

7. Consider the amount of time sales representatives spend on post-sale data entry

8. Ascertain how sales representatives can readily move specific customer findings and requests to other departments for action, thereby clearing their desks for more sales work (i.e., decrease turnover time)

9. Develop a qualification and prioritization procedure for inquiries stemming from visits with existing customers and prospects

10. Create an internal prioritization for communication

11. Identify sub-customers in and beyond the enterprise (e.g., multiple executives or b-to-b customers, attorneys, accountants, spouses, and others who advise on purchases or influence satisfaction)

12. Determine the level of impact each sub-customer might have on the relationship (keep it simple)

13. Look for links and dependencies between individuals

14. Note each individual's attitude toward your company, product, or service

Chapter Twelve

The One-to-One Call Center

HOW TO USE THE CALL CENTER TO HELP BUILD
YOUR 1TO1 ENTERPRISE

A s the world's most ambitious marketers recover from round one of "Web site frenzy" and look to the next horizon of individualized dialogue with customers, that horizon is closer than it looks. In fact, you can find it simply by picking up the telephone.

Traditionally housed in the basement, a corner of the warehouse, or across town from the glitzy headquarters of major corporations everywhere. Viewed as a near-evil, costly necessity. Managed by an erstwhile telemarketer in many cases, the call center is almost always a company's Rodney Dangerfield, lacking respect from senior corporate-management and marketing executives.

However, the call center is quickly getting a new lease on life, as Web sites and toll-free numbers invite customer comments, questions, and interaction. All those questions have to be answered by somebody, somewhere. And these days no one in the enterprise—except for the folks in the call center—ever seems to actually *talk* with customers on a regular basis. Talking with customers is an expertise usually found in the sales department, but it's increasingly mission-critical for those firms inviting more interaction with their customers. As a result, call centers are finally beginning to get some respect.

Almost any kind of company, of any size and in any industry, can effect dramatic improvements in its customer relationships, Share of Customer, and the incremental sale of products or services with help from a call center. Among other things, call centers provide marketers with a unique opportunity to learn from customers directly, without having to look through the filters of quantitative research, focus groups, or representative panels. The customers who call in to a center may be a self-selecting sample, but those called on a proactive, outbound basis certainly don't need to be. And every inbound call, properly orchestrated, can be a sales occasion as well—it is a marvelous share-of-customer opportunity. Don't just send me the manual or the spare part I requested. *Engage me* in a dialogue about your company and its services and the additional products I might find useful in my own individual situation.

The call center is an ideal medium for building relationships *one customer at a time*.

Many call centers grew inadvertently into their current roles after starting as help lines, hot lines, or maybe a spare- or replacement parts ordering service. Over time, the help line might have expanded on an ad hoc basis to accommodate the increasing needs of customers to communicate with the enterprise directly and quickly. As a result, the mission statement at a call center today, if it exists at all, is not likely to be well thought out. Most call centers are far more concerned with the measurable costs of talk time and calls handled per hour than they are with the harder-to-quantify benefits of customer satisfaction, complaint resolution, or loyalty. And almost no one outside the direct-marketing world dares to suggest that profits or increased customer value might result from the thousands of calls handled daily.

But today the call center at many firms has become more of an enterprise business center dealing with literally every aspect of electronic customer contact. Often integrating under one roof all activities dealing with inquiries, requests for support, and other interactions, the broader,

The Customer Interaction Center: Phone, Fax, Web

more comprehensive call center is these days more accurately called a "Customer Interaction Center." Here the lowly call center's role expands dramatically to make it the enterprise's fulcrum for all customer interactions.[1]

Customers can do anything they want at an interaction center using whatever communications medium they choose. Whether they are making a purchase, checking the status of their accounts, inquiring about current orders, asking for information about new products, or seeking technical support, the interaction center is often where their inquiries are handled. It's organized to help customers get the answers they need and resolve their questions with a single call, fax, mail, or electronic communication.

The ideal interaction center would deliver a one-to-one relationship for the enterprise's customers, one customer at a time. It would provide a single point of contact for addressing each customer's needs, creating a true "Customer Manager environment" to increase both the effectiveness and the efficiency of interactions. Orders would be placed faster. Shipping instructions would be predetermined based on customer profile and business policy. Many calls would be handled through automated, self-service interfaces, freeing live agents for more profitable customers, or for customers who prefer live interactions.

This is not science fiction. One system we've seen, from Palo Alto–based Chordiant Software, enables fully differentiated treatment of customers in both live and self-service interactions. Shipping options presented to a mail-order customer, for example, can be adjusted based on the customer's own previous purchase history and account status. VIP callers (or e-mailers or Web inquiries) might automatically have their orders delivered next-day air at no additional cost. Folks who've called for support more than three times of late will be auto-routed to a senior technician who's presented with a complete view of their service history. And, if the call lasts longer than a preplanned period of time

[1]Dr. Jon Anton, a researcher at Purdue University, has done research into customer service issues, especially as they relate to doing business by telephone, for years. He says that "teleweb" is becoming an increasingly popular term.

without a resolution, it is automatically escalated. When a customer's profile shows an overdue balance, the system might default to COD-only. A wealth of customer data and consistent service offerings allow telephone service reps to focus on listening to their customers and building relationships, providing added-value and cross-sell opportunities, letting the system handle the more routine tasks of messaging, fulfillment, and confirmation. Systems like Chordiant's even allow product mix, pricing, promotions, and service offerings to be changed—by region, by order size or type, or by individual customer, and these selection criteria can be managed and changed by the marketers, in an object-oriented environment, on the fly. No more trying to squeeze a project into the C++ programming queue.

Some outbound calling operations are relying on "data-infused dialogue" to create the potential for longer, more meaningful conversations. "Data-infused" calls are designed less to glean information or sell product than to build or expand upon a relationship between a company and a high-value customer. Sky Alland Marketing, which specializes in customer relationship management, has developed a capability called "Smart Talk." It stems from the premise that good dialogue is good marketing. In a Smart Talk scenario, information captured during previous contacts with the customer is fed into the calling script, creating the potential for a true 1to1 dialogue. Sky Alland relies on Smart Talk to build customer relationships for clients such as Porsche, Mitsubishi, and Owens Corning.

In the case of Mitsubishi, Sky Alland captures customer phone contacts verbatim, yielding a treasure trove of information that can be passed along to a local dealer or worked into the script of a future outbound call. Smart Talk empowers the caller to engage in a personal, intelligent conversation with customers about their specific concerns.

Turning a lowly call center into a more automated and capable customer interaction center creates an environment in which a true Learning Relationship can be cultivated with each customer. It also turns a low-paid customer-service rep into a directed, well-prepared salesperson for the enterprise, equipping him or her with a flawless, in-depth memory of each customer. But this approach flies directly in the face of most centers' modus operandi, which reads more like an engineering manual. Linear, operational data drives most traditional call centers, in large measure because they're viewed as cost centers.

"Reduce talk time 7 percent."
"Improve customer satisfaction 8 percent."
"Decrease call-abandonment rate to 19 percent."

The CFOs and COOs who often oversee the call center only glance occasionally at any data not related to cost-per-station or cost-per-call. Quite often they have no real clue about the potential marketing and relationship-building power hiding in that small, expensive, often problematic business unit in the basement.

To implement a 1to1 marketing program that truly leverages customer interactions, you need first to step back and shift your thinking 180 degrees, from cost to profit. Consider installing a customer interaction center not just as a cost of doing business, but as an opportunity to improve your business's profit. A customer interaction center can:

- Sell additional products and services, expanding your firm's share of customer
- Support complex or expensive products, reducing service costs
- Provide ongoing ancillary services, increasing your customers' loyalty to the basic product
- Prequalify sales leads, reducing your cost of sales
- Reduce the need to win new business with discounts, improving overall unit margins
- Perform low-cost market research, reducing the need for more expensive, outside research

Canadian Tire Acceptance Ltd. (CTAL), the financial services division of the $4 billion Canadian Tire Corp., Ltd., expects to increase sales and enhance customer retention systematically through a new effort to develop an integrated call center. It intends to eliminate annoying and time-consuming call transfers, ensuring that customers are treated on an individual basis.

Such efforts are expected to have an important impact on the entire enterprise. While CTAL was established to serve Canadian Tire's four million credit-card holders, it has become the company's primary call center.

CTAL is relying on Chordiant Software's Customer Communication Solution (CCS) as the foundation for its customer-centric efforts. The system—based in the call center—will enable it to build and act on sophisticated customer profiles. "The call center is a strategic asset," says Mary Turner, vice president of customer services at CTAL. "This is our main point of contact with the customer. We have to maximize it."

The demands are heavy. CTAL's ten call centers operate twenty-four hours a day, seven days a week, and respond to more than fifteen million calls a year. Call center representatives are expected to provide personalized service while handling a diverse set of customer needs—responding to more than two hundred types of customer requests. What CTAL intends to do is ensure that any rep can resolve any customer need without handoffs to other departments.

CTAL had several key business objectives:

- Greater customer loyalty to Canadian Tire as a result of enhanced service;
- Personalized customer attention and reduced transfers;
- Rapid introduction of new products or changes to existing business services;
- Reduced training requirements for customer-service representatives; and
- Integration of all customer touch points via a single system capable of handling Web, e-mail and call center interactions.

As Turner puts it, "Our primary goal was to create a customer service environment that enables a complete set of customer-focused services in which we understand customer behavior and needs, offer timely introduction of new services valued by Canadian Tire customers, and enhance existing services to meet changing customer expectations.

"When we began the project, we took a look at our operations and saw too many independent call centers," Turner continues. "It seemed that every time we introduced a new product or service, we set up a new call center. We decided to streamline operations to make it possible for customers to reach the right representative whenever they called."

CTAL chose Chordiant because it offered technology that would integrate data from multiple sources and media, and did not force the company to adopt inflexible business processes. "At first, we thought we could take an incremental approach," Turner adds. "Very quickly it became apparent that we needed to take a long-term strategic view. Otherwise, we would end up with a partial solution that would not serve us in the long run."

As this example illustrates, one of the key elements of a 1to1 strategy is developing an interaction center that immediately recognizes the individual customer and integrates data that reflects on the relationship. It can be a demanding and expensive challenge, but many companies have realized how critical such efforts are to customer loyalty and profitability.

The interaction center provides your firm with a crucial mechanism for interacting with customers and prospects. And, as we said in introducing the interaction concept, your interactions must be focused on not only cost-efficiency but also effectiveness. However, in the same way we approach managing channel relations, the direct sales force, and every other element of a 1to1 program execution, we're going to use the four-step implementation methodology for call centers, too—identify, differentiate, interact, and customize. These four implementation steps provide a valuable set of checkpoints for applying 1to1 marketing principles.

Identify Your Callers

The identification step seems almost too trivial to merit discussion in the context of an interaction center. Even a totally cost-oriented, product-based call center still can save significant costs by implementing some form of ANI or caller-ID technology, allowing the computer to look up a customer's record while the phone is still ringing. Sometimes costs can also be reduced by using automated ID to route each call to an appropriate node—whether it's an elite service rep for a complicated system installation or an IVR for an unidentified caller.

On the other hand, not all your customers will be calling in, and you may be in a business in which the *only* customers you can identify are those who choose to call in to the interaction center or identify themselves at your Web site. Your interaction center can actually provide a mechanism for identifying a larger proportion of your heretofore anonymous customers. So the first real principle in running a 1to1-oriented interaction center is to promote it to those customers you most want to identify. You want to ensure that at least your best customers have an ability to identify themselves to you, and maybe even an incentive to do so.

Rubbermaid's Little Tikes toy division is one of the world's largest automakers, with millions of "Cozy Coupe" foot-propelled cars sold over the years, and now available over the Internet. Little Tikes ambitiously encourages its customers to contact the company, not with an expensive incentive but simply by molding the company's 800 number into *every single product the company sells*. Need a spare wheel, a replacement part, or a hard-to-find toy your five-year-old just absolutely has to have? Little Tikes' 800 number is likely scattered all over your playroom floor. And every time a customer calls in, Little Tikes can identify another end user, storing the customer ID information in its database to make future interactions easier and easier with that customer.

Differentiate Your Callers

Even more antiquated call center operations enable some level of "call vectoring" or "skill-path routing," which allow incoming calls to be sent to a specific desk or individual. This relatively simple, powerful adjustment can yield tremendous benefits in terms of customer service and cost control.

American Airlines and many others provide differentiated numbers for gold, platinum, and "100K" fliers. These elite-level fliers are instantly recognized and connected to reps much faster than the typical customer. Moreover, the reps assigned to these callers are promoted from the ranks, well paid, and know to expect more complicated, more demanding calls from the airline's most valuable customers.

Dell Computer routes corporate customers calling the main 800 number to the specialist account manager who knows each company's terms, product specifications, purchase-order requirements, and more. As we've seen in "mystery shopper" calls to the company, the Dell corporate rep sometimes knows more about a customer's company and its PC requirements than the customer does. What makes this an especially appealing benefit is the simple fact that Dell uses the inbound phone call as a mechanism for differentiating one customer from another and sending each customer to the appropriate node at the interaction center.

Good information management is problematic for call centers and the databases responsible for their efficiency and success. Most IT and MIS managers boast of the wealth of data their multiterabyte systems can store about each customer. But customer data, all by itself, isn't very helpful in a high-speed call center environment. Customer *knowledge* is what's needed when an irate caller is on the line, seeking an immediate resolution. Putting that caller on hold while the rep scans page after page of history, purchase, and profile information can cause more damage than the problem triggering the call in the first place.

Besides simply routing a customer to one specialist or another, a good interaction center will also provide enough information to the service rep to know what is unique about this particular customer. The best, most automated interaction centers apply mass customization principles to modularize customer descriptions, developing customer profiles, or "buckets," that summarize the firm's relationship with each customer individually. This way, in a live situation, the service rep can gain instant knowledge of a particular customer's relationship with the firm and begin reflecting that knowledge in words and deeds starting with "Hello, how may I help you?"

GTE Teleservices has cracked the code on this issue. They provide technology solutions for cellular-phone companies, who often receive floods of irate calls from good and bad customers alike. GTE developed a data mining product called ChurnManager that scans all the data in a customer's file and summarizes it in an easy-to-use graphical interface that is prominent on the very first customer record screen displayed to the service rep answering the call.

Every customer's relationship with GTE is summarized with both graphical and numerical data to provide CSRs with instant notification of potential customer dissatisfaction, as well as customer value and vulnerability to leaving the service.

One to five bombs indicate a customer's probability of leaving. One to five moneybags show a customer's overall value to the service provider. A separate, individual bomb icon flags potential problems the customer may be experiencing, which reflects the number of complaints, service interruptions, or other issues the customer has recently reported.

Instantly, almost without thinking, the customer service rep knows this customer, intimately, simply by looking at the collection of moneybags and bombs prominently displayed on the customer profile screen. The best systems will screen-pop this kind of instant-recognition customer differentiation information into the rep's face just as the phone rings. If you're calling a GTE ChurnManager-equipped call center from your cell phone, as is most often the case, the hit rate is superb.

Nobody asks for your account number (which none of us remember) or your cell phone number (which some of us remember). "Good morning, Mr. Jones. Thanks for being one of our very best customers. How can I help you this morning?" Much smarter, friendlier, faster, and more cost-efficient than "Good morning, may I have your number, please? And, by the way, how long have you been a customer?"

Interact with Your Callers

Improving the interaction you have with your customers, as we've said, means working to improve both its cost-efficiency and its effectiveness. The more cost-efficient you are with interactivity, the more interactivity you'll be able to afford with your customers. And the more effectively useful information you can gain from these interactions, the more powerful a bond you'll be able to create with each individual customer.

Over time, the World Wide Web will help many retail consumers interact with the companies with whom they do business, just as today thousands of Cisco and Dell customers turn to the Web for product advice, configuration, and support. But for now consumers are demonstrably Web-deprived in most categories, and if you are going to keep your cost of sales low while improving the level of service you offer, one particularly good mechanism to consider is a capable, 1to1-oriented customer interaction center.

When it comes to the interaction center, interactivity's twin goals—cost-efficiency and effectiveness—are related to each other. On one hand, the cost of a "live" sales call continues to escalate, so driving more personal sales calls into an interaction center will pay dividends in the form of dramatically lower costs. On the other hand the likelihood of finding an intelligent, knowledgeable salesperson on the retail selling floor continues to decline in many consumer businesses, so driving even routine requests for information into a more controllable interaction center environment will improve the effectiveness of your interactions.

Efficiency is a traditional measure of call center success, but there is more to creating a relationship than simple cost control. When your customers call with questions, in need of help, or to learn more, encourage warmth, friendliness, respect, and a positive attitude on your company's end of the telephone. Your customer took time from his or her day to reach out to your company; welcome that outreach, embrace the customer. Make the call a positive, feel-good experience—something that can readily be accomplished at nominal incremental cost.

Attitude in the call center is as critical as technology. What's the work environment in your center, and how good does it make your newest or oldest rep feel about coming to work every morning? Recognize and reward the biggest smiles, which can be heard across phone lines for sure.

Most call centers define cost-efficiency success in terms of call duration, or how quickly the center gets the customer *off the phone*. But a 1to1 call center strives to talk more with interested customers, not less, and uses stopwatches and computers to measure the specific, incremental benefit of each extended conversation.

Little Tikes, for example, offers a weekly special in almost every call. It's a discontinued item, an overrun, or a product that doesn't violate its powerful retail channel. Vail Associates, Inc., sells lift tickets, which is a pretty obvious add-on sale for people who call the resort primarily to reserve condos. In addition to assuring that the customer will ski Vail instead of a nearby competitor, selling lift tickets on the phone shortens the lift-ticket lines, saving the customer some time and reducing the resort's costs. Other marketers add a friendly, simple customer-satisfaction question or two to an inbound phone conversation, or they probe for referrals to prospects the caller might suggest.

The cost and benefit of an expanded call duration is precisely measurable, simply by testing your policy against a control group. Make a special offer to every nth caller next month. Compare the gross profit on the offer to the incremental "talk time" cost and expand the program as the numbers dictate.

A crucial 1to1 fundamental for customer dialogue is to cultivate an institutional memory of your relationship with each customer. Said another way, if I've told you my shoe size is 13 EEE, don't ask me again. And tell me early in the conversation if you don't make this particular type of shoe in wide sizes—tell me before I start reading through code numbers, product descriptions, and prices.

Customize for Your Callers

When did your COO or marketing vice president last spend more than twenty minutes in the call center? Smart center operators circulate one-hour audiocassettes providing a random sampling of recorded calls, good and bad, to management each month. Smarter operators *require* management people to spend a few hours each month listening to calls on a supervisor's muted headset. The smartest operators insist that folks spend an entire shift staffing the call center personally.

One major pharmaceutical company makes the call center a mandatory stop on the career ladder for its best, most promising sales reps. After field sales success, they spend a year in the call center en route to a "cushy" job in headquarters. Sales reps are required to interact with customers—doctors in this case—firsthand, every day. The company feels that the experience will enable such upward-bound individuals to feel greater empathy for customers and contribute more at the executive management level.

Sometimes No Rules Are the Best Rules of All

One of the very highest-touch interaction centers anywhere is the American Cancer Society's National Cancer Information Center—dubbed the NCIC—in Austin, Texas. This ninety-seat center was built in late 1996 and handles more than a million calls a year. Inbound calls range from people making a ten-dollar contribution or seeking advice on how to stop smoking to the overpowering, "Hello. I've just been diagnosed with an advanced stage of cancer. Help me."

To accommodate this dramatic range of callers, and to serve its noble mission, the society threw out almost all the rules a call center normally runs by. Why? Its mission suggests that every customer is a Most Valuable Customer, whether the caller is contributing five dollars, working on a term paper, or coping with the devastating disease. In terms of call center operations, consider American Cancer Society's rules as you rethink your own:

- Every call is answered by a live voice, to make the center welcoming and warm, particularly for those callers in severe need
- Call durations are neither measured nor discussed
- Callers can be referred anywhere, and information specialists are encouraged to do one-off article searches and basic research to find any information a caller needs
- CSRs are encouraged to take breaks and walks regularly, and to spend an hour or so each day learning more about the "product" by poring through the center's extensive online databases

An enlightened view, for sure, and one that's no doubt brought considerable comfort to thousands of people in a time of great need. Congratulations, ACS, and thank you for giving us usually commercial types some ideas to learn from.

Anton, Jon, Jodie Monger, and Debra Perkins. *Call Center Management: By the Numbers* (Purdue University Press, 1997).
The authors provide an excellent primer on overcoming challenges and developing a successful call center. The book is loaded with practical advice as well as useful metrics and methodologies.

Zajas, Jay J., and Olive D. Church. *Applying Telecommunications and Technology from a Global Business Perspective* (Haworth Press, 1997).
Zajas and Church demonstrate how executives in many roles throughout an enterprise can capitalize on emerging telecommunications technologies. Their book provides an excellent survey of telecom technology and its impact on business.

Recommended Reads

CHAPTER 12: CALL CENTER

Activity 12A

Twenty Questions to Consider in Evaluating Your Call Center

Target Completion Date: _____

To think through the issues surrounding your company's use of its current and future call centers, work through as many of these questions as possible.

After answering them, begin the evaluation process. Where it's called for, consider using the columns on the right side of the page to indicate:

Acceptable performance: Use a check to indicate acceptable performance in this area.
Need for improvement: 1, 2, or 3 to indicate urgency of need for improvement (1 being the most urgent).
Ease of improvement: Use a "+" to indicate that the situation can be improved with existing equipment or software; use a "0" to indicate the need for further investigation and a "−" to indicate significant roadblocks ahead.

Work on improvements can begin with questions answered with a "1+." Use the scoring system to prioritize next steps beyond those immediately actionable improvements.

Question	Acceptable performance (✓)	Need for improvement (1 to 3)	Ease of improvement (+, 0, or −)
Call-Center Strategy and Business Applications			
1. Do call centers adequately support the entire geographic structure of your corporation? (Multidivisional enterprises should expand to evaluate each business unit and its strategy separately.)			
A. Headquarters location			
B. Major service center locations			
C. Manufacturing centers			
D. Processing centers			
E. Claims centers			
F. Retail locations			
G. Sales offices			
H. Independent distributors			
2. What are the lines of business in the corporation and your strategies for them?			
A. Within the lines of business, what are the functions and services provided?			
B. For the services provided, what are the origins of the customers?			

Question	Acceptable performance (✓)	Need for improvement (1 to 3)	Ease of improvement (+, 0, or −)
C. What is the identification, segmentation, and entitlement approach for the customers of each line of business?			
D. What is the business value and strategy for this line of business, e.g., growth, retention, entering new market, cost avoidance/reduction?			
3. What is the reporting structure of the lines of business and their service centers?			
A. Centrally managed?			
B. Geographically distributed management?			
C. Are the potential synergies across these areas adequately used?			
4. Describe growth needs and strategies, opportunities, and issues			
A. Growth by application?			
B. Growth by geography?			
C. Growth by services offered?			
D. Major business initiatives by date and phasing?			
E. Adequacy of infrastructure to support initiatives?			
5. Describe hiring, training, staffing, work-force scheduling methods			

Question	Acceptable performance (✓)	Need for improvement (1 to 3)	Ease of improvement (+, 0, or −)
A. What is the distribution of agent skills, and where do they reside?			
B. Does the firm balance its agents' skill use across the enterprise?			
C. Are labor rates, overtime, and time-zone shifts optimized?			
D. Are management of equipment and resources optimized?			
6. Are human resource approaches shared?			
A. Common hiring?			
B. Common training?			
C. Common online and offline support materials?			
Operations and Technology Questions			
7. What is the organization of customer-information technology?			
A. How are client record databases organized?			
B. Where are they physically located?			
C. How are the screen-based applications organized and offered to users?			
8. What is your communications infrastructure?			
A. What is the architecture of the current voice network?			
B. Common arriving traffic?			

Question	Acceptable performance (✓)	Need for improvement (1 to 3)	Ease of improvement (+, 0, or −)
C. Common internodal tie line?			
D. Virtual facilities?			
E. Numbering plan across sites?			
F. Adequacy of bandwidth for peak volumes?			
9. Review call management data: time-based performance statistics on all applications at the summary level by site			
10. Review "from" and "to" relationships for all cross-site transfers			
11. Review adequacy and currency of current disaster-recovery plan			
12. Review strategy for cross-site load balancing			
13. Overview time-of-day, day-of-week operational rules by site and application			
14. Map and evaluate voice-response infrastructure information			
15. Review usage data on VRU			
16. Describe skills distribution of calls and agent assignments			
17. Describe current management methods used for networking and ACDs, including management reports			
18. Describe major seasonality of traffic by site and application			

Question	Acceptable performance (✓)	Need for improvement (1 to 3)	Ease of improvement (+, 0, or −)
19. Assess computer telephony integration (CTI) applications, by flow and by application location			
20. Identify top five areas of management dissatisfaction with current call center operations			

Provided courtesy of Lucent Technologies, formerly the systems and technology units of AT&T. Developed by Joe Righter, Lucent Director of Call Center Advocacy.

Activity 12B

The Call Center "Health Check"

The most powerful assessment of any call center is provided thousands of times each day by customers. Thus the most powerful assessment of any call center's delivery will replicate the customer interaction experience to the greatest extent possible. In other words, mystery shopping is a powerful diagnostic tool.

Mystery shopping provides qualitative analysis that, when coupled with the center's statistics, provides a far more valid view of the call center through the customer's eyes. Policies and procedures manuals present call centers in an ideal state. Live tests demonstrate the extent to which those policies and procedures are (a) implemented and (b) delivering the best possible customer experience at present.

Target Completion Date: _____

Step	Description
1. Planning the "Health Check"	■ Choose a number of calls that will be achievable while providing a representative sample of call-center volume. Ideally the test should include at least 500 calls

Step	Description
	■ Schedule the test calls over a variety of time periods that fairly reflect call volumes (If half the calls are typically received between 8 A.M. and 11 A.M., make half the test calls during that time period)
	■ Be sure to include peak times, key break times, late nights, and weekends (If more than one center is employed, sample each proportionately)
	■ Create tests that represent different customer types and/or customers of different value or importance, to the firm. Observe the different levels of treatment, if any
	■ Recruit test callers who represent the caller population. Consider recruiting from outside the employee population, if necessary
	■ Don't forget that union rules may require employee notification when an audit is going on
	■ Assure service reps that *individual* performance is not being monitored as part of the study. If necessary, sanitize the record to exclude service representative identifying data
2. Benchmarking against competition	■ On at least a semiannual basis, conduct a scaled-down version of the assessment with each of your company's three to five most important competitors. Use objective questions that will provide directly comparable statistics to benchmark your call center against the competition

Step	Description
	■ Solicit information via mail, fax, or e-mail. Monitor your competitors' response times. Focus on the attitude, helpfulness, friendliness, and thoroughness of the competitors' responses. Consider using stopwatches to time total call duration and hold times
3. Developing an analysis tool	■ No two call centers are alike. Missions, operations, interactions of each are established to suit a company's needs. Develop a simple, single-sheet call assessment that can be used immediately on completion of each call. Keep the evaluation to no more than ten or twelve questions (See Activity 12C) ■ Make the questions quantifiable when possible—answered either yes-or-no or on a 1-to-5-point rating system so comparisons can be drawn between time of day, specific call center, customer type, etc.

Activity 12C

Checklist for Evaluating the 1to1 Quality of a Call

Listen to ten or more randomly chosen calls placed to your call center. (Be sure to let both customers and operators know you may be listening in.) Evaluate those calls based on the following criteria:

Target Completion Date: _____

Customer Identification

Did the representative reflect any knowledge of the caller or his situation?

Did the system automatically identify the caller and link to her customer record?

Was the welcome and problem definition brief, helpful, and to the point?

Was the greeting friendly and informative?

Were the prompts (options) clear and easy to understand?

Customer Differentiation

Was any unique or personalized welcome greeting employed once identification was complete?

Did the agent reflect any knowledge of the caller's prior relationship with the company?

Was customer information used to speed the process (e.g., "Shall I ship that to . . . ?")?

Were insightful questions asked to gain further knowledge of the customer's behavior toward, or relationship with, the company?

Customer Interaction

Was the call answered promptly and appropriately?

If a transfer was required, did it happen in a reasonable number of seconds?

Were there any "dead air," or extended hold, periods?

If so, was the "hold time" used to provide appropriate information?

Were "opt-outs" provided prominently where appropriate (e.g., "To reach a live operator . . ." or "To leave a message instead . . ."?

Did the first person to speak with the customer solve the problem completely?

Was the customer asked for any information that should have already been known?

How long does it take to respond to specific requests by postal mail, e-mail, or fax?

How long does it take for a salesperson to call, if asked?

Customization

Were agents empowered to vary from the scripts or rules at all? For valuable customers?

Did customer information transfer along with the call, or did the conversation start all over again with the new agent?

Were any special offers, concessions, or information provided as a result of the caller's prior interaction with the organization?

Did the agent provide options to further refine the company's service?

Will the call center respond in preferred ways—e-mail, fax, postal mail, or in person—or in only one specific format?

Chapter Thirteen

The One-to-One Web Site

CAPITALIZING ON THE POWER
OF THE WORLD WIDE WEB

Warren Buffett says the secret to good shareholder relations is the same as the secret to a good marriage: low expectations.

He may be right, but another secret to a good relationship is memory. Which is why it's useful to visualize a happy marriage, involving two people who have grown to know each other more and more intimately with time. Think about just the little things:

- Coffee's made the right strength every time; chocolate's stirred in on Sunday
- Every Thursday around eight you're handed the phone to call your mom
- He reads the metro and sports sections first, she gets page one and business
- Thermostats in every room are adjusted for your comfort
- You talk about how nice the Smiths are and voilà—they're on the social calendar!

Silly examples? Perhaps. But if we switch to a business environment, you realize right away that the secret to having a happy customer is more than simply low expectations. It's remembering the customer and adapting your behavior to the customer's needs.

This may be the most basic theory of one-to-one marketing, but nowhere will it be put to a better, purer test than on your corporate Web site. By its nature your Web site epitomizes the very essence of the capabilities needed for 1to1 marketing—it is an immediate and highly cost-efficient interactive channel. It can be customized to individual visitors. It can dispense complex product or service information, qualify sales leads, complete purchase transactions, perform customer service tasks.

So why isn't corporate America rushing to the 1to1 Web site? Because, like a great marriage, it's a lot of work. Much easier just to write the checks for video, games, Java animation, and other creative gimmicks on your site. To build a Web site that truly lives up to its 1to1 potential requires you to build one that:

- Identifies each visitor, or gives each an incentive to self-identify
- Differentiates each visitor, on every visit, based on past and future needs
- Figures all this out without administering long, difficult questionnaires
- Tracks and interprets clickstreams
- Retains a memory of all this
- Customizes itself to meet the individual preferences of individual visitors

This is hard work, but if you do it right, your Web site can drive your entire enterprise toward 1to1 marketing. Working out the various issues and conflicts involved in putting together a 1to1 Web site will focus your organization's managers on what it takes to treat different customers differently, in an integrated, rational manner.

Before you get captivated by all the nifty toys of the Web trade, ask yourself *why* your firm wants a Web site in the first place. When it comes online, what will be the *business context* of your site?

So many companies rush to design a site before they decide what they're trying to do with it. Designing a site is creative and fun, but setting objectives and agreeing on the metrics to decide whether those objectives are being met requires analysis and hard work. Nevertheless, establishing your business parameters is an absolutely critical first step. There are three basic types of objective for any company's Web site:

Setting Objectives

1. Direct revenue generation: selling products and services, collecting subscription fees or advertising payments;
2. Reducing costs or improving efficiency: usually self-help services for customers, employees, or partners; and
3. Generating indirect or long-term benefits for the firm: mostly improving brand awareness or image.

Build the metrics into your site at the very beginning to gauge your success at accomplishing whatever objectives you establish. And set a time goal for achieving these objectives. Just as advertisers shoot for an advertising-to-sales ratio and monitor the impact of one on the other, be sure the company knows how much it will be investing in the site and the relative upside it anticipates.

Your metrics should match your business model. If your business model is direct revenue generation, set specific targets. If, say, you want to increase the dollars each customer spends, how will you tally and track your results? If you want to generate more advertising revenue, will this mean selling ads to a larger number of advertisers? Or selling higher-priced ads?

If you want to reduce costs and improve efficiency, the most useful thing to concentrate on would be automating a few of your customer service functions and eliminating some steps. So think about what your customers need from you in terms of support and service, and consider how you can get them to help themselves. Then gauge your success by counting how many customers do help themselves. Sometimes, as with Cisco Online, for example, setting up online self-help services will allow a firm to cater to a whole different category of customer—a type of customer it *only* makes sense to serve because the Web makes it possible to do so without sales reps or telephone agents.

If you're trying to generate awareness or some other, indirect benefit, you can measure such things as the number of visitors per week or the time spent per visit. You can pay off a Web site's expense by reducing your mass media budget. Or you could track other variables, such as customer satisfaction levels among MVCs or the reduced cost of e-mail messages compared to snail mail.

Some of the other variables you might want to track, to the extent possible, include:

- First-time visitors versus repeaters versus visitors with charge accounts
- Technical versus nontechnical users of your product or service
- Senior executives versus middle managers or lower-level personnel
- People seeking product guidance or support versus those seeking purchasing specifications
- Advanced versus beginning users of your product or service

Reality Check   Now that you're getting ready to commit to the development of a true 1to1 Web site, you might want to face up to some serious issues first:

1. It may be cost-efficient, but it won't be inexpensive. Developing and maintaining an active 1to1 site for a significant corporation (say, for example, one with $100 million or more in sales) will require at least a six-figure annual budget, essentially forever. A seven-figure annual expense would be more realistic if you expect your site to execute transactions and aid in customer service. Is your company really prepared to commit this kind of money?
2. Get a grip and answer two questions:

(a) If you do this, will your customers care, or will they think more of you for your efforts on their behalf?

(b) Is your company *really* ready and able to concentrate on this complex, long-term task, or is it likely to be just the next "project du jour," destined to suffer the same slow, resource-sapping, death spiral that other such projects have suffered?

3. More than a Web site is at stake. Much more. Analyze the functions that offer the greatest value to your customers and your firm, along with those that can be implemented with the least cost or disruption. Any 1to1 site will be inherently multidimensional, requiring you to break down barriers between departments. Sales and shipping will have to talk to one another, digitally of course, on a moment-by-moment basis. Are you ready for this, and can your company deal with it?

4. Virtually *every* business that puts up a Web site, in *every* business category, soon reports that the site and its capabilities are revolutionizing the way the firm operates. Don't take our word for it. Open any business magazine and read the news for yourself. So when you launch a genuine, 1to1 Web site, be prepared for a bronco ride. But remember, it's better to be on the bronco yourself than to be watching one of your competitors coming at you on *his* bronco.

Identify Your Visitors

Assuming you've passed the gut check and despite all our cautions you've decided to plunge ahead and create a site that genuinely helps you maintain individual, 1to1 relationships with customers and prospects, the first step is to identify your visitors. This sounds easy on the Web, but it's not.

First the practical limitations. In order to recognize individuals, you will need to consider available Web-identification technologies, all of which have strengths and weaknesses. The most common way of identifying visitors and their activities on your site is through "cookies"—information stored in a text file of a user's computer that facilitates customization and user tracking. While this is a relatively easy and reliable way to track individuals, there is some concern in the Web community that the practice of "dropping" cookies on the user's hard drive is invasive and compromises security. "Digital certificates" (offered by VeriSign and other companies) represent another way of addressing the issue of identification—one that is completely voluntary from the perspective of the Web user. While this is generally considered a more secure technology for ensuring the authenticity of a user's ID (due to the technical difficulties of cracking an encrypted identification), the need to actively apply for it and ensure compatibility has limited the popularity of such approaches among general consumers.

Of course, companies must encourage their visitors to register at the site if they want to identify them as individuals. This can be a challenge in an environment like the Web, where requests for customer and prospect information are commonplace.

The surest way to identify visitors when they come to your Web site is to offer some sort of incentive for them to self-identify. You want a visitor to find it in her own interest to identify herself when she shows up. If your site is designed to dispense customized product or service advice, or to facilitate a customer's self-service, getting visitors to identify themselves is a no-brainer. You can't really run the site at all without providing a mechanism for customers to let you know who they are, individually.

But if, as is more often the case, your site is trying to attract visits from customers and potential customers in order to sell them products and services directly, or to provide information to them on a quicker and more cost-efficient basis, or to create better relationships with them, the identification issue is more difficult. Clearly, at the start of the relationship, getting the customer to identify himself is much more in your interest than his. You get access to the actual contact information for a real or potential customer, someone you might be able to sell more stuff to. But for him, simply telling you his identity means taking an extra couple of minutes, wasting a few more keystrokes, and (in the back of his mind anyway) thinking it would be awfully easy for you to abuse this information if he gives it to you—sell it to others, "spam" him with worthless e-mail messages and empty offers that waste even more of his time. No, getting a visitor to identify himself when he comes to your site is not usually a slam-dunk.

Drip-irrigation dialogue. One thing *not* to do is threaten the entire relationship in its infancy by unveiling a massive, complicated profile or questionnaire. Instead, gather the information that is useful for the current transaction, remember it, and build your relationship's context over time, little by little. Think of the task as a kind of "drip irrigation" for the relationship. Don't flood the relationship with massive doses of data, but instead build its context gradually, one item at a time.

If you want to encourage visitors to identify themselves, then start with what you can offer, in terms of increasing convenience, benefits, or even some form of discount or monetary compensation. One way to visualize the whole interactive process—the "clickstream" that defines a single visitor's session at your site—is to think of it in terms of swapping value for value. Give me a little information and I give you something in return. Give me a little more and I'll give you a little more. Step by step, shepherd the visitor through a series of successively beneficial and informative interactions.

At every step in the process, concentrate on gathering the information that will be useful to you. Don't bother the visitor asking for information that is of uncertain value to relationship development. Knowing the gender of a visitor is not going to be critical in selling that visitor more computer software, for instance. But knowing how skilled the visitor is in using software today would be immensely helpful.

Unfortunately, many Web site operators are still simply trying to gather the same demographic and other descriptive information that companies use for targeting their mass-media ads. And some operators gather the data but don't even use it for that!

Excite sells some $37 million of advertising annually on its search engine site, which is second only to Yahoo! as a Web site directory. But according to a review of 1to1 marketing initiatives in *Wired* magazine, Excite has yet to use any of this information even to target its ads better—despite the fact that it has been collecting names and zip codes from its Web visitors for two years.

In the same article, the author contends that, in terms of giving Web site operators personal information, consumers are a lot more resistant than many operators had counted on. But what else should we expect? If I take the time and keystrokes to give you personal information of any kind, and I never see that information used for my benefit—if I see no personal benefit from having given you that information—then why ever would I want to take the time to give you more information?

Differentiate Your Visitors

While ordinarily it's important to rank your customers by their value first, in order to direct your resources catering to the needs of those customers who account for most of your revenue, on the Web this maxim is not as important. Automated interactions on the Web are so cost-efficient that there is very little expense to allocate. Setup costs might be large, especially if they are spread over just a few customers, but setup costs can't really be allocated to particular tiers of customers anyway. And the transaction costs of handling a single interaction on the Web are virtually negligible.

The point is that the first task in customer differentiation on the Web is not necessarily to rank customers by value, but to differentiate them by their needs. The easiest way to do this is to provide different initial choices, designed to appeal to different communities of interests.

1. Visualize your customers in terms of their different types of needs. Think of the visitor, not the visit. Focus on the characteristics of a visitor that make him or her different, in terms of what needs that visitor will be trying to satisfy at your site;
2. Map out different features and benefits at your site, designed to appeal to these different communities of interest, and
3. Design a series of choices, options, questions, or routes that will channel your visitors into the appropriate community.

Once you have more data on individual visitors—after repeated visits or interactions—you can begin to use more sophisticated tools, mapping customers into finer and finer groups, with ever more precise insights into their own needs. Your goal is to make it more convenient for the visitor to come to your site and find what is needed, with every visit. With every visit, you want the visitor to think it was more convenient this time than it was the last time.

Matching engines. In order to encourage this interaction and continued refinement in the relationship, you have to be able to match your content to the visitor's needs. This will require a "matching engine." One kind of matching engine would be a simple profile-driven selection. Set up a number of different types of profiles to serve the needs of the different types of customers each profile represents. When a visitor arrives at your site, suggest that he choose the profile that best fits his own needs. Some sites use pictures of people to represent profile information more conveniently. A shopping site might refer to such profiles as "shopping assistants" or "personal shoppers," while an information site might call them "research assistants."

Regardless of what you call it, what you are really doing here is offering visitors the opportunity to designate an "agent" to represent her own personal needs and preferences. This type of agent is crude and approximate, but it allows a site to employ a better interactive business model than simply treating all visitors identically.

To become a *real* agent, the profile must be continually updated with a visitor's own record of purchases and interactions, so that the agent becomes smarter and smarter, the more it is employed by the visitor. In designing a 1to1 Web site, keep in mind how you interact with real-life, human agents in a variety of non-Web business situations. A travel agent, for instance, is someone you might rely on to help choose a vacation destination. When you call the travel agent, she'll interview you a bit to try to get a sense of what you're looking for. Then she might provide you with a selection of three possible vacation spots. You give her feedback (e.g., the second one looks best, but you really wanted more of an activities-based vacation). And she comes back with two or three additional suggestions.

The real dynamic that characterizes any agent-client relationship is feedback. There is a feedback loop between the agent and her client. Client requests something, agent suggests some alternatives. Client comments on the alternatives, agent uses this feedback to generate a new set of alternatives. With each such iteration the agent comes closer to the client's personal preferences. Moreover, the next time the client looks for something, the agent remembers what transpired the last time—so all the previous relevant feedback is incorporated in the next interaction as well. Obviously, the agent-client relationship is a Learning Relationship, with the agent being taught more and more by the client.

This is the dynamic you'll want to create to run a successful matching engine at your 1to1 Web site. If you can set up your site so that the matching engine uses a visitor's individual feedback to make it easier and easier for that visitor to find what he needs, then he'll always find it easier to come back to your site rather than to visit a competitor's site and have to reteach it his preferences. Once you have a travel agent who knows your preferences and has booked a few successful trips for you, it becomes risky and difficult to switch travel agents, right?

Another type of matching engine involves a technique more in vogue now on account of the tremendous interactive power of the Web—collaborative filtering. Collaborative filtering is a technique we called "community knowledge" in Chapter Nine of our book *Enterprise One to One*. If you have thousands of visitors, interacting with you in a variety of ways and seeking out particular content to meet their own interests, by examining the content most requested by the members of a particular visitor's community of interest, you can make smart, highly individualized recommendations to the visitor.

There are several firms today that offer collaborative filtering software solutions, including Net Perceptions and Firefly. One of the original examples of such technology being put to actual use was Firefly's music-selection site, where a visitor could ask for music recommendations. It would first ask the visitor to rate a number of different types of music, groups, and specific CDs. Then it would recommend a CD or a music group based on how that visitor's ratings compared with others' ratings.

Today you can find an excellent example of collaborative-filtering technology for selecting movies, with Moviefinder, a Net Perceptions application running on the E! Online site (http://www.moviefinder.com).

The site allows you to ask for a movie now playing in theaters, or a recently released video, or an old movie. You can specify you want a movie that you'll like personally or one that both you and your spouse will like. The basic concept is simple: Begin by rating a few movies you have seen, based on whether you found them to be highly attractive or not at all attractive. The more ratings you give the engine, the better a match it will likely find for you. Both Barnes and Noble and Amazon.com have collaborative-filtering engines available at their online bookstore sites, and Net Perceptions has ambitions for collaborative filtering that extend to intranets, online directories, knowledge management, and other applications.

Collaborative filtering technology has limitations, however. First, it is best suited for those types of interests and preferences that people have more trouble putting into words in the first place, which is one reason music and video selections represent early success stories for the technology. In each of these cases a user might find it easier just to name the types of movies or CDs he has liked in the past, rather than trying to explain why he liked what he did. On the other hand, if you can describe your interests reasonably well in simple language, a more reliable and quicker form of selection might be a basic directory/subdirectory cataloguing of subjects.

In addition, the mathematical techniques involved in collaborative filtering require a large number of data points. David Anderson, a mathematician who has worked on collaborative filtering problems, calls this the "cold-start" problem. You need a lot of data before you can provide much guidance to anyone. Not only do you need a number of ratings from a particular individual to be able to get an accurate fix on that individual's true interests, but you need ratings from a statistically significant number of people with somewhat similar tastes to compare. According to Anderson, one of the reasons for the success of collaborative filtering (he calls it "social filtering") in the video domain is that, compared to music or books, there are a relatively limited number of "big" movies that everyone has seen and can rate.

Regardless of the matching engine you use, however, the important thing is to employ the choices visitors make on your Web site to begin differentiating them early and in detail with respect to their needs. Start with communities of interest, but as you accumulate more data and experience, be prepared to break these communities into subcommunities and sub-subcommunities.

Ideally, the communities you map your customers into will be at least somewhat correlated with their value to you, so you can identify the most valuable few constituencies and implement extra services for them. It is almost always possible to correlate a customer's value with his or her needs, at least at some level, and if you can do so on your Web site, you have a vehicle for ensuring that special attention is paid to your most valuable customers.

In addition to mapping and tracking your visitors' "community needs," you will want to track their individual needs—names, addresses, credit-card numbers, and so forth—in order to make it easier for a visitor to order from you or to answer a questionnaire or survey.

In accommodating both community and individual needs, consider a travel Web site for booking airline reservations. A business traveler's community needs would encompass such things as schedule and connection information—including connections to and flights on other airlines—along with access to airline clubs and business facilities, business hotels, car service, even laptop plugs in airline seats. These are all needs that business travelers are likely to have in common with other business travelers—the needs that, in essence, define the "community" of business travelers.

A leisure traveler's community needs would be different, and would include such things as fare comparisons and destination information, family accommodations, baby seats, ground packages, and so forth.

In both cases—business and leisure travel—the traveler's individual needs might include things such as seat preference, special meals, phone numbers, frequent-flier account numbers, and so forth.

The truth is, we've just defined our "communities" in terms of the event rather than the visitor—that is, the same visitor to this travel Web site might be coming on one day to book a business trip and on the next day to book a leisure trip. But, for the most part, business travelers are more frequent, and identifiable, in their preferences. So defining our communities in this way is not a bad compromise, provided that we remember to make it possible for any visitor previously catalogued as a business traveler to specify he or she is traveling for leisure on a particular trip.

You can identify the community to which a particular travel-site visitor belongs by the choices she makes when first entering the site. If she goes right for the schedules or the business arrangements, she's probably in the business-traveler group, but if she starts by trying to find the least expensive fare, she's more likely to be in the leisure group. If it's indeterminate, you can always simply ask the visitor to specify whether she's planning a business or leisure trip. The point is, your 1to1 Web site should be set up so that any visitor's first few clicks begin to reveal the nature of the visitor.

A Web site is of course an ideal venue for interacting with customers. Every click at your site is in fact an interaction. But so are calls to the call center and transactions at the point of purchase. When you think about this third implementation step and how it applies to Web sites, remember that while the Web accounts for just one type of interaction, it is almost always the most cost-efficient type. On one hand, this means you should be careful to link interactions with a customer at your Web site with all the other forms of interaction available to the customer. You might consider "call me" buttons on your site, or "chat" buttons, for instance.

Interact with Your Visitors

Second, you need to encourage as many interactions on the Web site as possible, moving them off more costly vehicles such as the call center. In the initial stages, at least to generate your first traffic from your most frequent customers, you might want to consider a financial incentive to encourage use of the Web site rather than the call center, for instance, to make a purchase or conduct a transaction.

But in the long run you have to make interaction on your Web site absolutely as easy for the customer as is humanly possible—so easy that the customer will prefer a Web-based interaction for his own convenience. Every conceivable type of customer request or initiative should be accommodated on your Web site. In *Enterprise One to One*, Chapter Ten, we suggested that one way to begin the journey to becoming a 1to1 enterprise was to do an "interaction inventory," documenting all the different media by which customers interact (Web, phone, sales call, etc.) and matching each medium up against the different substantive reasons for the interaction, whether the interaction was initiated by the customer or by the enterprise.

But Web sites are by their nature *inbound*-interactivity vehicles. Customers initiate a Web-site interaction, or else the interaction doesn't occur. Therefore, in evaluating your own Web site for the type of utility it offers visitors, make a list of all the reasons a customer might want to initiate an interaction with you, and be sure you can accommodate all those interactions.

Your customer should be able to come to your Web site and order a product, purchase the product, check the status of his account, request service for his product, specify or configure his product or service, obtain information or suggestions on the proper use of his product, inquire as to the availability of a product or the status of a previously submitted order, lodge a complaint, make a suggestion, dispute a bill, or submit a fan letter. In initiating any of these interactions, your customer has a right to expect that you will remember all his previous interactions and respond to him in such a way that he never has to repeat himself. So, if you intend to run a 1to1 Web site, make plans to accommodate and process all these forms of inbound interactions. It will obviously require you to integrate the operation of your Web site with a number of other systems at your firm, ranging from inventory management to product specification and billing.

In addition to accommodating these types of interactions, you may also want to consider allowing customers to contact other customers (or at least reference sites), or make side-by-side comparisons with competitive products and services sold by other firms.

If you've done your differentiation job correctly, a visitor will come to your site and fairly quickly map himself or herself into a profile of some type—a profile that will be continually updated, as survey information is processed and as the visitor's own clickstream is tracked. Because the Web is such a richly interactive interface, it is important to allow your visitors to maintain as much control over their own profiles as possible. When you put your site together, show a "profile update" button on the menu bar, so a visitor can alter the way he presents himself and his needs to you at any time. Human beings are fickle creatures. What I told you yesterday may not be true today, either because I didn't really understand the question, or because I was visualizing a different role for myself, or simply because I changed my mind. Regardless of the reason, your Web site has to be flexible.

Customize for Your Visitors

Remember the game "Twenty Questions"? You try to guess what I'm thinking about, and you get to ask up to twenty yes-or-no questions. The fewer questions you ask before you guess the answer, the higher your score will be.

This game is a good analogy for creating a successful 1to1 Web site. The better you become at listening to a customer, processing the information, and then customizing your next interaction, the faster you succeed. Here are a few lessons inspired by the game Twenty Questions:

- A customer's answer to your most recent question should shape, or perhaps eliminate, your next question. If your customer tells you she's thinking of something that is alive, don't then ask if she's thinking about a mineral. If she tells you it's smaller than a breadbox, don't ask whether you can skate on it.
- Ask only one or two questions at a time, using the drip-irrigation methodology. Don't try to get every shred of information at once. Don't leap to premature conclusions, and don't assault your visitor with more questions than you reasonably need the answers to right away.
- Ask the fewest possible questions necessary to satisfy a customer's needs.
- Make specific suggestions only after you have enough answers to support an educated guess. Guessing prematurely results in absurd attempts at customer satisfaction: "Our super-deluxe personal search engine has found 7,657 products that meet your criteria. Would you like to see the first 10?"

The true secret to customizing your Web site lies in employing mass customization principles. Rather than get bogged down trying to accommodate every conceivable difference among all your visitors, you should be modularizing your site and the way it renders itself. The choices your customer makes can then be used to render individually different pages and Web site configurations.

There are a number of firms that have emerged to address the challenges of mass-customizing the Web site. BroadVision One-to-One sets the de facto standard for robust, differentiated 1to1 interactions on the Web and has installed more than one hundred 1to1 Web engines. Broad-Vision's sophisticated "dynamic command center" technology enables business managers to rapidly change applications and business rules to address the individual needs and preferences of their customers. Such capabilities facilitate cross-selling, up-selling, and customer retention efforts by personalizing content based on profiled information, session behavior, and other types of input. The company is focusing on e-commerce, financial services, and knowledge management markets and has a broad array of impressive clients now putting its technologies to work.

SMART Technologies is an Enterprise Relationship Management vendor. Its eCustomer solution is designed to engage the individual effectively and facilitate customized, dynamic, real-time interaction. SMART is focused on providing a "single, integrated, customer-driven connection point" that reaches into all departments within a company to enable individuals to access information that is rich and personally relevant. The company uses SMART Touchpoints and its SMART DNA architecture to produce Web solutions that recognize different users, levels of access, preferences, and other profiled elements. Meantime, Vignette Corp. is positioning itself as a relationship management solution provider, downplaying the role of dynamic publishing and playing up the need for personal profiling, business intelligence and decision support tools that enable companies to interact more effectively with their customers.

Clearly there is an extraordinary amount of innovation occurring in this space. The aspiring 1to1 enterprise will eventually need to consider and eventually adopt such solutions if it is to capitalize on the tremendous relationship-building opportunities afforded by the Web.

Allen, Cliff, Deborah Kania, and Beth Yaeckel. *Internet World Guide to One to One Web Marketing* (John Wiley & Sons, 1998).
The authors provide an excellent overview of issues facing companies that are trying to build 1to1 relationships on the Web. It looks at some of the key technologies that firms must consider and addresses key business and strategic issues. With a title like this, our only wish is that the book had gone into more of the "how to" behind 1to1.

Bayne, Kim M. *The Internet Marketing Plan: A Practical Handbook for Creating, Implementing, and Assessing Your Online Presence* (John Wiley & Sons, 1997).
This book provides the foundation for a Web marketing strategy, and includes a diskette containing documents, checklists, spreadsheets, and other materials to help the marketer develop a plan.

Brady, Regina, Edward Forrest, and Richard Mizerski. *Cybermarketing: Your Interactive Marketing Consultant* (NTC Business Books, 1997).
Brady, Forrest, and Mizerski provide an excellent collection of articles exploring the challenges and opportunities of interactive and Web-based marketing. The book offers a powerful overview of trends that need to be considered as companies develop their own customer relationship and interactive media strategies.

Godin, Seth. *eMarketing: Reaping Profits on the Information Highway* (Berkley Publishing Group, 1995).
This comprehensive guide to electronic-marketing opportunities, which features essays from Don Peppers and Martha Rogers, explores the potential associated with a range of technologies. Among them: the Internet, fax on demand, bulletin boards, CD-ROM, infomercials, and audiotext. The essays explain in clear layman's terms how these technologies work and how you can use them to dramatically enhance the way you do business.

Schwartz, Evan I. *Webonomics: Nine Essential Principles for Growing Your Business on the World Wide Web* (Broadway Books, 1997).
Schwartz outlines some of the key trends that companies must address in a

Recommended Reads

networked business environment where consumers demand to be compensated for their information. It's primarily a good, high-level overview of the coming impact of Web commerce.

Sterne, Jim. *Customer Service on the Internet: Building Relationships, Increasing Loyalty, and Staying Competitive* (John Wiley & Sons, 1996).
Recognizing the pressures toward individualized, 24 × 7 customer service that the Web both encourages and facilitates, Sterne offers a compelling picture of where customer service is headed. The book is loaded with intelligent case studies and practical advice.

Vassos, Tom. *Strategic Internet Marketing* (Business Computer Library, 1996).
Vassos offers practical advice, case studies, and specific information for making marketing decisions and implementing your Internet marketing plan. Supporting his book is an online site that offers in-depth reference material with additional facts, notes, and resources.

Activity 13A

Web Issues for Your Transition Team to Discuss

Target Completion Date: _____

1. Elevator Speech: As you set up a one-to-one Web site, you will need to break down barriers between departments. Your site will be inherently multi-dimensional and will require various functions and divisions to speak to each other constantly and electronically.

Analyze the functions that offer the greatest value to your customers and your organization and how best to integrate them for your site. Once your team has discussed this issue, prepare an Elevator Speech that explains to anyone in your organization (a) why this integration is necessary for a successful Web site and (b) how you will accomplish it.

_____

_____

_____

_____

2. Decide what the basic objective for your Web site will be. You will probably choose one or more of the following three possibilities:

   O Direct revenue generation: selling products and services, collecting subscription fees, or advertising payments
   O Reducing costs or improving efficiency: usually self-help services for customers, employees, channel members, or partners
   O Generating indirect or long-term benefits for the firm: mostly improving brand awareness or image

_____

_____

_____

_____

3. Is your company really ready and able to concentrate on this complex, long-term task? Where will the six- or seven-digit annual support budget come from?

_____

_____

_____

_____

4. How will your organization have to change to accommodate Web interaction with your customers?

_____

_____

_____

_____

5. Who will be in charge of your Web site?

_____

_____

_____

_____

Web Checkpoint

Answer yes or no to the following questions. Repeat this activity one year after the initial date you complete it.

Target Completion Date: _____

Question	Now	One Year from Now
Do you have a Web site?	○Yes ○No	○Yes ○No
Do you identify each visitor?	○Yes ○No	○Yes ○No
Do you give each visitor an incentive to self-identify?	○Yes ○No	○Yes ○No
Do you differentiate each visitor, on every visit, based on needs as you understand them?	○Yes ○No	○Yes ○No
Have you determined how to differentiate visitors without administering a long, difficult questionnaire?	○Yes ○No	○Yes ○No
Can customers interact with you at your site?	○Yes ○No	○Yes ○No
Can they interact in real time (e.g., chat lines or phone links)?	○Yes ○No	○Yes ○No
Can customers purchase products or services directly from your site?	○Yes ○No	○Yes ○No

Can a customer check the status of his order at your site?   ○Yes ○No   ○Yes ○No

---

Is a customer's product or service configuration information available to   ○Yes ○No   ○Yes ○No
her at the site?

Does your site give a customer the ability to lodge a complaint or address ○Yes ○No   ○Yes ○No
a product-specific inquiry?

Do you have a system that will automatically alert customers about   ○Yes ○No   ○Yes ○No
products, services, or information in which they have expressed interest?

Can you use links to different pages on your site to cross-sell?   ○Yes ○No   ○Yes ○No

---

Do you have a proportion of your customers' e-mail addresses? Estimate   ○Yes ○No   ○Yes ○No
percentage:——

Activity 13C

Identify and Differentiate Visitors to Your Web Site

		Identify		

Target Completion Date: _____

Who Will Do It? (init.)	By When? (date)	Task	75% Done (✓)	100% Done (✓)
		Develop an incentive for your Web visitors to self-identify		
		Develop a privacy protection policy for your home page that specifies protection and disclosure of information		
		Design a method for drip-irrigation dialogue so you don't have to ask a lot of questions for the first, or any, visit		
		Determine whether you need password protection, and if so, install it		
		Determine whether there are other security issues and how to resolve them		

		Differentiate		

Target Completion Date: _____

Who Will Do It? (init.)	By When? (date)	Task	75% Done (✓)	100% Done (✓)
		Develop a method to visualize your customers in terms of their different types of needs. Focus on the characteristics of a visitor that makes him or her different, in terms of what needs he or she will be trying to satisfy at your site		

		Map out different features and benefits to your site, designed to appeal to different communities of interest		
		Design a series of choices, options, questions, or routes that will channel your visitors into each one's appropriate community		
		Explore the use of matching engines—profile-driven selection, collaborative filtering, or other		
		Figure out how to incorporate ongoing feedback from your customers		

Activity 13D

Web Interaction and Customization

Target Completion Date: _____

Who Will Do It? (init.)	By When? (date)	Task	75% Done (✓)	100% Done (✓)
		▪ Determine how to promote your site		
		▪ Create a long-term site promotion plan		
		▪ Capture every click from each identified visitor and incorporate that into his or her record		
		▪ Determine how to measure the frequency of repeat visits (cookies?)		
		▪ Determine who monitors, edits, and refreshes discussion-group information		
		▪ Connect to call-center point-of-purchase (POP) transactions, if they involve the same visitor		

- Determine how to handle incoming messages, queries, and complaints on your Web site

- Determine a maximum response time

- Reward your customers for using the Web more, as Web interactions will reduce your cost

- Track and compare the relative cost of various functions in their traditional mode versus the Web mode (e.g., invoicing, data entry and update, product configuration, purchase orders, and order status)

- Consider setting up your MVCs with a computer and Web browser, or WebTV, and perhaps even subsidize it for them

- Determine what resources channel members should have access to and whether they should have access to their customers' information

- Develop a method to alert customers when a product, service, or piece of information in which they've expressed an interest becomes available

- Ensure that your Web site is connected to the required internal information systems

Chapter Fourteen

Advertising and Marketing Communications for the One-to-One Enterprise

HOW TO USE TRADITIONAL MASS MEDIA TO GENERATE BETTER CUSTOMER RELATIONSHIPS

Now, what's a nice chapter like this doing in a place like *The One to One Fieldbook*? Isn't one-to-one marketing all about how to compete in the age of addressable, interactive media?

Yes, but nonaddressable, noninteractive media—ranging from television and radio to print and outdoor—will be with us for a very long time. Companies will continue to find it necessary to put their messages in front of large numbers of unknown prospects in order to entice them into customer relationships. Reaching an audience of millions, or tens of millions, will continue to be something achievable in any practical way only with mass media, so don't go shorting stock in those cable TV and magazine publishing companies just yet.

In addition, branding—imposing a single, commonly accepted brand image on a product or service that can be understood the same way by everyone—will continue to be important in the interactive age, partly because clinging to the safety of a well-known brand is one way a consumer can deal with the storm of information and choice that now surrounds us all. And even if this storm were to abate, "badge" brands will still want to advertise to *everyone,* including those who aren't in the market for the badge. After all, at least part of the fun in wearing a new pair of Nikes is likely to derive from having your friends see you wearing them.

In other words, advertising and other noninteractive marketing communications are alive and well, and will continue to thrive, even as other forms of media become more interactive.

Nevertheless, in implementing a 1to1 marketing program, there are some things you should think about with respect to how your largely nonaddressable, noninteractive marketing communications programs are managed. In this chapter we're going to discuss how to use broadcast, print, and outdoor media, as well as direct mail, brochures, collateral, kiosks, and other forms of non-mass media. We'll also review how some of the more traditional marketing tasks—such as product launches—should be adjusted to account for your 1to1 marketing program.

WHAT IS THE ROLE OF A BRAND?

Throughout the Industrial Age, companies have focused more and more on differentiating themselves from their competition. One important element of this effort has been "branding." Brands became important when mass marketing became the dominant form of competition among consumer businesses. One way to look at a brand is to think of it as a large company's substitute for the relationship that a small, mom-and-pop company used to have with its customers. The brand symbolizes a company's promise to deliver a good product to customers who have no personal relationship with the people who work at the company. It is also a mechanism for pulling a consumer through a retail environment and creating demand for a product that is represented as living up to the standards of the brand.

In the age of mass marketing, brands differentiated companies from one another. A smart marketer could even differentiate its product purely by referring to brand values, without respect to the actual characteristics of the product. Two very indistinguishable commodities could have—and often did have—entirely different brand personalities.

But a brand is not a relationship. An individual may identify with a brand. It may even give her confidence in an unknown product or service. The company behind the brand, however, doesn't necessarily know anything about that individual. In other words, a brand is no substitute for learning a customer's particular needs and preferences and then addressing them.

On the other hand, it is still vitally important to take into account the strengths of a brand in introducing a 1to1 marketing program. The individual relationships you set up with your customers should leverage the strengths of your brand where possible and point to your brand's personality. But the primary role of your brand is to serve as a vehicle for carrying a message to that vast majority of people who are not your customers yet and who have no other relationship with you by which to gauge your merit.

Identify, Differentiate, Interact, and Customize

If you're like most firms, your objectives in advertising are going to be some combination of promoting sales, awareness, and a positive brand image. But if you're also launching a 1to1 marketing program—if you're trying to cultivate individual relationships with increasing numbers of customers at the same time you're mass-advertising to them—it's worthwhile to step back for a minute and consider just how your advertising program might help you implement your 1to1 program.

Since traditional advertising vehicles are for the most part nonaddressable and noninteractive, it isn't really necessary to know the identities of your advertising audience before you launch a campaign. Nor is it possible to use advertising to differentiate customers one from another, except to the extent that a customer's individual characteristics can be used in combination with similar traits among other customers to define smaller and more refined niche markets.

But an ad campaign *could* help you identify and differentiate your customers, if the ad message itself were to generate a response. So one key issue to consider, in terms of how to put advertising into the service of 1to1 marketing, is generating such a response—using the advertising to cultivate feedback with individual customers. Other key issues involve how your own firm's behavior toward different customers is managed. Can you figure out how to treat different customers differently, either on the front end of the ad campaign, by using different messages to appeal to different customers, or on the back end, by ensuring that any "fulfillment" activities related to your ad campaign are as prompt, accurate, and automated as possible?

So, given these considerations, we're going to reframe our four-point implementation strategy, as it applies to advertising. Whether you're looking at the use of outdoor, print, broadcast, or any other type of media, the key methods for employing these media in the service of launching a 1to1 marketing campaign can be summarized into three basic activities: versioning, cultivating feedback, and fulfillment.

Versioning

The first thing to concern yourself with is doing what you can to ensure that the most relevant messages get to the right customers for those messages. In print media anyway, reaching individual readers with individual versions of a message is a practice that has been around for a while.

Agricultural firms have been creating specific versions of print ads for farmers at least since the early 1970s, when publications such as *Farm Journal* and *Ohio Farmer-Stockman* pioneered the use of selective binding and localized sections ("signatures," in printer's parlance). Meredith Custom Publishing produced more than 3,700 versions of *SUCCESSFUL FARMING* in its February 1998 issue. This enabled a company to sell corn herbicides to corn growers in the upper Southeast with dry soil, for instance, or to promote different chemicals in different regions, delivering distinctive ad messages to, say, farmers who plant more than a thousand acres a year. More recently, the mainstream magazines have discovered selective binding and digital printing. Thus, *Time* can now run a four-color Buick ad inviting you to test-drive a Buick Regal at Bob's Motors on Elm Street in your town, coupling it with a response device containing the subscriber's name and the names and locations of the nearest dealers.

One thing to steer clear of, when you start creating different, addressable versions of a print ad, is personalizing it for no good reason. Simply greeting a magazine reader by name in an advertisement within the magazine, while it might momentarily stop the reader, is not likely to advance your 1to1 marketing program. So if you need a good mass-media trick to get your message read, then fine. But if you're looking to begin a relationship you'll have to use the individuality of the ad to provide some benefit to the customer or prospect.

Producing versioned brochures and collateral material is easier than producing versioned magazine or print ads, because you control your own production process when it comes to brochures. And producing versioned pieces of direct mail is a well-developed science today. But whether you're considering a print ad, a brochure, or a piece of postal mail, there generally are only two good reasons to personalize:

Relevance. Personalization reflects additional knowledge of the recipient that might be either tangibly or intangibly valuable to the reader of the ad. People do like a personal touch. They pay a bit more attention when they encounter their own name, a fact that salespeople have been using since Dale Carnegie's *How to Win Friends and Influence People.* So, to a certain extent anyway, simply reminding a reader that you know her and remember her can be helpful in your selling effort—even though she knows darn well it's a customer database doing most of the work.

But take care to personalize the ad in such a way that it amounts to more than just the "playback" of a name. To make a personalized message relevant, you must introduce a fact that differentiates this reader from all other readers, *in addition to* the reader's name. "As a five-year customer, you are one of only 1,100 to receive this special offer. . . ." says a lot, as does "Because your warranty expires in three months, you might find the enclosed offer particularly attractive. . . ."

Convenience. A Learning Relationship can be cultivated if every time a customer deals with you it is easier than it was the last time. So, besides ensuring that an ad message is relevant, you should try to provide a convenience to your reader or customer. Your goal is to make it easier for her to do business with you due to your current knowledge of her.

If you're asking for feedback or input from the reader of the ad, you can use personalization to make providing that feedback easier. Fill in the return form with the reader's name and account number, or put that information on the coupon being offered. Create a "suggested" option for new orders or value-added services, and use the information you already have about this customer to make it easy for the customer simply to "sign on the dotted line."

You can use versioning and segmenting principles to test one offer or message against another. Print and mail, though not exactly interactive, allow you to test your ideas on one small population at a time, gradually honing your offer to achieve the best result. And large broadcast direct marketers know that you can test the success of a spot as well—putting different phone numbers on different messages and comparing the results. (This will never be as statistically precise as direct mail, but it usually serves the purpose.)

The principal weakness of most advertising and media vehicles is that they aren't interactive, and therefore you get no feedback from individual customers. But, if you're careful, you can figure out how to generate at least some feedback, even if you have to provide a financial incentive to a customer to generate it.

Cultivating Feedback

Insurance and financial services providers have applied this technique for some time, although their offers have occasionally been rather transparent. "Send us your current list of investments and we'll provide a free portfolio analysis" is a fairly common stockbroker solicitation. It implies a tangible value to the security evaluation, which may or may not provide value; it certainly encourages an investor to "raise his hand" if he's a potential customer.

"A free guide to IRAs" or *"The Wall Street Journal* Guide to Investing" and similar offers of third-party products with a more objectively measured value ("retail price, $29.95," for example) provide a clearer explicit bargain. They involve the trade of an objectively valued commodity like a book or a free calculator, perhaps, for a consumer's willingness to announce him- or herself as a prospective customer.

You should ensure that every outbound communication encourages a customer response through as many different response devices and vehicles as are practical. Listing URLs, phone numbers, and postal addresses on billboards or in TV spots may be impractical, but listing either phone or URL—depending on the type of customer base you're appealing to—can usually be accommodated with minimal impact on the creative look of the ad.

In generating feedback, it's important also to pay attention to the kind of information you really want. Solicit more feedback than name, address, and phone number. Obtain some useful customer differentiation data in the initial interaction. Insurance companies regularly ask the respondent's age, which is, for them, a very helpful but relatively nonthreatening differentiator. Stockbrokers ask for an approximate level of invested funds (soliciting ranges rather than specific dollar amounts).

ADVERTISING ON THE WEB

One of the best vehicles for doing interactive advertising is, of course, the World Wide Web. While we devoted a whole chapter to the subject of using your Web site to build better, more profitable relationships with your customers or prospects, what about putting ads on the Web to sell your products? What about banners and clickthroughs, site sponsorships, contests, promotions, incentives, and so forth?

The Web is generally acknowledged to be more efficient as a tool for stimulating direct sales and generating customer loyalty than for building overall brand awareness. Different firms take different approaches to Web advertising, depending on their attitude toward these two types of activity. Recent studies of Web advertising have shown that companies selling low-priced consumer goods or household products tend to concentrate more on brand-building, while sellers of high-priced merchandise or services spend more money developing their own sites.

Jupiter Communications' recommendation is that if you sell indirectly, you should allocate 75 percent of the overall budget to buying Web advertising, with the remainder of your budget allocated to your own site. If you sell directly, then split your budget evenly.

While this book should not be considered a primer on Web advertising (many of those are already out), there are a couple of other practical considerations when it comes to putting an actual ad campaign on the Web. First, while widely accepted measurement standards have grown up around traditional print and broadcast media, allowing marketers to compare the relative benefits of buying ads on different programs or in different media vehicles, such standards have not yet appeared for measuring the effectiveness of Web advertising.

This is a real drawback when you're trying to decide how to allocate your budget. We can argue about what activity the Web is better at—generating sales or increasing awareness—but without a useful standard of comparison we still don't really know how to compare the benefit of buying a banner ad on one site or another. Standards will certainly develop over time, but it might take a while yet.

Another issue has to do with the regulatory restrictions that surround advertising, as a business activity. In the United States the Federal Trade Commission enforces "truth in advertising" rules that require advertisers to substantiate the claims they make in their ads. But what about claims made on the Web at non-U.S. sites? Suppose you do business in the United States and one of your U.S. consumers visits your company's South African Web site, where he sees an ad claim that would not be allowed without substantiation in the United States? Are you liable? And what about press releases? Advertising regulations in the United States don't generally apply to press releases, but what if your press releases are posted on your company's Web site, available not just to reporters but to consumers?

Advertising on the Web will also be affected by the European Union's new rules governing their own consumers' privacy, due to go into effect in 1999. These rules are very restrictive, generally prohibiting *any* use of an EU citizen's information without the express, written consent of the citizen in advance. But do they apply to the Web? If a German clicks through on one of your Web ads and then fills out a profile to help you fulfill his electronic orders faster, are you now bound by the EU's privacy rules with respect to using his information in the future? (The correct answer is, "probably.")

Fulfillment

If there's one most frequently overlooked secret to running a successful Web business or direct-marketing company it is this: fulfillment.

The biggest single problem for most companies, when it comes to stimulating dialogue with their customers using mass media vehicles, is poor fulfillment. Be absolutely certain, before you make an offer, that you really can ship that brochure or mail out that report on a timely basis. Your back office will not automatically take care of itself. It will definitely require attention.

The need to ensure rapid and high-quality fulfillment will put a damper on your efforts to version your advertising. The more versioning is done, the more complex the back-office operations will be.

When you're trying to manage the content or the fulfillment streams for different versions of an ad, brochure, or some other vehicle, you should rely on the principles of mass customization. First divide your versioning and fulfillment options into nonconflicting content modules. Ensure that the modules fit together easily—that is, make sure you know which modules can be configured with which other modules. Any "connecting language" needed for an ad—the language that goes between the modules—should either already be in the message or be easily and automatically dropped in. Otherwise you'll be spending time and resources manually adjusting your process.

By focusing on individual modules first, however, you can avoid the kind of version pollution that might otherwise occur. Using individual data without first designing the modules would generate an unwieldy, unmanageable number of copy permutations.

In addition, focusing on the modules first lets you cut to the chase in terms of evaluating the real payoff for your effort. It's important to consider both the production and fulfillment sides of your versioning equation because, while the costs of individualized copy production are certainly dropping, the cost of managing and coordinating a widening set of possible customer responses is not declining nearly so rapidly.

One way to keep an eye on your own fulfillment is to "mystery-shop" your own firm constantly. Respond to an ad or a brochure. Request the sales material or the phone call. Find out how long it takes and how rough the service is.

The truth is, there are two separate revolutions that have made 1to1 marketing possible for direct selling organizations. One is the revolution we've been highlighting in all our books, the information technology revolution. But just as important to companies like Amazon, Dell, Lands' End, or Cisco is the logistics revolution. If you deal in physical products at all, chances are that FedEx, UPS, and other delivery and fulfillment companies around the world are nearly as critical to your continued success and prosperity as Moore's Law.

RETURN OF THE KIOSK

With few exceptions, the 1980s was a tough decade for retail kiosks. Despite lots of enthusiasm, most kiosks just didn't work. But integrated, cost-effective hardware solutions and local dial-ups to the Internet have given kiosks a new lease on life, facilitating on-site interactivity at increased speed and decreased cost.

On the other hand, even though kiosks are now more capable advertising and relationship marketing vehicles than ever before, most marketers don't pay enough attention to the actual interaction, often concentrating instead on the aesthetic design of the physical kiosk. According to kiosk guru Scott Randall of New York–based Media Designs, "Many marketers spare no expense trying to make the kiosk cabinet look like a banana, but then pay little or no attention to the part of the kiosk that actually engages the banana customer and motivates a sale. To be effective, kiosk software needs to be designed from the customer up."

Until recently, kiosks were viewed primarily as a one-way, broadcast medium. But today's Internet-linked kiosks make truly inexpensive consumer interaction possible, and can be used to give a customer the opportunity to update his profile or collect detailed information from a central database.

Kiosks can, in fact, serve as elegant, interactive data collection points, capturing customer-specific information right at the actual point of purchase. If you have retail locations, or partners with retail locations, and obtaining customer-specific information from consumers is something you need to be doing, you should consider using kiosks to collect data in your high-traffic locations. Supermarkets and mass merchandisers should welcome the opportunity to learn customers' names and addresses, and perhaps gain share of customer or preference data in the process. Service organizations such as airlines and hotels could use their own premises to gather opinion, share of customer, and preference data far less intrusively and more cost-effectively than they could with a phone or mail survey.

Intouch Group, the music-sampling database company and the originator of the "i-Station" kiosk in music stores, now also offers an Internet-based kiosk solution for retailers in a variety of fields. Imagine, for instance, having your customer come into your store and use a kiosk permanently connected to the Web to look up the book or CD, or the hardware tool, or the camera she came to purchase. The Web site she browses would be branded with this retail-store location's identity. Once she finds what she's seeking, either the Web site would direct her to the proper location in the store or, if the product was not carried, the customer could swipe her credit card and it would offer to ship the product directly to her home. When she leaves the store, she can use her membership or user profile ID to access the same site from home later, either to order other products directly or to search for them in the store without having to get into her car. Intouch provides a turnkey solution.

LAUNCHING A PRODUCT

One-to-one marketing operates in the customer dimension rather than the product dimension, so asking how to launch a product using 1to1 marketing is actually a nonsensical question. You can't launch a product with a 1to1 marketing program any more than you could launch a customer relationship using a product promotion.

On the other hand, the fact that you are trying to cultivate 1to1 relationships with your customers does not mean that your firm will not also be launching new products. In truth, the closer your relationships with individual customers, the more new products you might be considering. So how exactly do a product-launch program and a 1to1 marketing program relate to each other? Are there additional steps you could take during a product launch to improve your customer relationships?

The first question a 1to1 marketer must answer is this: Is your new product or program:

(a) An opportunity to increase share of customer, at least with some customers

or

(b) A replacement product of some kind, for a product you already make

or

(c) Neither.

If the answer is (a) or (b), and, for most companies, at least 90 percent of the time it is, the advantage to be gained by marketing this product to your existing customer base should be obvious—that is, provided you already know your customers' identities and differences, and you are able to contact them to explain the new product.

For any new product, however, you should be thinking "complete solution." When you begin thinking beyond the physical goods your firm is about to produce, or the core service your firm will soon offer, it may be possible to create new, profitable services to accompany the launch. Not only will such services create added revenue streams for your business, they also have the potential of locking in your customers' loyalty to the new product itself.

So ask yourself whether some groups of customers or prospective customers might appreciate customization of the services surrounding the base product. Is there a group of heavy users that might want 24×7 service capabilities for this new product, even though this capability might not be important for your other products? Or would some new purchasers be interested in paying for training? Can you customize the product guide, the instruction manual, or other collateral material that will be shipped with the product?

Above all, don't forget to plan the launch of this product in such a way as to allow you to obtain the identities of, and at least a little bit of differentiating information about, the product's purchasers. This might mean asking customers to register the new product, or to make a connection at the Web site, or it might mean offering a premium or a rebate to them—but the important thing is to plan the launch so that you can make as many new-customer connections as possible.

Some questions you should consider when launching a product:

- How will you track purchases?
- What is your feedback loop with the purchasers of this new product?

- Have you ensured that data on this new product's purchasers will correctly and efficiently be entered into your customer database?
- Are your best customers prospects for this new product?
- Are some of your existing customers willing to migrate to the new product over time? Do you know which ones?
- Can the product be customized, post-purchase, through the addition of options or services?
- Can the product be customized in any way by channel members?
- Are there really two or more products that need to be "launched separately"?
- Are there any special packaging requirements for certain customers?
- Will there be any special shipping needs?
- What language or cultural differences are you managing as part of the launch?
- Do you already know some customers who would be right for this product?
- Will the product lend itself to identifying more customers?
- Will different customers use the product to satisfy different needs, and if so, are there additional products or services, related to these different needs, that could also be offered?

Novak, Thomas P., and Donna L. Hoffman. "New Metrics for New Media: Toward the Development of Web Measurement Standards," *World Wide Web Journal,* Winter 1997, 2(1), pp. 213–246.
The authors examine the different types of economic models that are emerging on the Web. They compare Web-based advertising to conventional advertising. The piece also proposes ways of measuring and researching the effectiveness of Web advertising.

Percy, Larry. *Strategies for Implementing Integrated Marketing Communications* (NTC Pub. Group, 1994).
Percy provides a strategic framework for integrated marketing communications, and discusses planning issues and tools as well as tactics and case studies.

Rossiter, John R., and Larry Percy (editor). *Advertising Communications & Promotion Management* (McGraw-Hill, 1997).
Rossiter and Percy lay a valuable foundation for advertising-communications efforts. They show how to plan, budget, and implement them.

Recommended Reads

Activity 14A

Nine Checkpoints in One-to-One Communications Planning

While very little print advertising truly provides a two-way dialogue today, the following are some considerations to accelerate the movement of print ads and collateral materials in the one-to-one direction. Most of these issues apply to all 1to1 marketing communications.

Target Completion Date: _____

Checkpoint	Description
1. Don't ask for information you won't use	■ Consumers and businesspeople alike share a limited appetite for providing information to marketers ■ Be sure that all information you gather will be used before it perishes—generally within a year's time
2. Scan if possible	■ Work in advance with a local scanning supplier to plan the graphic treatment, paper stock, and spacing required for an optimum "hit rate" or readability by optical character reader (OCR) scanners ■ The cost savings can be dramatic, as well as the advantage that comes from capturing and digitizing more useful customer information
3. Evaluate the incremental CPM compared to increased profit goals	■ This is not a drill. Use sound business judgment to "pencil out" the incremental response rates anticipated from individualized or portfolio-focused messaging, as well as the incremental gross margin yield—before and after the added costs of personalization

4. Calculate production costs on an "all-in" basis	■ This includes copywriting, production, and management time as well as the higher CPM ■ Consider 1to1 relationship enhancement as a fringe benefit or allocate a monetary value to the potential improvement in customer lifetime value
5. Avoid long copy	■ The natural temptation of copywriters using a number of individual data fields is to "write long," and often to "show off" all the individualized information ■ In any other medium besides direct mail, this may create a barrier to readership that offsets the entire gain to be realized from individualization (In direct mail, longer copy often pulls a *higher* response)
6. Beware of incomplete data sets	■ Review customer data files before designing copy ■ Assure that, for each field used, differentiating data is available for at least 75% of customers, ideally more ■ Marketers who only know the preferred leisure activities of a third of their customers will have only a one-in-three chance of employing this data field for incremental effectiveness
7. Show me you know me	■ Demonstrate through text and tone that the data you are feeding back to an individual reader is information you've learned, not guessed at ■ This will invariably add impact to the message
8. Eschew cosmetic customization	■ Laser-jetting "John Doe has just won $1,000,000" is as old as direct marketing itself ■ Whatever customization you add should enhance the *substance* of your offer

9. Customize the call to action	■ Whenever possible, stress the option of using the customer's preferred response mode (fax, phone, e-mail)

Getting 1to1 Benefits from Your Mass Marketing Materials

Before launching a 1to1 advertising or marketing communications initiative, review the following criteria:

Creative Considerations	
	Target Completion Date: _____
Criteria	**Description**

1. Ensure copy clarity	■ Review a representative sample of the many copy iterations individually. Check for:
	  ■ Clarity
	  ■ Appropriateness
	  ■ Key points not obfuscated by the integration of reused paragraphs or data fields

2. Beware of cosmetic customization	■ If a data field is inserted or repeated just "because it's there," delete it ■ Check to be sure each customer data field adds value to the "conversation" each time it's included
3. Don't be overly creative	■ When a printed communication contains powerful individual information, there is less need for high-cost production, with four-color foldouts and the like
4. Protect privacy	■ Consider a brief but firm privacy pledge toward the end of each personalized mailing

- Consider building a promise of privacy into the running text as well as highlighting it graphically

5. Test copy for the value of customization	■ Be certain that each individualized data field adds value and impact to the message ■ Small-cell testing is the best defense against careless customization ■ Compare the increasingly customized mailing to a control group of standardized offers before launching large-scale 1to1 efforts

Production Considerations

Target Completion Date: _____

Criteria	Description
1. Protect personalized information	■ Don't ask customers to put sensitive or confidential data on business reply cards ■ Don't ask for confirmation of data you already know ■ Tell customers how you will, or won't, use the information to serve them better
2. Consider economies of scale	■ Don't let the use of individual data produced yield an unwieldy, unmanageable number of copy permutations ■ Assess the incremental cost and potential return from an increasing number of versions ■ Consider both the production and response sides of this equation, since the costs of individualized copy production are dropping far faster than the human, error, and training costs of responding to a widening set of possible customer responses

3. Assess production ability	■ Matching inserts to letters, letters to envelopes, offers to letters, and so forth is getting easier, but it is hardly a perfect science ■ Use the right tools, such as bar codes
4. Heighten production-quality-control efforts	■ Spot-check multiple versions of everything that is versioned ■ Don't let anything into a content database that isn't proofed twice

Activity 14C

Generating the Right Customer Feedback

Using information provided by a customer to make his or her life easier helps to build Learning Relationships. Use accurate customer-provided data to reduce the amount of physical energy or thinking required of a willing respondent.

To optimize customer response to requests for data, follow these rules:

Target Completion Date: _____

Rule	Description
1. Keep asking new questions	■ Recognize that 1to1 marketing is a holistic, iterative process that strives to keep the "conversation" going ■ Each use of information should encourage customers to provide further data
2. Ensure that copy encourages response to the feedback solicitation	■ Express enthusiasm for learning more about each customer, whether or not an order is enclosed ■ Propose the customer benefit for responsiveness

3. Remember "drip-irrigation" dialogue	■ Customers, especially MVCs, will often balk at extensive and intrusive fact-gathering efforts, even when an explicit bargain or reward is offered ■ Since the relationship-building process is ongoing, gather individual facts a few at a time
4. Fill out the forms	■ Once an ink-jet or laser system is online, the incremental cost of filling out the forms is often, if not always, nominal, especially compared to the impact ■ When a business-reply card or other response device already includes the customer's name, address, account number and other nonconfidential information, response is far easier ■ As an added benefit, processing errors are reduced dramatically as well
5. Keep the options simple and reflective of your customer knowledge	■ The fewer questions, the better ■ Minimizing the number of options enhances response, provided the options presented are based on real customer knowledge ■ Where shipping and billing addresses have differed in the past, get confirmation rather than soliciting the addresses themselves
6. Retain and use source code data	■ Recognize the offer and the medium it appeared in as valuable tools to stimulate future response ■ By storing the source codes for offers attracting an individual customer's response, marketers can often reduce total message frequency to that customer by eliminating other types of mailings

Activity 14D

Ideas for "Versioning" Your Media Messages

Many of the ideas presented here are more clever than cost-effective, more segmentation-enabling than 1to1 enabling. Be extremely sensitive to the relative ease with which many marketers become enamored of these new technologies. But here are some ideas that might help you figure out when and how to "version" your mass-media messages:

Target Completion Date: _____

Steps	Description
1. Check that the features, advantages, and benefits of your product or service are varied enough	■ They should appeal differently to varied audiences, by a significant-enough margin to merit versioning in the first place
2. Calculate the "best guess" sales improvement rate and the gross margin throw-off from 1to1 activity before proceeding	■ Remember to calculate hidden production costs (e.g., copywriting time) and to subtract the cost of comparable traditional marketing that's already built in to the product's P&L
3. Don't be overly optimistic	■ Study the best single promotion or marketing event or "lift" your firm has generated to date and use some fraction of that number as the best possible result for your first trial
4. Start by identifying "sweet spots" that warrant immediate testing and measurement	■ Brainstorm with this chapter and assess the ideas that surface to pick several with the greatest potential impact and highest likelihood of profitability
5. Test one to three individualized marketing activities at a time	■ A rule of thumb is to try to motivate 200 individuals to act, an old direct marketing saw ■ Test 10,000 mailing pieces if a 2% response rate is anticipated

6. Be brave

■ Find solace in the way the Franklin Mint, one of America's most ambitious direct marketers, operates. After their M.B.A.'s finished weeks worth of writing plans and crunching numbers, one managing director invited his best and brightest to regular meetings where marketing trial ideas were developed and tested purely on business judgment. Totally absent were modeling, statistics, or forecasting

Chapter Fifteen

Next Steps

WHERE TO GO FROM HERE

Now that you've come all this way in the book, we at least owe you a plan for how to put into actual practice what you've read, and that's what we'll try to provide you in this last chapter. We'll make it as short and to the point as possible.

In this chapter we're going to assume you are basically starting from scratch, and that you want to ensure that your company has the best possible chance to improve its one-to-one relationships with customers and protect its unit margins over the long term.

We recommend a ten-step, iterative approach, beginning with department-specific or division-specific projects and progressing gradually to a broader and more ambitious set of initiatives. In brief, the plan works like this:

1. Get senior management to buy in. Without senior management support you won't get to first base.
2. Establish your team. It needs to be multidisciplinary, and it will have to operate on a long-term basis.

3. Develop a plan. Include short-term goals for particular departments and divisions as well as a long-term vision for the greater enterprise.

4. Define a specific set of strategies for your MVCs and MGCs. Apply the four implementation steps to both these groups, in order to define particular programs for retaining them and growing them.

5. Define a specific set of strategies for your BZs. Outline any decreased activity or cost reductions with BZs that might help fund new 1to1 initiatives.

6. Evaluate particular projects prior to implementation. From the strategies identified in Steps 3, 4, and 5, decide which initiatives should be implemented first.

7. Begin implementing particular projects. Set objectives and metrics for each project, including the responsible managers, expected outcomes, timing, and so forth.

8. Document your successes and share the learning across the enterprise. Create some mechanism, perhaps an intranet site, to ensure that the learning acquired in one department is shared across other departments.

9. Make a transition to more comprehensive, corporate metrics. As you gain experience, begin compiling information that is more oriented to measures of customer Lifetime Values and share of customer, across all divisions and departments.

10. Go back to Step 4. As you accumulate better and better information about your customers' value across the whole enterprise, redefine your MVCs, MGCs, and BZs, and create more cross-divisional programs for creating 1to1 relationships with them.

Step 1. Get Senior Management to Buy In

Because a 1to1 initiative operates in the customer dimension, while most businesses are organized for operating in the product dimension, any effort to implement a 1to1 program is destined to cross a large number of departmental and divisional lines.

It's vital that you have a senior executive's imprimatur and blessing on your efforts. Without the active assent of the CEO and his or her senior management, you might as well hang up your hat because the programs you come up with will be chopped up early on by the buzz saw of interdepartmental rivalry. No matter how team-oriented and well-intentioned your overall enterprise may be, it won't be simple to introduce a 1to1 initiative in the first place. There will be a need to resolve disputes, quell conflict, and make choices among equally deserving budgets and departments. So if you don't have senior management participation on the front end, save your money.

On the other hand, in our experience it isn't usually that hard to get senior management approval. Senior executives usually *want* their organizations to operate in a more integrated, customer-oriented dimension. The biggest problem will occur if they give their approval to your effort without fully realizing the magnitude of the conflict and change you might generate. So at some point you have to have a long, serious discussion with someone in your company's senior management who really "gets it" with respect to 1to1 issues.

This is the first step. Before doing anything, you have to have the support of the CEO or a very senior executive who is knowledgeable about 1to1 marketing and willing to go to the mat to get some things accomplished.

Step 2. Establish Your Team

Because any 1to1 initiative will inevitably become an interdepartmental issue, you have to have people on your team who represent a variety of functions and who have expertise in many different disciplines, not just marketing or sales.

Try to recruit volunteers rather than "leftovers." Identify the hard-charging, can-do people in your organization, communicate the corporate commitment to this ongoing initiative, and show them the career capital that success will bring. Senior management sponsorship will be a powerful benefit in recruiting the right team.

Tell people up-front exactly what's involved. Planning and coordination sessions might easily consume a day or two per week for a serious corporate effort, not counting the time a team member spends back in his or her department, implementing and supervising specific 1to1 programs.

REQUIREMENTS FOR TEAM MEMBERS

1. *Make them senior enough* in the organization to "make it happen," yet not so senior that other priorities can keep them away from the regular meetings or from enthusiastic involvement in the process.

2. *Use known stars wherever possible:* Send signals throughout the enterprise that this effort isn't just another one of those here-today, gone-tomorrow undertakings. Ask the sponsoring execs to hand-pick their best and brightest for the task.

3. *Be sure they have the time* to participate enthusiastically. This involves meeting time, for sure, but also considerable time demands for the assessment, implementation, and oversight processes about to happen in the executive's home division.

4. *Require a base level of 1to1 expertise:* At a minimum, *Enterprise One to One* and *The One to One Fieldbook* should be required reading.

5. *Look for computer savvy, creativity, and enthusiasm for customer service issues:* Your team will be devoted to differentiated, individualized customer treatment in a wide range of forms. New technologies will be important, and new definitions of customer service and satisfaction are likely to be explored. Folks with enthusiasm in these areas will fare best.

WHO SHOULD BE INVOLVED

Every department that touches customers should be represented in some way on the team. We suggest ten to fifteen active team members for best results, drawn from as many of these departments as appropriate.

Primary	Secondary
Marketing	Manufacturing
Sales	Finance
Service (e.g., repair, aftermarket)	Advertising
Customer service (call center)	Market research
Customer information or database	Product planning

Information technology

Interactive services (Web site)

Channel management

THE FIRST TEAM MEETING

All required reading should be completed by the first meeting. Team members should bring the activities for each chapter of the *Fieldbook* with Chapters One and Two completed. Ask team members to identify two sets of activities from their own areas of expertise and to come to the meeting prepared to discuss them:

- Programs that seem to be 1to1 that are under way at present
- One-to-one programs that have been contemplated or discussed, but are not under way at present

Your team leader should prepare an overview of 1to1 strategies and their application at the enterprise. Either the team leader or (even better) the sponsoring senior corporate executive should make this presentation as a kickoff event, followed by discussion of the need to apply 1to1 strategies throughout the enterprise.

An agenda for the first team meeting might be as follows:

I. Introduction of team members, including their disciplines and roles

II. Process rules (meeting schedules, attendance, minutes, location)

III. Kickoff presentation of 1to1 principles

IV. Discussion and evaluation of each department's current and contemplated 1to1 initiatives

V. Determining how, and when, the group will outline a short-term and long-term plan

Bring lots of doughnuts. This agenda covers a great deal of ground.

You and your team will need to write a long-term-vision statement that neatly encapsulates the objective (to become a 1to1 enterprise) and briefly explains why it's imperative to make this effort. The vision statement should include a concise description of the ideal culture and organization that will evolve over the course of your implementation. The statement should be short and to the point. When it's finalized, post copies on every bulletin board in the company. Post it on your corporate intranet site. E-mail it to every employee. Send a voice mail from the CEO to every employee. Let them know the revolution has begun!

You also need to take swift action on a series of short-term goals. As early as possible, your team should begin developing a list of immediate achievables, activities that can be launched and followed through with a minimum investment of time and resource. Here are the general guidelines:

1. *Keep it simple.* Don't involve too many people, changes, or departments. The goal of any Quick Start program is fast, measurable success, and the easier it arrives, the better.
2. *Don't overload any single department.* Your information technology people often get socked with long to-do lists, since many 1to1 programs involve them. Strike a balance across as many departments as possible. Make sure every department is involved in at least a few initiatives.
3. *Make the programs measurable* so the early results can be quantified and reported, in order to build enthusiasm for additional 1to1 activity going forward.

Look for quick visibility among customers and staff alike. Try to build satisfaction with the general direction of this new, customer-centered strategy for your firm.

If you're searching for ideas, go back carefully through Chapter Two, "Quick Start." Put your team through the Quick Start brainstorming exercise outlined in Activity 2B. You should also assign someone to compile a list of 1to1 tactics employed by your company's peers and competitors. Not only will this list be useful to you, it might serve as a wake-up call to the fence-sitters and naysayers.

Remember, this is the phase when you want to hit the ground running. Think of your short-term plan as a kick start that gets the engine going and sets the larger processes in motion.

Step 4. Define a Strategy for MVCs and MGCs

Okay, you've rolled out the plan internally and your people are starting to climb aboard. Now it's time to concentrate on the most important audience—your customers. Here are the two customer types that should receive the lion's share of your attention:

Most Valuable Customers (MVCs): the people who generally give the enterprise most of their business already. You want to retain their business, reward them for their loyalty, and make certain they receive the highest level of service. Train your people to recognize them, understand their value to the company, and anticipate their needs.

Most Growable Customers (MGCs): the people most likely to become MVCs. Recognizing good customers and evolving them into great customers is the Holy Grail of 1to1. It's also a wonderful way to drive up profits dramatically. The trick here is learning to recognize your MGCs. Unlike MVCs, who are relatively easy to spot and track, MGCs can lurk in any corner of your customer database. They might be loyal customers of a subsidiary or a far-flung office that's slipped beneath your radar. They might be single-product customers or even lapsed customers. Train your people to search for them as intensely as equities analysts search for undervalued stocks.

A word to the wise: Defining these two customer types in your own terms (and in as few words as possible) is mission-critical. All those in your company who interface with customers will need the skills and understanding to recognize an MVC or an MGC as soon as they see one. And they'll need to know what to do next, too. There's no reason a bank teller shouldn't ask a checking account customer with a large balance if she has an IRA, for instance.

Aligning 1to1 programs and tactics with customer types is what the 1to1 implementation process is all about. The more focused you make your customer-type definitions, the easier it will be to align specific programs around the customer's exhibited and anticipated behavior.

Disseminating the key customer-type definitions is essential in operating environments as well. Airline staffs are instructed to favor the carrier's most frequent fliers, just as hotel staffs kowtow to senior, out-of-town executives from the companies headquartered nearby.

Try to create a set of customer definitions that are short and objective. To the extent possible, your customer definitions should be both quantitative and actionable. By these criteria, MGCs are the hardest customer types to define, and they are often the hardest for front-line people to recognize. But here are two examples of how different firms might define their MGCs:

Airline: MGC
- Flies more than twenty business trips a year
- At least ten trips per year on our airline
- Purchased at least 50 percent of tickets undiscounted
- Participant in our own frequent flier program
- Elite-level participant in a competitive frequent flier program

Manufacturer: MGC
- Buys more than $30,000 of product per year
- Buys at least six different products
- Buyer is a director or higher at the company
- Enterprise is one of three or more suppliers in category
- Credit rating of B+ or above

Step 5. Define a Strategy for BZs

Compared to traditional marketing, 1to1 techniques tend to require greater labor and place heavier loads on information systems. Unlike traditional models, however, 1to1 is designed to increase each customer's value, not necessarily product market share. So for most companies it is inherently a better driver of profit. But the piper must be paid. If you plan to devote more resources to your MVCs and MGCs, you'll have to obtain those resources somewhere.

The best short-term way to fund a 1to1 program is to shift resources away from serving customers who don't return a profit and have little or no hope of ever returning a profit—your BZs, or "Below Zero" customers.

So it is extremely important not only to identify your BZ customers early on but also to identify the services and benefits that go to BZs. Once you've identified these services, you can eliminate some altogether to reduce cost, or you can charge a fee for some to generate revenue. Not only will this free up financial and human resources, it will send a clear message internally that leadership is not expecting the increased attention paid to MVCs and MGCs to come from additional hours worked by the staff.

Caution: Before reducing service to one business unit's BZs it is vital to ensure that the same customer is not an MVC or MGC for some other unit.

When defining an MVC or MGC, you can comfortably rely on a single business unit's criteria—specifying widely different customer types in different units, where that's applicable. Later in the process, when it comes time to begin aggregating your single-customer data across business units to roll your efforts up to a more enterprise-oriented view, your initiatives with respect to MVCs and MGCs will change considerably, but naturally. You may discover additional, enterprise-wide high-value customers, but you won't have foreclosed any options with respect to each individual unit's customers.

However, this process is *not* the best way to handle BZs. Your business units can identify their own BZs, but *before reducing any services or taking any action at all with respect to a particular BZ,* be sure to ascertain that the customer in question is not on some other unit's VIP list.

Once you've cleared this hurdle, there are several distinct approaches to reducing the energy and resources a company devotes to its BZs:

Reduced service: Provide fewer options, less choice, slower methods of shipping.

Alternative service: Use "virtual" representatives for sales, customer service, or support. Divert inbound calls from BZs to the voice response unit through the creative use of ANI, or automatic number identification.

Charge for services: Charge for services that were once free. This helps make the customer more profitable, at least for the short term. *Reduce communication:* Decrease the frequency of catalogue mailings and other direct mail offers, or perhaps eliminate them entirely. Encourage BZ customers to migrate quickly toward electronic channels. Seek opportunities to bill customers less frequently, eliminate billing inserts, or identify other cost-saving avenues.

Defining and disseminating the attributes of the BZ customer type often proves challenging. The process often runs cross-grain to current corporate culture, particularly at very large firms, which might operate on the unspoken belief that all customers should be treated equally, regardless of size, potential, or any other metrics. The issue is likely to provoke strong debate early in the planning process. Look at this debate as a discussion that is not only healthy but also provides an excellent forum to review the reasons behind your company's decision to become a 1to1 enterprise. Use it to educate your people with respect to the fundamental differences between 1to1 and traditional systems. Let's be honest: If you treat all your customers equally, how can you treat each one differently?

By this point, you and your team will have developed a list of possible 1to1 initiatives. Review them carefully and decide which ones should be launched first. As you are evaluating each initiative, apply these questions:

Step 6. Evaluate and Prioritize Specific Projects

> A. *If we do this, will our customers notice?*
> B. *Can we implement this program with relative ease?*
> C. *Will the program, if successful, improve customer retention, stimulate customer growth, or increase profit in some other way?*

Assign a ranking of one, two, or three to each question for each program, with three indicating "absolutely" and one pointing toward "highly unlikely."

Now add them up! Nines and eights indicate the best, most logical starting points. Lower scores belong in subsequent quarters or years, varying with the group's enthusiasm. Don't overengineer this process, since each idea you relegate to a future period will be reevaluated and compared against newer ideas that emerge as you move on down the road. And by all means, continue to encourage people to come up with new ideas.

Step 7. Begin Implementing

You've made your choices, now it's time to start launching the rockets.

First you'll need to assign someone to be responsible for managing each initiative—someone who can be held accountable for the program's planning, launch, and operation. Set firm deadlines with enough lead time so that nobody is pushed to the wall. Encourage weekly progress reports to make sure no one falls too far behind.

Next it's essential to track the progress of each initiative as carefully and as thoroughly as possible. Remember, you picked these initiatives largely on the basis of their likelihood to succeed, so don't pass up an opportunity to bolster your success stories with plausible (and, we hope, impressive) metrics. In this type of process, anecdotes are good, but numbers are better.

Therefore it's important, early on, to create the right metric of success for each program, based on 1to1 principles. You could measure the customer service department, for example, on customer satisfaction scores among MVCs and MGCs, perhaps, rather than simply measuring satisfaction across the board. You could recognize inside salespeople for increased contact frequency with MGCs, or perhaps for incremental SKUs purchased by that group. You could count the number of MVCs identified for the first time. You could calculate the cost savings from reduced BZ services, or the profit gained by serving fewer BZs overall. Or you could simply tally the increased percentage of accurate and updated customer records in your database.

Ideally the measures should be as individualized as possible. Global metrics, such as "percentage of calls answered by the third ring" or "number of customer visits per quarter," can be useful, but don't allow them to get in the way of the very critical customer differentiation elements of your plan. And unless a particular 1to1 project is specifically aimed at some global increase in the level of customer service, such a metric won't be very helpful.

Break your objectives into two components: an operational view and a customer view. Measures of things such as satisfaction, interaction, and cross-selling are inherently customer-focused. But operational measures still can have a powerful impact on customer value, even if only indirectly. "All service inquiries handled the same day" or "MVCs recognized personally and offered special service on each visit" are operational metrics by nature, yet relatively easy to measure and, ultimately, certain to deliver impact.

Be careful not to overmeasure. Where the entire benefit of a program can be measured in a single, unarguable statistic, use it. If "increasing the number of MVC orders per year by 25 percent or more" is the goal, then great.

Avoid warm and fuzzy goals, but set targets that can be met without superhuman effort, too. You'll need to build enthusiasm and momentum for the 1to1 migration, and the best way to do this is to show a continuing stream of individual, quantified program successes.

One-to-one marketing is new and uncharted territory for most businesses, and you are essentially a frontier explorer. You want to send postcards back to your friends, let them know what it looks like. You want to draw a map for those who will follow in your footsteps. Don't make the people who come after you relearn what you are learning. Don't make them vulnerable to the same mistakes and wrong turns.

So start spreading news about your successes by posting your numbers (and anecdotes) on a dedicated page of your company intranet site. Or create a newsletter to publicize and reinforce your efforts. At the very least, you should send regular updates via e-mail to all management employees. As more and more people get involved in the overall process, you'll start getting more valuable feedback, more useful ideas, and greater acceptance. You might even consider creating contests and awards to stimulate more company-wide involvement.

Step 8. Share the Learning

Step 9. Analyze and Document Issues Affecting the Broader Enterprise

As your enterprise gains experience in a variety of limited areas, the projects will begin broadening of their own accord. The people in Division A who implement a program designed to maximize their relationships with certain MVCs will soon want to influence how Division B treats those same MVCs. The sales reps who make better contacts with and collect more useful dialogue information from the company's MGCs will soon want to see the production folks do something with this information to tailor the firm's products for some of these MGCs.

It's been our experience that implementing even a relatively limited 1to1 project has a natural tendency to motivate a company to take a more integrated, enterprise-wide view of its customers. String a few of these projects together and pretty soon you're going to have a real series of enterprise issues to deal with. People in different functions and from different business units will be working together more frequently on an ad hoc basis. Managers on one project will be trying to relate their metrics to the outcome of other projects.

As you begin to take a more naturally integrated view of the enterprise, organizational questions will begin to come up, so you're going to have to be ready for them. Some examples of issues that will come up soon:

- If you measure a customer's value across more than one division, is someone going to be placed in charge of that customer's relationship, and if so, how is it going to be structured?
- Should the enterprise set up or modify its key account-selling system?
- Should the enterprise underwrite a more comprehensive information system, standardizing customer data across every division?
- Should the firm be thinking about a data mart or a data warehouse?
- Should the sales force be better automated, and if so, then who should set the strategy for how sales reps interact with particular customers?

- Are different sales forces for different divisions as important now as they were before?
- Is it possible for the various Web sites and call centers operated by the company to work together better?
- Should the company package more services with the products it sells, and if so, how should those services be delivered?
- Should the firm seriously explore investing in mass-customization manufacturing facilities?

To deal with issues like these, you need to begin encouraging a more integrative, working-together attitude. So concentrate some effort now on programs that will facilitate the process. Create a multidepartment committee to agree on a standard way to report customer information, for instance. Agree on a cross-divisional standard format for customer service calls. Come up with a weighted measure to rank enterprise customers by their overall value, across more than one division.

Now is the right time to escalate the discussion of 1to1 at the corporate level, too. Be sure your senior-level corporate sponsors know what's happening and remain prepared to deal with these issues.

With every new enterprise-wide initiative or standard, you have another chance to ratchet up your effort. So use the issues of enterprise metrics to go back now and redefine your MVCs and MGCs. Define them this time not just with respect to a particular business unit or function, but with respect to a broader, more integrated group of business units within your enterprise. Or look at the value of your individual customers for the enterprise as a whole, if you're ready.

Use the broadest possible definitions of MVC and MGC to prioritize your enterprise-wide, 1to1 marketing initiatives. For cross-divisional programs the project budgets won't be as easy to generate, but in the same way that you defined cross-divisional MVCs you can probably identify cross-divisional BZs as well.

"Difficulty at the beginning," said the philosophers of ancient China. That observation is as true today as it was three thousand years ago. The

Step 10. Go Back to Step 4 and Begin Again

Setting Out on the Journey

initial stages of your 1to1 journey are quite likely to prove the most arduous, precisely because that's when you'll encounter the strongest opposition. The primal thinkers likened such difficulty to the struggles of a newly sprouted blade of grass pushing its way upward through the earth and out into the sunlight.

You are free to devise your own analogies as you proceed, but remember this: What you've set out to accomplish is nothing short of a revolution. You have embarked on a mission to change the culture and organization of your company. So don't be surprised, hurt, or demoralized when you get some push-back. It's an inevitable part of the process. If the blade of grass can succeed, so can you.

Every revolution needs a good team of chroniclers. Take responsibility for chronicling your company's progress and for sharing what you've learned with your peers and colleagues. Write the history of your revolution as it gathers speed and wins followers. When the smoke clears, you'll have plenty of material for internal and external use. You might even have enough material for a book of your own.

By now you've probably noticed that we have squeezed as much information into this *Fieldbook* as humanly possible while still making it readable. There's still more information on the Web site, along with updates culled from events that transpired after the *Fieldbook* went to press. You can become part of that ongoing update process by sharing your experiences with us via e-mail. As you chronicle your own firm's progress, let other pioneers in on it. Tell us about your problems, the solutions you devised, and the unexpected speed bumps you encountered along the way.

Our final, step-by-step advice:

Step 1: Reread this book.
Step 2: Print out the checklists from our Web site.
Step 3: Get moving.

We may be out of space, but now you're out of excuses.

Recommended Reads	Bayers, Chip. "The Promise of One to One (A Love Story)," *Wired*, May 1998, pp. 130–187.

The author catalogues some of the hurdles faced by companies that are struggling to develop a 1to1 marketing strategy. While the piece does not undermine the case for building a 1to1 enterprise, it does give practitioners some ideas of the challenges they will face.

Fournier, Susan, Susan Dobscha, and David Glen Mick. "Preventing the Premature Death of Relationship Marketing," *Harvard Business Review,* January/February 1998, pp. 42–51.
The article is interesting primarily for its discussion of the anxieties and concerns that now run through the minds of consumers as they are barraged with marketing messages and requests for information. But we don't agree with the premise that relationship marketing efforts are generally failing. We think the examples the authors cite are symptomatic of "faux relationship marketing," which does not coincide with the principles of 1to1 marketing.

Activity 15A

Making the Transition to a 1to1 Enterprise: The Project Plan

Target Completion Date: _____

1. Who is the primary project planner? (Note: This person will oversee the completion of tasks by each team member and will keep the group up to date on progress.)

Name and Title: _____

2. Where will you get your resources for this project?

_____

_____

_____

_____

3. List all of the team members who will be responsible for accomplishing the tasks listed throughout this *Fieldbook*. You will want to consider having the team include three to fifteen people total, from

some or all of the following areas: marketing, sales, customer service, finance, production, delivery and logistics, product management, and information systems.

	Name	Initials	Department
1.			
2.			
3.			
4.			
5.			
6.			
7.			
8.			
9.			
10.			
11.			
12.			
13.			
14.			
15.			

Activity 15B

Step-by-Step Project Plan

Use this step-by-step project plan to keep a record of who is responsible for making sure that each task is completed and deadlines are met. We've set up a two-stage completion process, because we know from our own experience that task lists look less daunting when you can mark areas where you have made considerable progress, but can't quite check the "100% done" box.

Target Completion Date: _____

Who Will Do It? (init.)	By When? (date)	DESIGN TASKS	75% Done (✓)	100% Done (✓)
		Step 1: Get senior management to buy in		
		Provide reading material		
		Conduct an "orientation workshop" in 1to1		
		Prepare a first-principles business case for 1to1		
		Have a face-to-face meeting		
		Step 2: Establish your team		
		Define requirements for team members		
		Complete Activity 15A		
		Identify candidates		
		Get departmental approvals		
		Organize the first team meeting		
		Step 3: Develop long-term vision and short-term goals		
		Craft a 1to1 vision statement		
		Get approval for the vision statement		

Circulate and publicize the vision

Collect information on all short-term projects
now being planned

Conduct Activity 2B, "Quick Start
Brainstorming Session"

Compile a list of 1to1 tactics employed by
your firm's peers and competitors

Step 4: Define a strategy for MVCs and MGCs

Define these customer types, using different
definitions for different business units in your
enterprise, if necessary

Create understandable profiles for these
customers, suitable for front-line service
personnel

Refine your definitions again, to ensure that
they are concise and objective

Step 5: Define a strategy for BZs

Define this customer type, using different
definitions for different business units in your
enterprise, if necessary

Screen each business unit's list of BZs against
every other business unit's MVC and MGC
list, and eliminate duplicates from the BZ list

Consider reducing services for BZs

- Reduce options

- Remove choices

- Ship products less expensively

- Other——

Consider providing alternative, less expensive
services for BZs

- "Virtual" reps for sales or support

- Divert inbound calls to VRU

- Other——

Consider charging for services

- Transaction fees

- Subscription fees

- Service or maintenance agreements

Consider reducing your communications costs

- Reduce catalogue mailings

- Switch customer to e-channels

Prepare a cultural-education program to
acquaint the enterprise with the merits of this
policy

Prepare a plan to handle negative PR issues,
if they arise

Step 6: Evaluate and prioritize
specific projects

Rank your projects in terms of:

- Will your customers notice?

- Can you implement?

- Will it contribute to profit?

Create a roll-out plan for implementing all
appropriate projects

Step 7: Begin implementing

Assign a project manager for each program

Choose appropriate metrics to gauge each program's success

Set customer-specific metrics for each program

Set operational metrics for each program

Step 8: Share the learning

Create an intranet site to capture results

Disseminate anecdotes and success stories to managers and employees. Consider:

- A multidivisional 1to1 newsletter

- E-mail bulletins

- Bulletin boards

- Other——

Step 9: Analyze and document issues affecting the broader enterprise

Compare initiatives taking place in business units with overlapping customer bases, and look for common customer types or policies

Take note of jurisdiction issues, such as who owns the dialogue with a particular customer, or who manages the interactions at a Web site serving more than one unit

Continue to educate the enterprise with respect to the integrative nature of 1to1

Raise the appropriate infrastructure questions with your senior corporate sponsors, such as:

- Modify the sales system?

- Obtain a data mart or data warehouse?

- Integrate various corporate Web sites into one?

- Other issues——

Step 10: Go back to Step 4 and begin again

Redefine your MVCs and MGCs, this time with a more integrative, enterprise-wide perspective

Get the financial folks involved to construct better, more enterprise-wide funding mechanisms for cross-divisional 1to1 programs

Appendix

The One-to-One Nonprofit

HOW TO STRENGTHEN RELATIONSHIPS
WITH MEMBERS, DONORS, STUDENTS,
PATIENTS, AND CITIZENS

Many not-for-profit organizations recognize right away that the principles and strategies of the one-to-one enterprise apply to them too. Every organization, no matter its orientation and objective, can benefit from identifying and differentiating its "customers," learning more about them through ongoing interactivity, and building strong, individualized Learning Relationships with them.

In the not-for-profit universe there are all sorts of organizations, including foundations and associations, colleges and universities, health care institutions, and government agencies. Each has its own particular constituencies. Each has special opportunities to individualize its offerings. And while such organizations are not focused on generating profit, they do face tough competition. Therefore, 1to1 approaches are as critical to their long-term success as they are to firms in for-profit businesses.

Consider professional associations. If you want to enhance your relationships with members, you will need to become increasingly relevant to them. You need to identify which ones are the most likely to make a valuable donation or to purchase your products and services. You then can focus on offering special treatment to them. How about individualized e-mail updates that address their particular concerns? How about providing a matching service that will link members who share a mutual interest? How about personal invitations to special events? Members who participate the most and who help recruit new members can be considered the most valuable. You can win their loyalty by learning their needs and then helping them grow professionally and personally.

For charities and other goodwill organizations, the "customers" are (1) those who use your services, (2) volunteers (who contribute time), (3) donors (who contribute money). With hundreds of worthy causes vying for attention, the successful organization will learn what is appreciated by each of its constituencies and appeal to the needs of individual constituents. In addition, understanding what types of interactivity work best for each constituent is critical.

Aware that many of its donors were frustrated by its frequent mailings, Botton Village—a Florida residential and employment community for the handicapped—simply *asked* its donors how often it should contact them. Most donors opted for the once-a-year fundraising campaign. As a result, Botton Village saved itself a tidy sum in printing and mailing costs that year and the following holiday season, and it still achieved a higher response rate and higher average donations than ever before.

Or consider health care. This is one industry that certainly could benefit from some 1to1 thinking. In recent years, the business often has been focused on cost-cutting—a goal that it has accomplished through standardization.

Gary Adamson, president of Medimetrix/Unison Marketing in Denver, says the goal of a health care provider should be to create a perpetual, interactive relationship with the customer-patient—one that does not simply revolve around events that occur between admission and discharge. He points out that *the real power of health care integration lies in creating the ability to do things differently for each customer—not the ability to do more of the same for all customers.* One of his clients, Community Hospitals in Indianapolis, is implementing a 1to1 initiative, which it calls "Patient-Focused Medicine," concentrating on four constituent groups: patients, physicians, employees, and payers.

What Community has discovered is that most medical practitioners literally customize the "care *for* you" part of their treatment by individually diagnosing and treating medical disorders. But Community also intends to individualize the "care *about* you" component—the part that makes most patients feel like a member of a herd. Recognizing that random acts of kindness by a dedicated nursing staff are great but still not the same as customization, Community's challenge is to treat different customers differently, in a cost-efficient and well-planned manner.

Even governments could benefit from 1to1 approaches. While there will be notable restrictions on the ability of government agencies to operate in a 1to1 fashion (due to concerns about privacy, discrimination, and corruption), there are many important benefits that can come from looking at things from the citizen's (as opposed to just the government's) perspective. One of the key objectives is finding ways to spend the taxpayer's money more effectively, productively, and even fairly.

Take a city like Toledo or Phoenix, for instance. What if every citizen who wanted one was assigned an identification number and a City-Card—something that would permit easy identification, facilitate record-keeping, and support transactions.

Here's the concept: Every time a citizen uses a city-operated service—such as a bus, a park, a library, or perhaps an after-school program—he or she is identified and the interaction is tracked. As the government learned who is using which services, and in what quantities, it would be able to make better decisions with respect to resource allocation. It could inform individual citizens about activities that may be of particular interest. That benefits everyone. It enables the government to correctly identify and promote services that are in demand, while reducing the waste associated with trying to tell everyone everything, all the time.

Of course, privacy will have to be protected too, and governments are not at the top of everyone's list when it comes to thinking through this very important issue. As just one example, there is growing concern about how the New York State government will use the information it gathers from its EZ-PASS system, which permits faster movement through auto tolls but also enables database tracking of an individual's whereabouts. While the transit authority maintains that the information will be protected, the fact is that its privacy policy is quite fluid.

On the other hand, EZ-PASS provides an excellent tool for the government to use individual information to improve itself and the efficiency of its services. If you are a frequent NYC bridge traveler, the system already customizes its service to your prepaid usage needs, charging your credit card in amounts automatically calculated to cover your needs. Of course, governments must take steps to ensure that citizens are comfortable with their handling of individual information if such promising initiatives are to succeed.

Clearly, adopting 1to1 approaches in the not-for-profit sector would be beneficial. Everyone wants to be treated as an individual—and loyalty and participation are directly connected to an organization's ability to provide such treatment.

Recommended Reads

Hoben, John W. (editor). *1998 Guide to Health Care Resources on the Internet* (Faulkner & Gray, 1997).
This valuable book includes articles on the business trends and technologies that promise to shape the health care business in the coming years. It also includes links to and reviews of top Web sites in the health care field. Among the articles in the book is one by Don, Martha, and Gary Adamson entitled "The One to One Future of Health Care Systems."

Maxwell, Margaret (editor). *Marketing the Non-Profit: The Challenge of Fundraising in a Consumer Culture* (Jossey-Bass Publishers, 1997).
This book includes an array of excellent essays examining how organizations should apply new marketing principles and techniques to the nonprofit sector. It includes a Peppers and Rogers essay called "The One-to-One Future of Fundraising."

Moore, Gwendolyn, John Rollins, and David Rey. *Prescription for the Future* (Knowledge Exchange, 1996).
The authors, all from Andersen Consulting, provide a powerful vision of how

new technologies will transform medicine in the coming years, suggesting that the quality of care can increase even as costs drop.

Sagalyn, Raphael. *The Great American Web Book: A Citizen's Guide to the Treasures of the U.S. Government on the World Wide Web* (Random House, 1996).
This is an excellent resource for individuals seeking out governmental organizations and information on the Web. Sagalyn offers an easy-to-use guide that summarizes the types of information that are available and provides links to the sites.

End Notes

Chapter 1

Page 2: This discussion about "Who Is the Customer?" reminds us of a classic quotation by Peter Drucker that reads: "Business has only two basic functions—marketing and innovation. Everything else is just cost." (Drucker, Peter F., *The Practice of Management; A Study of the Most Important Function in American Society,* Harper & Row, 1993 revised edition.)

Page 3: The discussion about "Learning, Loyalty, and Profitability" was introduced in an article Don and Martha wrote in *Harvard Business Review* with Joe Pine called "Do You Want to Keep Your Customers Forever?" (*Harvard Business Review,* March/April 1995, pp. 103–14). See also Gilmore, James H., and B. Joseph Pine II, "The Four Faces of Mass Customization," *Harvard Business Review,* January/February, 1997, pp. 91–101.

Page 5: Stan Davis coined the term "mass customize." See Davis, Stan, and Bill Davidson, *2020 Vision: Transform Your Business Today to Succeed in Tomorrow's Economy* (New York: Simon & Schuster, 1991) and Davis, Stan, *Future Perfect* (New York: Addison-Wesley Publishing Company, Inc., 1996).

Page 6: We learned about Hewlett-Packard's 100 separate 1to1 initiatives in a series of meetings with Lane Michel, Relationship Initiative Manager, and Andy Danver, Senior Consultant at Hewlett-Packard, during the spring of 1998. Lane also said that Hewlett-Packard president Lew Platt has used the term "Hoshin Plan," short for the Japanese hoshin kanri process, for MBO-like planning that has apparently been in place at Hewlett-Packard for many years. Lane added that Lew Platt articulates his breakthrough objectives, which are equivalent to hoshin objectives, in terms of "Creating Customer Intensity Everywhere in HP" (Lew Platt, January 1998). Peppers and Rogers Group has consulted for Owens Corning.

Chapter 3

Pages 25–26: Owens Corning has been working on building one-to-one relationships with customers since March 1996. We spoke with Steve Smoot, director of customer-information services, by phone on March 19, 1998. He confirmed details about the challenges Owens Corning faces for us by fax on April 16, 1998.

Page 29: Peppers and Rogers Group partner Bruce Kasanoff reported that Mitchells uses an IBM AS/400 computer database to track its customers in a story he wrote in *INSIDE 1to1* on March 6, 1997. (http://www.1to1.com/articles/i1-3-6-97.html#a3). The information was confirmed by Jack Mitchell, owner of Mitchells of Westport, by phone on March 30, 1998.

Page 29: We spoke with Chris Zane, owner of Zane's Cycles, for a story that appeared in *INSIDE 1to1* on April 9, 1998. In addition, we referenced articles from *Nation's Business* (Barrier, Michael, "Ties That Bind," *Nation's Business,* August 1997, pp. 12–18) and *Inc.* Magazine (Fenn, Donna, "Leader of the Pack," *Inc.* Magazine, February 1996, pp. 30–38).

Page 30: The numbers used to describe Groupe Casino's frequency marketing programs were confirmed by Guillaume Pellet, SDW (scalable data warehouse) sales specialist at NCR France, on April 6, 1998.

Page 32: Daniel Nissan is president of New York City-based NetGrocer, which was founded in 1997. Peapod is based in Skokie, Illinois, and was founded in 1989 by brothers Andrew and Thomas Parkinson. Streamline, a

Westwood, Massachusetts-based company, was founded in 1995. Tim DeMello is president. Two of Peppers and Rogers Group's partners have made personal investments in Streamline, a privately held company.

Pages 33–35: We spoke with Patrick J. Kennedy, CEO of La Mansion del Rio, about Preferred Hotels and Resorts Worldwide and Guestnet on February 26, 1998. He confirmed the information about guest preference cards by fax on April 28, 1998. Guestnet is a privately held company with multiple shareholders based in San Antonio, Texas. Don Peppers serves on its board of directors.

Page 37: We spoke with Dave Ropes, director of corporate advertising and integrated marketing, on March 16, 1998, about the consolidation of Ford Motor Company's overall customer-oriented marketing efforts. The information was verified by Sandra Nicholls, advertising coordinator, corporate advertising, Ford Motor Company, on May 4, 1998.

Page 38: We interviewed Bruce Hamilton of customer focused marketing at 3M and confirmed our discussion about 3M's databases by e-mail on June 25, 1998. Peppers and Rogers Group has consulted for 3M.

Pages 39–40: We first wrote about Mobil's Speedpass program in our weekly e-mail newsletter (Peppers, Don, and Martha Rogers, Ph.D., "Fill 'er up with Mobil Speedpass"). The information was confirmed by fax by Jeanne Mitchell, former senior public affairs advisor, Mobil, on May 15, 1998.

Page 40: We read about the Dutch PTT in an article that appeared in *AMS Connections,* a publication of the AMS Telecommunications Industry Group. The article was called "Electronic Commerce: Breaking Boundaries" and appeared in the winter/spring 1997 issue on pages 2–3. We subsequently wrote a couple of stories about Dutch PTT in *INSIDE 1to1* (Peppers, Don, "On the Money: Dutch PTT Plans a Nationwide Smart Card," *INSIDE 1to1,* January 23, 1997, http://www.1to1.com/articles/i1-1-23-97.html) and (Peppers, Don, "Dutch Redux: 1to1 Phone Bills for Businesses," *INSIDE 1to1,* February 6, 1997, http://www.1to1.com/articles/i1-2-6-97.html#a1). Ache Miedema of the Chipper Company, based in the Netherlands, added that it is developing additional uses for the (Chipper) kiosk.

Pages 41–42: Be on the lookout for a retinal scan device and fingerprint scanner, as well as 3-D Body Measurement. Martha Rogers saw these technologies demonstrated at a retail technology conference hosted by Dr. Raymond Burke of the Center for Education and Research in Retailing at Indiana University in Bloomington, Indiana, on May 29, 1998. The conference was called "Knowledge-Based Retailing: Using Technology to Tailor the Physical Store to the Needs of Individual Customers."

Pages 43–44: Our discussion about Hewlett-Packard's Test and Measurement Organization was confirmed by Lane Michel, Relationship Initiative Manager at Hewlett-Packard, by phone on June 24, 1998.

Page 45: We first wrote about Schwab in our weekly e-mail newsletter (Peppers, Don and Martha Rogers, Ph.D., "Schwab Builds Powerful Customer Relationships," *INSIDE 1to1*, March 26, 1998, http://www.1to1.com/ articles/i1-3-26-98.html#a1). We interviewed Mary Kelley, vice president, database and relationship marketing, at Schwab in March 1998 as well. She confirmed by e-mail on June 28, 1998 our discussion about Schwab using phone and online connections to do the majority of their business.

Chapter 4

Page 60: We wrote about FedEx in our electronic newsletter (Peppers, Don, "FedEx Focuses on Profitable Customers," *INSIDE 1to1*, November 20, 1997, http://www.1to1.com/articles/i1-11-20-97.html#a1). We learned about the details of the success of FedEx's customer value differentiation program from an article in *Fortune* magazine by Linda Grant: "Why FedEx Is Flying High," November 10, 1997, pp. 86–89, (http://pathfinder.com/ fortune/1997/971110/fed.html).

Page 60: Our discussion of Roden Electrical Supply tiering its customers by the most recent year's actual sales volume and third-party information to assess strategic value was confirmed by Mike Smith, vice president of operations at Roden Electrical Supply, by e-mail on June 25, 1998.

Pages 61–62: Beth Rounds, senior vice president at Custom Research Inc., confirmed our discussion about CRI's MVC treatment and Malcolm Baldrige National Quality Award by fax on April 6, 1998.

Page 61: We spoke with Steve Weingrod, senior development consultant at Great Lakes Communications, on March 31, 1998. He confirmed the material about Harry W. Schwartz Booksellers by e-mail on March 31, 1998. He can be reached at sweingro@gl-nbc.com.

Page 61: We spoke with Patrick J. Kennedy, CEO of La Mansion del Rio and president and chairman of Guest Information Network, Inc., about Boston's Charles Hotel and its Distinguished Guest Program in a phone interview on February 26, 1998. He confirmed the information by fax on April 28, 1998.

Page 67: Our discussion of the most visible influencers at Pitney Bowes was verified by Tom Shimko, former Vice President, Marketing, U.S. Mailing Systems, in our Stamford office on June 24, 1998. Tom is now a partner and senior consultant at Peppers and Rogers Group. Peppers and Rogers Group has consulted for Pitney Bowes.

Pages 69–70: Our discussion about customer differentiation at Hewlett-Packard and "HP-At-Home" was confirmed by Lane Michel, Relationship Initiative Manager at Hewlett-Packard, by phone on June 24, 1998.

Page 70: Sanjay Choudhuri, director of mass customization at Levi Strauss & Co., confirmed in June 1998 that Levi's manufactures 227 waist/hip combinations and 25 leg sizes in its Levi's® Original Spin™ program. Choudhuri said Levi's can therefore deliver one of more than 5,700 jeans options. In addition, each jeans combination can be made in one of six denim colors and can be made with either zip or button fly. Altogether, there are 68,000 possible combinations.

Page 72: Our discussion about 3M's differentiation by profile types was confirmed by Bruce Hamilton, in charge of customer focused marketing at 3M, by e-mail on June 25, 1998. We interviewed Bruce by phone in March 1998.

Page 72: We first wrote about Franklin University in our weekly newsletter (Rogers, Martha, "The University of Relationship Management," *INSIDE 1to1,* December 4, 1997, http://www.1to1.com/articles/i1-12-4-97.html). Linda Steele, vice president of students at Franklin University, confirmed our discussion about Franklin's student service associates by e-mail on April 2, 1998.

Pages 74–75: Our discussion about 3M's integrated solutions was confirmed by Bruce Hamilton, in charge of customer focused marketing at 3M, by e-mail on June 25, 1998. We interviewed Bruce by phone in March 1998.

Pages 79–80: Patrick J. Kennedy, chairman and president of Guestnet, spoke to us about Looking Glass, Inc., and Guestnet on February 26, 1998. He confirmed the information by fax on April 28, 1998.

Chapter 5

Page 95: The article cited in our discussion of overinteraction with customers appeared in the January/February 1998 issue of *Harvard Business Review* (Fournier, Susan, Susan Dobscha and David Glen Mick, "Preventing the Premature Death of Relationship Marketing," pp. 42–51). The article acknowledges the rise of relationship marketing, but equates RM with better targeted harassment, rather than the ability to use individual customer information to serve a customer better and thus to keep that customer longer and make him more valuable. We responded to the article in *INSIDE 1to1* (Peppers, Don, and Martha Rogers, Ph.D., "The Truth About Faux Relationship Marketing," *INSIDE 1to1*, January 15, 1998, http://www:1to1.com/articles/il-1-15-98.html#a1) and in a *Harvard Business Review* editorial (Peppers, Don, and Martha Rogers, Ph.D., "Letters to the Editor," *Harvard Business Review*, May–June, 1998).

Page 101: We spoke with Paola Benassi, product operations manager at TRUSTe, on June 30, 1998, at which time she confirmed the information for the sidebar. We also wrote about TRUSTe in our electronic newsletter ("TRUSTe—Branding Privacy on the Web," *INSIDE 1to1,* June 19, 1997, http://www.1to1.com/articles/il-6-19-97.html).

Page 102: Our discussion of Cisco Systems came in part from its Web site, http://www.cisco.com. In addition, we referenced two articles: Matson, Eric, "What's Online at Cisco," *Fast Company,* February/March 1997, pp. 34–36; and Peppers, Don, "Cisco's Customer Connection," *INSIDE 1to1,* March 5, 1998, http://www.1to1.com/articles/il-3-5-98.html#a1.

Page 103: We spoke with Steve Smoot, Owens Corning's director of customer-information services, by phone March 19, 1998. He confirmed details for us by fax on April 16, 1998.

Page 103: We first wrote about BuildNet, Inc., in our electronic newsletter (Rogers, Martha, "Building Houses in the Information Age: Construction That Works," *INSIDE 1to1,* July 24, 1997, http://www.1to1.com/articles/il-7-24-97.html#a3). Founded fifteen years ago as a support board for contractors software, BuildNet has become the largest provider of information to professionals in the building industry, with a Web site (http://www.buildnet.com/) in excess of 900,000 pages. BuildNet is also geared to help home improvement enthusiasts, and architects are guided toward the search engine, BuildNet AEC Construction.

Pages 103–104: We spoke with Dave Ropes, director of corporate advertising and integrated marketing, on March 16, 1998, about the consolidation of Ford Motor Company's overall customer-oriented marketing efforts. The information was verified by Sandra Nicholls, advertising coordinator, corporate advertising, Ford Motor Company, on May 4, 1998.

Pages 104–105: Peter Fisk at PA Consulting Group in the United Kingdom confirmed our discussion about First Direct's lemon program and AT&T's customer clusters by e-mail on June 26, 1998.

Page 105: We first wrote about Schwab in our weekly e-mail newsletter (Peppers, Don and Martha Rogers, Ph.D., "Schwab Builds Powerful Customer Relationships," *INSIDE 1to1,* March 26, 1998, http://www.1to1.com/articles/i1-3-26-98.html#a1). We interviewed Mary Kelley, vice president, database and relationship marketing, at Schwab in March 1998 as well. She confirmed our discussion about Schwab differentiating its customers based on their trading activity and investable assets on June 28, 1998.

Page 107: We first wrote about the Northwestern Medical Faculty Foundation (NMFF) in our weekly e-mail newsletter, when our editorial staff interviewed Greg Padovani, director of marketing at NMFF (Niehaus, Tom, "Let the Healing Begin," *INSIDE 1to1,* March 19, 1998, http://www.1to1.com/articles/i1-3-19-98.html). Greg Padovani confirmed our discussion about "Health Notes" by e-mail on June 28, 1998.

Pages 108–109: We first wrote about British Airways in our electronic newsletter (Peppers, Don, "Overheard Overhead: The Hazards of Identifying MVCs," *INSIDE 1to1,* January 30, 1997, http://www.1to1.com/articles/i1-1-30-97.html and "British Airways May Soon Have Everything You Want on Board Every Time," *INSIDE 1to1,* April 3, 1997, http://www.1to1.com/articles/i1-4-3-97.html). In addition, we confirmed facts with a British Airways executive by phone on April 17, 1998.

Page 110: We spoke with Steve Smoot, Owens Corning's director of customer-information services, by phone March 19, 1998. He confirmed details for us by fax on April 16, 1998.

Chapter 6

Page 126: Sanjay Choudhuri, director of mass customization at Levi Strauss & Co., confirmed the numbers for Levi's Original Spin program by phone on June 26, 1998.

Pages 131–132: Our discussion of GameTime Playground Company and its sophisticated computer-aided systems was confirmed by Kathryn Dawson, Advertising Manager at GameTime, by fax on April 27, 1998.

Pages 134–135: We first wrote about British Airways in our electronic newsletter (Peppers, Don, "Overheard Overhead: The Hazards of Identifying MVCs," *INSIDE 1to1,* January 30, 1997, http://www.1to1.com/articles/i1-1-30-97.html, and "British Airways May Soon Have Everything You Want on Board Every Time," *INSIDE 1to1,* April 3, 1997, http://www.1to1.com/articles/i1-4-3-97.html). In addition, we spoke with a British Airways executive by phone on April 17, 1998, who confirmed facts.

Page 135: Patrick Kennedy, CEO of La Mansion del Rio and chairman and president of Guestnet, told us about his goals for his client hotels in a phone interview on February 26, 1998. He confirmed the information by fax on April 28, 1998.

Pages 135–136: We first wrote about the Northwestern Medical Faculty Foundation (NMFF) in our weekly e-mail newsletter, *INSIDE 1to1,* when our editorial staff interviewed Greg Padovani, director of marketing at NMFF (Niehaus, Tom, "Let the Healing Begin," *INSIDE 1to1,* March 19, 1998, http://www.1to1.com/articles/i1-3-19-98.html). Greg Padovani confirmed that there are 50,000 versions of "Health Notes" by e-mail on June 28, 1998.

Pages 137–138: We spoke with Steve Smoot, Owens Corning's director of customer-information services, by phone March 19, 1998. He confirmed details for us by fax on April 16, 1998.

Page 138: Lane Michel, Relationship Initiative Manager at Hewlett-Packard, confirmed our discussion about divisional integration and HP's Test and Measurement Organization by phone on June 24, 1998.

Pages 139–141: Our discussion of the three types of product groupings (integrated solution products, needs-related products, and production-related products) will cover most situations. Technically, there is a fourth category as well—for totally unrelated products. For the most part, however, when these are produced by the same enterprise it is only because the enterprise itself is a large, loosely controlled conglomerate.

Page 141: Bruce Hamilton, in charge of customer focused marketing at 3M, spoke with us about the chairman's initiatives by phone in March 1998. He confirmed the information by e-mail on June 25, 1998.

Page 143: Our discussion about America's Big Three auto companies and the Automotive Network Exchange was drawn, in part, from the Automotive Network Exchange's Web site, http://www.aiag.org/anx/. In addition, we wrote a story about Web-based competition in our weekly electronic newsletter (Peppers, Don, "Web-Based Competition Threatens Business-to-Business Relationships," *INSIDE 1to1,* January 22, 1998, http://www.1to1.com/articles/i1-1-22-98.html#a2).

Page 144: Our discussion about Cisco's reseller partners came from Cisco's Web site, http://www.cisco.com. We also wrote about Cisco in our weekly electronic newsletter (Peppers, Don, "Cisco's Customer Connection," *INSIDE 1to1,* March 5, 1998, http://www.1to1.com/articles/i1-3-5-98.html#a1).

Pages 144–145: We wrote about Great Plains Software and its CORE program in our weekly electronic newsletter (Peppers, Don, "The Elements of an Effective Channel Strategy," *INSIDE 1to1,* September 25, 1997, http://www.1to1.com/articles/i1-9-25-97.html). Don Nelson, general manager of CORE, verified our discussion about CORE by fax on June 29, 1998.

Chapter 8

Pages 172–173: Our information about Oxford Health Plans came from several articles: Smith, Lee, "Can Oxford Heal Itself?" *Fortune,* December 29, 1997, pp. 238–240; Winslow, Ron, and Scot J. Paltrow, "A Regulator's Ultimatum," *The Wall Street Journal,* April 29, 1998, p. A1; Perman, Stacy, "Health: Code Blue at Oxford: A Computer Glitch and a Quarterly Loss Trigger Bloodletting at What Had Been the Healthiest HMO," *Time Magazine,* November 10, 1997, p. 82; Hammonds, Keith H., and Susan Jackson, "Behind Oxford's Billing Nightmare," *Business Week,* November 17, 1997, p. 98. Peppers and Rogers Group has consulted for Oxford Health Plans.

Page 173: Steve Wiggins of Oxford Health Plans has admitted in the press that the company's IT system grew faster than the firm's ability to manage it. But before the implosion of its data systems forced the devaluation of its stock, Oxford's adoption of 1to1 practices not only contributed to the company's unprecedented growth, but also influenced patient-friendly practices at other health care organizations around the country, and played a role in raising the bar for the way managed health care is delivered. Oxford pioneered customer management in the health care field, making one employee responsible for settling a customer's claims and solving that customer's problems without passing the customer off to someone else. Oxford called it the Dedicated Service Manager program. If you were an Oxford customer, your assigned DSM could track and remember your issues, and work individually with you to resolve your health and billing problems.

An eight-person interdisciplinary task force led by Oxford executive VP Bob Smoller worked full-time for nearly two years to effect a comprehensive reengineering of the HMO around its most valuable asset—its individual plan members. The team worked to torque up the technology while Oxford VP/director of customer relations Blythe Hamer shepherded the individualization of messages. Oxford developed the ability to identify and interact with individual plan members through any medium, including kiosks, the Web, and EDI. In addition, Oxford pioneered programs for individual members that sometimes allowed use of chiropractors and other alternative medical practices, and provided members with online and IVR doctor bios and credentials to aid in their selection. By revamping the measures of success for the call center, Oxford simultaneously reduced costs *and* improved customer satisfaction in call handling and complaint resolution.

Although Oxford ran into serious problems as a result of its explosive growth, that positive growth can be partly attributed to 1to1 marketing initiatives.

Pages 174–175: Bob Dorf learned that wire woven through the ceilings of airports would only move limited amounts of data at a reasonable speed at a conference at the International Management Centre in Saint-Paul-de-Vence, France, in 1995. The conference was titled "Cut Airline Costs *and* Increase Customer Loyalty: Customerize."

Page 182: Peppers and Rogers Group has no business affiliation with *GoldMine* Software Company.

Chapter 9

Pages 204–206: The facts in our discussion about Hewlett-Packard's integrated organization structure were confirmed by Lane Michel, Relationship Initiative Manager at Hewlett-Packard, in a meeting on April 7, 1998, at our Stamford, Connecticut, office. He confirmed the material by phone on June 24, 1998.

Page 207: We spoke with Iones Montepietra, procuratore (product manager) at Credito Emiliano, by phone on May 29, 1998. He confirmed the information about tiering and differentiating customers by fax on May 30, 1998.

Page 208: We spoke with Bruce Hamilton, in charge of customer focused marketing at 3M, by phone in March 1998. He confirmed his comments about customer focused employees at 3M by e-mail on June 25, 1998.

Chapter 10

Pages 229–230: We wrote about Great Plains Software and its CORE program in our weekly electronic newsletter (Peppers, Don, "The Elements of an Effective Channel Strategy," *INSIDE 1to1,* September 25, 1997, http://www.1to1.com/ articles/i1-9-25-97.html). Don Nelson, general manager of CORE, confirmed our discussion about CORE by fax on June 29, 1998.

Page 233: We spoke to Rick June, director of professional and pharmaceutical sales, North America, at Procter & Gamble Health Care on June 30, 1998, at which time he confirmed that Fayetteville, Arkansas, houses one of Procter & Gamble's largest field offices and that Wal-Mart is its top customer.

Page 233: We learned about Cisco's reseller-specific information for its channel partners on its Web site, http://www.cisco.com. We also wrote about Cisco in our weekly electronic newsletter (Peppers, Don, "Cisco's Customer Connection," *INSIDE 1to1,* March 5, 1998, http://www.1to1.com/articles/i1-3-5-98.html#a1).

Page 233: The information about BroadVision's channel partners is available on its Web site, http://www.broadvision.com. Peppers and Rogers Group has a significant ongoing business relationship with BroadVision.

Page 234: Edward Feitzinger and Hau L. Lee argued that a producer can postpone the final assembly of a product by modularizing the basic manufacturing process in an article they coauthored in the January/February 1997 issue of *Harvard Business Review* ("Mass Customization at Hewlett-Packard: The Power of Postponement").

Chapter 11

Pages 250–251: Peppers and Rogers Group partner Tom Shimko spoke to the managing director of a Netherlands-based distributor of office products. We think the "Left or Right" story provides distilled reasoning for automating the sales force.

Page 251: Bob Runge, vice president at Pivotal Software, contributed to our discussion about what automating and synchronizing a sales force entails by e-mail in June, 1998. Peppers and Rogers Group has a significant ongoing business relationship with Pivotal Software.

Page 252: Bob Metcalfe, inventor of Ethernet, founder of 3Com, and technology pundit for the International Data Group, confirmed our discussion on Metcalfe's Law by e-mail on June 30, 1998.

Page 255: See *Life's a Pitch, Then You Buy* (Currency/Doubleday, 1995) by Don Peppers, Chapter Ten, for a discussion of "make me rich" or "make me famous" personalities.

Page 257: We are indebted to suggestions from Guy Pressault, of Presso.com, for reminding us about the way door-to-door life insurance salespeople were paid commissions throughout the seventies.

Page 258: Ian Thompson, former manager of education and training at *Midrange Computing,* sent Don Peppers and Martha Rogers an e-mail in response to an *INSIDE 1to1* article about compensation and customer loyalty that ran in the February 12, 1998, issue. http:www.1to1.com/articles/il-2-12-98.html#al.

Pages 258–259: We received an e-mail message from Eric Cohen, VP and managing director at CACI, on February 12, 1998, that responded to an article on compensation and customer loyalty that ran in the February 12, 1998, issue of *INSIDE 1to1* (http://www.1to1.com/articles/i1-2-12-98.html#a1). He confirmed the information by fax on June 24, 1998.

Pages 259–260: Barry Wrighton of Vanguard Consulting Ltd in the United Kingdom sent us an e-mail in February 1998 in response to an article on compensation and customer loyalty that ran in the February 12, 1998, issue of *INSIDE 1to1* (http://www.1to1.com/articles/i1-2-12-98.html#a1). In his message, he told us the story about the U.K. motor finance company.

Pages 263–264: Don Peppers first learned about Astra Merck in a teleconference with Kim Jacobs, Ken Medan, Nancy McDonald, Bob Harrell, and Patrick Blair from Astra Merck, which took place on January 23, 1998. Astra Merck has since become part of Astra Pharmaceuticals LP. Bob Harrell, Astra's director of communications, confirmed the information on June 30, 1998.

Pages 264–265: We first wrote about Schwab in our weekly e-mail newsletter (Peppers, Don, and Martha Rogers, Ph.D., "Schwab Builds Powerful Customer Relationships," *INSIDE 1to1,* March 26, 1998, http://www.1to1.com/articles/i1-3-26-98.html#a1). Our editorial staff interviewed Mary Kelley, vice president, database and relationship marketing, at Schwab in March 1998, at which time she shared her thoughts about how customers like to interact with Schwab. She confirmed the information by e-mail in June 1998.

Pages 265–266: Rich Bulat, Hartford Insurance's marketing director for Major Commercial Lines, confirmed our discussion about Hartford Insurance on June 8, 1998.

Pages 268–269: Marilyn Keyes, Marketing Communications Manager for the harvest partners Preferred Customer Program at American Cyanamid, confirmed facts and helped us with the details in our discussion about American Cyanamid's sales force. We spoke with Marilyn by phone on July 1, 1998. Special thanks to Dave Euson at Carlson Marketing Group for his help coordinating discussions between American Cyanamid and our research team.

Pages 269–270: Mark Ryan, general manager of North American sales at IBM, confirmed our discussion on the IBM Gold service program by phone on June 30, 1998.

Chapter 12

Page 282: Peppers and Rogers Group has a significant ongoing business relationship with Chordiant Software.

Page 283: Peppers and Rogers Group has a significant ongoing business relationship with Sky Alland Marketing.

Page 287: We spoke with Lorrie Paul Crum in Wolfgang Schmitt's office, Chairman of the Board and CEO of Rubbermaid, on July 1, 1998. She confirmed that Rubbermaid includes its 800 number on all of its toy parts. Rubbermaid's Web site is http://www.rubbermaid.com. Peppers and Rogers Group has consulted for Rubbermaid.

Pages 288–289: We first wrote about GTE Teleservices in *INSIDE 1to1* (Dorf, Bob, "To Transform Data Into Information, Create a Summary," *INSIDE 1to1,* April 10, 1997, http://www.1to1.com/articles/i1-4-10-97.html). Rusty Carter at GTE confirmed the discussion about GTE's ChurnMaster program by e-mail on June 26, 1998.

Pages 290–291: Chris Jarnot, Director of Advertising at Vail Associates, Inc., confirmed our discussion by phone on June 25, 1998. Rob Perlman at Vail Associates, Inc., added in an e-mail he sent us July 2, 1998, that the company's call center staff can also sell callers air and ground transportation to the resort as well as ski school lessons and other activities individually or as packages. Perlman said additional revenues are generated through commissions on airline tickets and rental car bookings and increased business volumes for the ski school and other activity centers. Selling lift tickets and ski lessons over the phone also shortens lift ticket and ski school enrollment lines, saving the customer time and the company costs. Customers also save time if they haven't already made other vacation arrangements through a travel agent or directly with an airline or rental car company. Peppers and Rogers Group has consulted for Vail Associates, Inc.

Page 292: David Houston, marketing director of donor relations at American Cancer Society, confirmed our discussion of American Cancer Society's NCIC by phone on June 30, 1998. Peppers and Rogers Group has consulted for American Cancer Society.

Chapter 13

Page 308: VeriSign, Inc., is a leading provider of digital authentication services and products for electronic commerce and other forms of secure communications. It is based in Mountain View, California (http://www.verisign.com/about/about vs.html).

Page 309: The information about Excite collecting customer information came from the cover story of the May 1998 issue of *Wired* magazine (Bayers, Chip, "The Promise of One to One [A Love Story]," *Wired,* May 1998, pp. 130–87).

Page 312: Net Perceptions is a company based in Minneapolis, Minnesota, that provides advanced Recommendation Engine technology. Firefly provides products and services for relationship management and advanced personalization. It is based in Cambridge, Mass.

Page 312: We wrote about Moviefinder in our weekly electronic newsletter (Peppers, Don, "Moviefinder.com Provides Personalized Film Tips," *INSIDE 1to1,* October 16, 1997, http://www.1to1.com/articles/10-16-97.html#a1). The information can be found at the Moviefinder Web site at http://www.moviefinder.com.

Page 313: You can check out Barnes and Noble's collaborative filtering software at its Web site, http://www.barnesandnoble.com, and don't miss Amazon.com's Web site at http://www.amazon.com.

Page 313: David Anderson, a former professor, shared his thoughts with us about social filtering and the "cold-start" problem in an e-mail he sent to Don on November 3, 1997. Additional thanks to Pehong Chen at BroadVision.

Page 318: Deborah Long, director of marketing communications at SMART Technologies, Inc., reviewed our discussion about SMART eCustomer and SMART DNA by e-mail on June 30, 1998. SMART is a leading vendor of customer-driven Enterprise Relationship Management software. It was formed in 1995 and is based in Austin, Texas.

Page 318: Allen T. Cervi, regional manager at Vignette Corporation, confirmed our discussion about Vignette's Web site (http://www.vignette.com) by fax on June 29, 1998.

Chapter 14

Page 331: Our discussion about *Time* magazine's ability to target Buick ads for individuals was confirmed by Katie Kiyo, Detroit advertising manager for *Time,* by phone on June 29, 1998.

Pages 334–335: Information about "Advertising on the Web" came from a Forrester Research study on Web advertising (Maddox, Kate, "CMP Conference Explores Online Branding, *Advertising Age,* May 4, 1998, pp. 42–44). A

January study by Jupiter Communications was cited in the same article. See *Recommended Reads* at the end of Chapter Fourteen for related articles by Donna Hoffman.

Pages 336–337: Scott Randall, president of New York City-based Media Designs Interactive, confirmed that kiosk software needs to be designed from the customer up at a meeting in our Stamford, Connecticut, office on June 29, 1998.

Page 337: Josh Kaplan, president and CEO of Intouch Group, confirmed our discussion on Internet-based kiosk solutions for retailers, by fax on June 24, 1998. Don Peppers is on the board of directors for Intouch, a privately held company.

Appendix

Page 372: Medimetrix/Unison Marketing, a health care communications agency and consultancy, is based in Denver, Colorado. President Gary Adamson confirms that Medimetrix/Unison Marketing owns or manages over three hundred hospitals nationwide. Peppers and Rogers Group has consulted for Medimetrix/Unison Marketing.

Index

Groupe Casino (France), frequency
    marketing program, 30
GroupLens software, 212
Growth potential. *See* Most Growable
    Customers (MGCs); Strategic value
    (customer)
GTE Teleservices, 288–89, 389–90
Guest Information Network, Inc.
    (Guestnet), 34–35, 79–80, 135, 379

Halal, William E., 217
Hallberg, Garth, 81
Hamer, Blythe, 386
Hamilton, Bruce, 38, 72, 74, 141–42,
    208, 379, 381, 385, 387
Hammer, Michael, 217
Harrell, Bob, 389
Harry W. Schwartz Booksellers
    (Milwaukee, Wis.), 61
Hartford Insurance Company,
    individualized sales presentation,
    265–66
Harvard Business Review, 95
Heskett, James L., 81
Hessan, Diane, 157
Hewlett-Packard, 216
    cost-efficiency of Web site, 103
    customer information standards in, 38
    customization by, 138, 234–35
    differentiating customers, 70
    end user identification, 43–44
    gradual implementation strategy, 204–6
    "Hoshin Plan," 378
    privacy policy, 100
    success of, xxii, 6
    value of end users to, 3
Hiebeler, Robert, 217
Hiring strategies, 210–12
Hoben, John W., 374
Hoffman, Donna L., 10, 112, 339, 391
Hoshin kanri process, 378
Houston, David, 390
How to Win Friends and Influence People
    (Carnegie), 332
Hughes, Arthur Middleton, 185

IBM, 38
    Gold Service customization, 269–70
    Web site privacy policy, 101
Identifying customers (implementation
    step 1)
    advertising and, 330, 333–34

call centers and, 285–87, 300–1
channel members vs. end users, 2–3, 4,
    25–26, 35–36
in consumer marketing businesses, 3,
    26–38
database systems for, 25, 27–28, 33–35,
    36–39, 179–80, 190–91
defined, 4, 24–25
flexibility in, 45–46
handling key influencers, 67–68
in nonprofit organizations, 371–72
quick start self-assessment worksheet,
    159
quick start suggestions, 19
in sales departments, 42, 44–45,
    248–50, 278–79
specific identifiers for, 25, 38–42,
    48–49
through frequency marketing programs,
    28, 30–33, 39
on Web sites, 212, 304, 307–10,
    316–17, 325
worksheets, 19, 47–55
Implementation steps. *See* Customizing
    products/services (implementation
    step 4); Differentiating customers
    (implementation step 2; Identifying
    customers (implementation step 1);
    Interactions with customers
    (implementation step 3)
Indigo Restaurant (Atlanta, Ga.), 30
Individual needs
    defined, 62–63
    differentiating customers through, 72
    tracking on Web sites, 314
    See also Customer needs
Information technology (IT)
    collaborative filtering, 312–13, 391
    cookies, 307–8
    customer identification systems, 29, 31,
        32–33, 39–40, 379–80
    electronic data interchange (EDI),
        121–22, 130, 143
    e-mail, 121–22, 308–9, 359, 372
    enhancing customer interactions,
        102–4, 107–9, 269–70
    essential role of, 15, 184, 211
    extranets, 143, 269
    intranets, 269, 359
    matching engines, 311–14
    rate of change in, 170–72
    self-assessment worksheet on, 161–62

Most Valuable Customers (MVCs)
  customization for, 108–9, 128, 129,
    130, 134, 142
  defining, 59, 87–89, 249
  enhancing loyalty of, 29, 61
  gaining identifying information about,
    41
  priority of interactions with, 98, 202
  reducing client list to, 60
  strategies for, 29, 83, 206–7, 269–70,
    354–55, 356, 358, 361
Moviefinder, 312–13, 390–91
Multidivisional enterprises
  differentiating customers, 69–70,
    73–74, 83
  divisional integration in, 136–42,
    384–85
  functional integration in, 131–36, 141,
    207, 307
  identifying customers, 27–28, 36–38
  internal conflicts, 15–16, 110, 141–42,
    350
  separate or unified sales departments in,
    266–67
  transition teams guiding, 7–8, 359–61

NASA, 216
National Cancer Information Center
  (NCIC), 292
NCR, 144, 171, 378
Needs-related products, customization of,
  140, 384–85
Nelson, Don, 145, 385, 387
Net Grocer, grocery delivery program, 32,
  378
Net Perceptions software, 212, 312–13,
  390
Newell, Frederick, 10
Newsletters
  customer differentiation and, 69–70
  personalized, 107, 126, 135–36, 384
New York Times on the Web, web site
  privacy policy, 101
Nicholls, Sandra, 379, 383
Niehaus, Tom, 383
Nissan, Daniel, 378
NMFF. See Northwestern Medical Faculty
  Foundation (NMFF) (Chicago, Ill.)
Non-cash benefits, measuring
  success/failure through, 17–18
Non-paying customers, 67–68
Nonprofit organizations, 67, 292, 371–74

Northwestern Medical Faculty Foundation
  (NMFF) (Chicago, Ill.), personalized
  newsletter, 107, 126, 135–36, 384
Norton, David P., 157
Novak, Thomas P., 10, 112, 339

Ogilvy, David, 81
Ohio Farmer-Stockman, 331
1-800-FLOWERS, success of, 104
One-to-one enterprises, defined, 2
One-to-One Future, 56, 97, 206
One-to-one marketing
  commitment to, 141–42, 203, 349–50
  customer management. See Customer
    managers
  defined, 1–2
  gradual implementation strategies,
    201–6, 235
  hiring strategies, 210–12
  infrastructure worksheets, 218–24
  measuring success of, 17–18, 214–15,
    358–59
  product launches and, 337–39
  quick start strategies. See Quick start
    strategies
  sales departments. See Sales
    departments
  self-assessment worksheets, 158–65
  short-term funding strategy, 355–56
  strategy mapping worksheets, 165–69
  training. See Training
  transition teams for. See Transition
    teams
  See also www.1to1.com
Online application processing (OLAP),
  178
Online services, 42, 45, 100, 101, 312–13
  See also Information technology (IT);
    World Wide Web (WWW)
Oracle database software, 179, 265
Outdoor Life, 70
Owens Corning, 378
  cost-efficiency of Web site, 103
  customer identification, 25–26
  customization by, 137–38
  interactive marketing by, 73–74
  resolving internal conflicts, 110
  success of, xxii, 6
Oxford Health Plans, data conversion
  disaster, 172–73, 385–86

Packaging, as customizing strategy, 128

Padovani, Greg, 107, 383, 384
Parkinson, Andrew, 378
Parkinson, Thomas, 378
Partnerships. *See* Alliances, strategic;
    Channel members/management
Parvatiyar, A., 11
Passwords, personal, 41–42
Payment terms, customization through,
    130
Payne, Adrian, 10
Peapod, grocery delivery program, 32,
    378
Peck, Helen, 10
Pellet, Guillaume, 378
Percy, Larry, 339
Perkins, Debra, 293
Perlman, Rob, 390
Personal computers. *See* Information
    technology (IT); *specific companies*
Personal digital assistants (PDAs), 250
Peters, Tom, 10, 217
Petersen, Glen S., 270
Picket fences, around Most Valuable
    Customers, 202
Pine, B. Joseph, II, 9, 10, 147, 210,
    234–35, 387
Pitney Bowes, success of, 6
Pivotal Relationship software, 183
Pizza Hut, 41
Platt, Lew, 378
Portfolios, customer, 91–92, 206–9
Posner, Barry, 217
Postponement manufacturing processes,
    234–35
Preferred Hotels, 33–34, 379
Pressault, Guy, 388
Press releases, 67, 335
Price competition
    customer acquisition through, xxi
    frequency marketing plans as, 32
Pricing, functional integration facilitating,
    133
Print advertising, 70, 331–33, 340–42
Privacy protection
    by governments, 335, 373–74
    customer identification and, 41, 308
    customer interactions and, 99–101
    European Union rules on, 335
Processing costs, customer convenience
    and, 17, 18
Procter & Gamble (P&G), channel
    relationships, 233, 387

Product expertise, customer expertise vs.,
    72–75
Production-related products,
    customization of, 140–41, 384–85
Product launches, advertising and, 337–39
Product management
    divisional integration facilitating,
        137–41, 384–85
    functional integration enhancing, 133
Product services, customizing, 5, 57,
    127–30, 139–41
Professional organizations
    differentiating customers in, 66
    nonprofit, 371–72
Profit margins, xxi, 17
Prospects. *See* Customer acquisition
Prusak, Laurence, 218

Quickcount, 178
Quick start strategies
    customizing products/services, 21–22,
        160
    differentiating customers, 19–20, 159
    identifying customers, 19, 159
    interacting with customers, 20–21, 96,
        106, 160
    for transition teams, 22–23, 158–60

Radio
    individualizing advertising, 333
    See also Advertising/marketing
Radio-frequency information chips (RFI),
    39–40
Randall, Scott, 337, 391
Rapid application deployment (RAD), 174
Rapp, Stan, 46
Registration systems, electronic, 205
Reichheld, Frederick F., 81
Relationship marketing
    one-to-one marketing compared to, 1
    overinteractions with customers as, 95,
        382
Responsibility for implementation
    by customer managers, 109–10,
        115–16, 203–4, 205–6, 209–10
    conflicts and, 15–16, 154, 350
Return on investment (ROI)
    personalized communications and, 107
    See also Cost-efficiency
Rey, David, 374
Ritz Carlton, customer interactions, 109
R. L. Polk, 28

numbers for identification, 40–41
preconfiguration as customization, 128
See also Call centers
Television
individualizing advertising, 333
See also Advertising/marketing
Tesco (U.K.), frequency marketing program, 30
Thermal technology, identifying customers, 31
Thissen, Carlene, 112
Thompson, Ian, 257–58, 388
3Com, 252
3M
customer identification database, 38, 379
differentiating customers, 72
participation by upper management, 141–42
product and customer expertise, 74–75, 208
success of, 6
Tichy, Noel M., 236
Time magazine, 331, 391
Training
by database firms, 196
call center operators, 104–5, 211, 212, 285, 290, 291
company-wide strategies for, 213–14
for customer identification, 28, 33
salespeople, 251, 252–53, 254
Transaction costs. *See* Cost-efficiency
Transition teamschannel management worksheet, 237
customer identification worksheet, 47–48
customization issues worksheet, 148–49
database system worksheet, 186–87
developing visions and goals, 353–54
differentiation issues worksheet, 82
first meeting, 352–53
infrastructure worksheets, 218–24
interactivity issues worksheet, 113–14
1to1 Gap Tool worksheet, 161–65
makeup of, 7–8, 350–52
overview issues/worksheets, 12–14, 350–62
project plan worksheets, 363–69
quick start strategies/worksheets, 19–23, 158–60

sales issues worksheets, 272–73
strategy mapping worksheets, 165–69
Web site worksheet, 321–22
TRUST, Web site privacy protection, 101, 382
Turner, Mary, 285–86

United Parcel Service (UPS), as channel member, 336
Unit margins, xxi, 17
Unix, 170, 171
Up-selling, measuring success/failure through, 17, 18
USAA, 27
call center, 104
success of, xxii, 6, 104
U.S. Post Office, customization by, 128–29

Vail Associates, Inc., 290–91, 390
Value-added incentives, at Ford Motor Company, 37
Value-added resellers, 144–46, 226, 227
See also Channel members/management
Value of customers. *See* Customer valuation; Lifetime value (LTV); Most Growable Customers (MGCs); Most Valuable Customers (MVCs); Strategic value (customer)
Van Asseldonk, Ton, 148
Vassos, Tom, 320
VeriSign, Inc., 308, 390
Versioning, individualizing advertising/marketing, 331–33, 335–36, 340–42, 346–47
Vignette Corporation, 318, 391
Voice Response Unit (VRU), 18

Wacker, Watts, 11
Wal-Mart, 143, 233, 387
Warranty services
customer data from, 27, 180
customization through, 129
enhancing loyalty, 29
Wayland, Robert E., 11
Web sites. *See* World Wide Web (WWW)
Weingrod, Steve, 380
Wells Fargo, success of, 6
Wevers, Jasmine, 270
Whiteley, Richard, 157
Wiersema, Fred, 11

ABOUT THE AUTHORS

Don Peppers and Martha Rogers founded Peppers and Rogers Group in 1992. Together they wrote *The One to One Future: Building Relationships One Customer at a Time* (1993) and *Enterprise One to One: Tools for Competing in the Interactive Age* (1997). Bob Dorf joined the company in 1993 as Managing Partner and is now President.

You can reach the authors at 1to1.com or visit the Web site at www.1to1.com